THE POLITICS OF C INFRASTRUCT

Spaces and (In)Equality

Edited by
Peter Cox and Till Koglin

P

First published in Great Britain in 2021 by

Policy Press, an imprint of
Bristol University Press
University of Bristol
1-9 Old Park Hill
Bristol
BS2 8BB
UK
t: +44 (0)117 954 5940
e: bup-info@bristol.ac.uk

Details of international sales and distribution partners are available at
policy.bristoluniversitypress.co.uk

British Library Cataloguing in Publication Data
A catalogue record for this book is available from the British Library

978-1-4473-4515-2 hardback
978-1-4473-4517-6 paperback
978-1-4473-4518-3 ePub
978-1-4473-4516-9 ePDF

Cover design: Liam Roberts
Front cover image: ChiccoDodiFC © iStock

Bristol University Press and Policy Press use environmentally responsible
print partners.

Printed in Great Britain by CPI Group (UK) Ltd, Croydon, CR0 4YY

FSC
www.fsc.org
MIX
Paper from
responsible sources
FSC® C013604

Contents

List of figures, tables and box

Figures

Tables

Box

Notes on contributors

Andrew Barnfield is a coordinator at EuroHealthNet where he leads on implementing best practices to reduce health inequalities. Andrew's research is at the intersection of public health and cultural geography and explores how to make cities more equitable, sustainable and healthy.

Tadej Brezina works at Vienna University of Technology's Research Centre of Transport Planning and Traffic Engineering. He is a civil engineer by education with a strong ecological background. His interests lie in a) understanding the time and spatial aspects of human mobility systems in interdependence with settlement systems over various scales; b) public transport user and cyclist behaviour and corresponding solutions; c) the general interaction of social and technological regimes and d) GIS and transport.

Peter Cox is a Professor of Sociology at the University of Chester, UK. In 2014–15, he was awarded a Leverhulme International Academic Fellowship to work at the Rachel Carson Centre for Environment and Society in Munich, where he focused on developing mobile research methods to better understand how people interact in public spaces of mobility. He was a founding member of the Cycling and Society Research Group and co-edited *Cycling and Society* (2007). He is the author of *Moving People: Sustainable Transport Development* (2010) and *Cycling: A Sociology of Vélo-Mobilities* (2019), and editor of *Cycling Cultures* (2015).

Marjolein de Lange is an expert in cycling, walking and road safety. She works on research, planning and policy. Recent work on cycling includes research into measures for (over)crowding on bike routes and Relaxed Routes for cyclists in Amsterdam. She is involved in Fietsersbond Amsterdam, Amsterdam's Cyclists' Union, in the strategy team and the infra team. Fred Feddes and Marjolein de Lange co-wrote *Bike City Amsterdam* (2019).

Martin Emanuel is a historian of technology and also undertakes research in the transdisciplinary fields of science and technology studies (STS) and mobility studies. He holds a PhD (2013) from the Royal Institute of Technology in Stockholm, Sweden and is a researcher at the Department of Economic History at Uppsala University, Sweden.

He co-edited *Cycling Cities: The European Experience: Hundred Years of Policy and Practice* (2016).

Fred Feddes is a journalist and writer specialising in spatial planning, landscape, urbanism and history. His publications include an acclaimed introduction to the spatial history of Amsterdam, *A Millennium of Amsterdam* (2012), as well as *Bike City Amsterdam* with Marjolein de Lange (2019).

Malene Freudendal-Pedersen is a Professor in Urban Planning at Aalborg University, Denmark and has an interdisciplinary background linking sociology, geography, urban planning and the sociology of technology. Her research has been strongly inspired by the mobilities turn. Previously, her work was primarily focused on investigating everyday life praxis' of mobilities and in the book *Mobility in Daily Life – Between Freedom and Unfreedom* she focuses on the importance of comprehending the interrelations between praxis, technologies and societies. Currently her research focuses on understanding the interrelation between spatial and digital mobilities and its impacts on everyday life communities, societies and cities. For many years she has co-organised the International Cosmobilities Network linking mobilities researchers in Europe and beyond. She is the co-founder and co-editor of the Routledge journal *Applied Mobilities* as well as the co-founder and co-editor of the book-series *Networked Urban Mobilities*, also published by Routledge.

Till Koglin holds a PhD in transport planning. He is a Senior Lecturer in Transport and Mobility Planning at Lund University, Sweden. His research mainly deals with mobility, transport and urban planning with a strong focus on the marginalisation of cycling in urban space. Within his research, he combines critical theory with transport and mobility in order to shed light on injustice issues within transport planning and transport systems. Till Koglin's research interests relate, on a theoretical level, to mobility, planning and power theories. On a more empirical level, he mainly works with qualitative methods in the area of mobility and planning.

Helmut Lemmerer is a research fellow at Vienna University of Technology in the Research Centre of Transport Planning and Traffic Engineering. The change from a car-oriented approach to a transport system in which people and their environment are at the forefront forms his basis for sustainable transport planning. His main research interests are active mobility, child-friendly and barrier-free mobility.

Ulrich Leth has been researching and planning human-centred mobility solutions for over a decade. His fields of interest include mobility masterplans for cities (SUMPS), cycling as an everyday means of transport and the relationship between the built environment and mobility behaviour.

Katja Leyendecker recently (2019) completed her doctoral thesis, an autoethnographic account of women activists campaigning for cycleways in the UK (Newcastle) and in Germany (Bremen). She is a civil engineer. Frustrated with the slow progress in sustainable transport planning, she co-founded the Newcastle Cycling Campaign in 2010 to hold decision makers to account and address the lack of safe space for cycling. She now lives in Berlin.

Letícia Lindenberg Lemos is a PhD student at the University of São Paulo, Faculty of Architecture and Urban Planning, and will be a visiting scholar at Eindhoven University's Department of Technology, Innovation and Society (TIS). She is working on her thesis about the development and implementation of cycling policies in São Paulo, Brazil from the perspective of social-state interactions and how these have reproduced and reinforce the socio-spatial segregation. She has trained in sustainable mobility in developing countries at the United Nations Institute for Training and Research. She is conducting research from a gendered perspective on sustainable mobility, focusing on active modes, in particular urban cycling, and how these have been shaped by rules, regulations and policies.

Njogu Morgan is a postdoctoral researcher in the History Workshop at the University of Witwatersrand, Johannesburg, South Africa. His overall research interest pertains to theoretical, conceptual and empirical aspects of sustainability transitions from a spatial comparative perspective.

Anna Plyushteva is postdoctoral research fellow in the Department of Geography, Vrije Universiteit Brussels. Her current research explores gender relations and affordability in the context of urban transport and mobility, and the intersections of transport infrastructure with other urban infrastructural systems.

Marco te Brömmelstroet holds the Urban Mobility Futures Chair of the University of Amsterdam. The Chair aims at strengthening the social-scientific perspective on mobility innovations. He is the founding Academic Director of the Urban Cycling Institute that is a part of the Centre for Urban Studies. The Institute leads research into the reciprocal relations between cycling, society and cities and is also actively involved in international dissemination of Dutch cycling knowledge.

John Whitelegg is a Visiting Professor in the School of the Built Environment at Liverpool John Moores University, UK. In recent years he has held professorial appointments at Lancaster University (Geography), Roskilde University (Transport), Essen University (Geography) and York University (Sustainable Development). He is the editor of the journal, *World Transport Policy and Practice*, a member of the International Advisory Board of the Wuppertal Institute for Climate, Energy and the Environment, Germany and a member of the Advisory Board of the Chandradeep Solar Research Institute (CDSRI) in Kolkata, India. He also is a member of the Board of Directors of the US organisation, Transportation Choices for Sustainable Communities Research and Policy Institute.

Introduction

Peter Cox and Till Koglin

The cycling situation today

Transport systems dominated by motorised traffic experience severe problems in congestion, pollution, social exclusion and health issues (Banister, 2005; Nuhn and Hesse, 2006; van Wee, 2007), in addition to being a major contributor to climate change. As an active mode of transport, cycling offers a range of benefits: it contributes to the health of its users, is an inexpensive way to travel, it takes up less space than motorised traffic and it does not contribute to CO_2 or other emissions (Garrard et al, 2012; Fishman, 2016; Götschi et al, 2016). Thus many cities are working on improvements for cycling conditions (Pucher and Buehler, 2008; Garrard et al, 2012; Handy et al, 2014; Lanzendorf and Busch-Geertsema, 2014; Fishman, 2016; Pojani et al, 2017).

Due to its positive effects, cycling is currently positively promoted across Europe as a contributor to a number of policy agendas. Cycle use as transport is seen to contribute to ease congestion, contribute to carbon reduction, improve urban air quality, and further benefits in individual health, economic efficiency and liveable cities are linked to its promotion (see Grafl et al, 2019). Research has repeatedly shown the positive effects of cycling, however, there are still many cities, like Stockholm in Sweden for example, that have failed to increase cycling as a percentage of trips (Koglin, 2015a). Other cities struggle to maintain high levels of cycling, or they observe decreases in cycling levels (Copenhagen, for example see te Brömmelstroet et al, forthcoming). The reality of current schemes building cycle-friendly cities is frequently framed around the provision of specific hard infrastructure.

In addition to the proliferation of policy studies, academic texts on cycling research are also expanding rapidly (Pucher and Buehler, 2017). A dominant theme among these is the use of infrastructure measures (hard and soft) to assist the promotion of cycling as part of a movement towards sustainable mobility systems (Béland, 2014; Mrkajić and Anguelovski, 2016). As part of these academic reflections on cycling practices and policies, there have been cycling-specific academic conferences and a considerable number of specialist panels on cycling in other network conferences, in fields such as mobilities studies, transport history and transport studies. Discussions between the editors of this volume developed over the course of a number of these meetings where the volume of papers that dealt directly or indirectly with issues of infrastructure was notable. In conversation the editors noted the frequency with which infrastructure (or lack thereof) was treated as a given, subject only to appropriate design and implementation, rather than a product of political contestation. Consideration of cycling infrastructure appeared to be distanced from the wider discussions and the growing number of publications on the politics of infrastructure. In order to explore more critically the subject of cycling infrastructure, a number of authors whose previous work had touched on these dimensions were invited to take part.

This volume and the broader conversation on cycling infrastructure

Physical infrastructure is currently posited as the primary key to unlock cycling's potential as a primary mode of sustainable transport (see, for example, Pooley et al, 2013; Pucher and Buehler, 2017). This centralisation of infrastructure has a number of dimensions, the first being advocacy. Leading groups, such as the European Cyclists' Federation (ECF), or individual national bodies (such as Sustrans in the UK) have long campaigned for the construction of cycleways and cycle tracks as a means to boost cycling numbers. Alongside the provision of specific routeways upon which to ride, human infrastructure in the form of cycle training schemes (for both children and adults) is part of the provisions made by these national representation groups. When not directly responsible for provision, these bodies have been heavily involved in drawing up the curricula and training standards. Second, there are academic studies that identify the lack of (quality) infrastructure as a major impediment to cycling growth and, conversely, those that celebrate the effects of quality infrastructure provision (Pucher et al, 2010; Basua and Vasuvedan, 2013; van Goeverden et al, 2015). To this end, we see a third category of publications concerning cycling infrastructure in the form of professional engineering-based guidance (CROW, 2007; Parkin, 2018). Against this background, the editors identified a number of gaps in understanding that prompted specific contributions for this volume.

Individual studies rarely stand together to be read back to back, in order to allow comparison between them. Oldenziel et al (2016) provide a useful measure of comparative city cycling histories that illustrate trends, but these are too brief to unpick the complexities of specific infrastructural measures and the processes by which decisions were made in given cases. The privilege of academic conferences is that they allow the attendee to compare and contrast different academic agendas and concerns of researchers, and to engage in conversation with them. The aim of this volume is to bring a selection of those parallel voices together and to initiate that dialogue for a wider audience.

Of course, this is limited by the number of contributions that can be incorporated into a single volume. However, a deliberate attempt has been made to cross between different networks and disciplines to allow conversation and comparison between authors whose work and theoretical frameworks might not be initially familiar to each other. The focus is largely urban and geared towards the use of cycles as transport. A decision was made to exclude the infrastructures of sport, tourism and leisure cycling, which deserve their own separate study. Infrastructure includes both physical and social provisioning. The latter is tangentially mentioned and forms the specific focus of one chapter in this work. The valuable role of training in the politics of social infrastructures remains largely unexplored here. Another conscious omission, and one that is most definitely an important dimension to the politics of cycling infrastructure, is that of the non-urban. There are valuable stories of social inclusion and exclusion to be explored in relation to non-urban mundane cycling practices and the infrastructural provisions made (or not) outside of cities. Again, space prohibits the current project from further exploration of these, and the authors eagerly anticipate the day when non-urban cycling is treated to a similar analysis of its infrastructuration.

As noted earlier, the contributors chosen for this volume come from a range of disciplines. Importantly, consideration was also given to approaching authors at a range of career stages of researcher. As part of the writing process, each contributor shared preliminary versions of their chapter so as to open up the dialogic process. Common themes emerged as we assembled and read the various contributions. First, and perhaps most obvious, was the messiness and contradictions of the processes of infrastructuring. No blueprints or universal best-practice regimes emerge. Each responds to the particular conditions of its local operations and broader political frames in which it operates. Processes are often chaotic, contradictory and imperfect. Planning is one element of the operation, but what results is often very different from even the most comprehensive strategic imagination. Underlying this chaos, however, is a lurking sense that the broader lessons of infrastructure provision for cycling need to be connected with the political analyses of infrastructuring derived from wider studies. There is no single utopian destination, no perfect infrastructure design. Indeed, even more clearly, infrastructure creation, provision and implementation is always an ongoing process. No final destination is possible. Spaces are always being remade, contested, conflicts over space are always unfinished as the process of politics is always unfinished. Infrastructuring is an ongoing process, taking place even when no physical or material environment is being created as people utilise the physical spaces that exist and provide them with new sets of meanings and contend the ownership and belonging of different mobile subjects to those spaces.

Contents

In light of the development of cycling and the rather slow increase of cycling in cities' mode share, this volume casts a critical gaze on current practices and on the relationship of cycling to other forms of urban mobility, especially within the context of sustainable and liveable cities.

The geographical focus is Europe but understood through acknowledgement of its colonial and imperial extension. There is already considerable literature about classically non-cycle-friendly countries (like the US, the UK or New Zealand) and how cycling is marginalised (Furness, 2010; Aldred, 2013; Smith, 2016). However, even in European cases celebrated for high cycling modal share, cycling continues to encounter marginalisation, hence the concern of this volume. Cities such as Copenhagen are frequently cited as examples of best practice but the issues cyclists face in their everyday mobility in 'cycle-friendly' cities and countries are seldom, if at all, the subject of analysis (Pucher and Buehler, 2008). This book sets out to challenge easy assumptions of European homogeneity and to extend the studies of infrastructure, (both hard and soft) beyond existing dominant foci, and to engage with the multiple policy drivers that shape infrastructural provision. It considers the issues and problems cyclists face, in infrastructure and mobility contexts and adds to a growing critical investigation of European cycle infrastructures (Freudendal-Pedersen, 2015; Koglin, 2015b).

This volume extends the arguments around the revitalisation of cycling as transport, with a strong focus on a critical analysis of current practices and the ways in which exclusions and inclusions are formed. Its aim is to link existing work on the value and opportunities presented by cycle planning (its contribution to sustainability, carbon reduction targets, health, and so on) to the broader problems of the continued dominance of motorised traffic. The volume disseminates new thinking and research in the field to a cross-disciplinary audience. Moreover, through the empirical focus on Europe and countries within Europe that are less dominant within scientific publications this book offers a new empirical foundation for theoretical developments within the field of cycle research and will offer new insights from 'cycle-friendly' countries.

This collection draws together an international group of scholars involved with mobility studies and cycling studies. It critically engages with two interlinked questions. First, how and why cycling remains marginalised in many transport systems, and second, it considers how this marginalisation relates to the continued maintenance of motorised transport dominance, even in countries where cycling is part of the everyday mobility (for example, Denmark, Germany or Sweden). Its contents draw from both quantitative and qualitative approaches to the study of mobility, and from a range of disciplines. This scope, from planning to sociology, makes full use of the interdisciplinary emerging in contemporary cycling studies. The focus, however, is not only the politics of cycling infrastructure, but also of the broader contexts of those infrastructures, shaped as they are by the dominance of motor traffic and the simultaneous marginalisation of other modes of transport.

Structure of the book

The opening chapters move from the examination of the historical construction of infrastructure and the legacies of its framing to an examination of how these legacies and path dependencies in thinking are experienced today, pointing ultimately toward examples where such limitations have been overcome, and transformational models of change enacted. They commence with an overview of recent theorisations that assist in secondary consideration of points raised in subsequent chapters.

Cox's opening chapter sets out some of the issues of political theory that arise in relation to infrastructure. He highlights a number of disparate and sometimes disconnected strands of theory around the politics of infrastructure and the politics of space and draws them together to show that consideration of a politics of infrastructure is a politics of spatial justice. These themes cross disciplinary boundaries, drawing on perspectives in sociology, political theory, geography and (post-)development studies, showing how discussions of cycling infrastructure are necessarily entangled with deeper questions about cities and citizenship. The chapter serves as a background to many of the following chapters, exploring themes subsequently explored through individual chapter case studies. Its particular contribution is to show how infrastructure acts as an apparatus of its own, with its own subject-making (interpellative) function. Moreover, similar material infrastructure can have different interpellative effects, depending upon the constellation of social relations of which it is reflective. These processes re-stress the importance of spatial justice and the need to consider how physical spaces of cycling created by infrastructural intervention may provide particular critical political perspectives.

Morgan concretises the political theory approach by a material historical case study of a single road in Johannesburg that illustrates many of the points made in the opening chapter. Showing how these political forces play out in practice, Morgan's chapter exposes the manner in which infrastructure gives material expression to ideology. He maps the changing fortunes of the cycle lane, its use and users, on this one road to chart how different groups of non-users perceived those using it, and of the expectations of who those users were, both in composition and in citizenship. The institution of the cycle lane, and its removal can be read as expressions of power and the power to render others invisible or undesirable. Simultaneously, Morgan also makes us aware of the presuppositions that underlie those decision-making processes, a theme taken further by Brezina and colleagues (Chapter 5). In Morgan's case, the historical legacy of other infrastructure management, based on fluid mechanics applied to water and waste management, is revealed to be an inadequate way to model human interactions. Reducing human movement to flow obscures the power dimensions and the structural relations between the very different constituent elements (physically and politically) of the traffic flow. The unreflective equation of cycle use with racialised definitions of the black population lends a further dimension to the understanding of infrastructure segregation. Cycle lanes or tracks could even be justified in order to maintain motoring as a white privilege and thus maintain socio-political control through control of mobility.

Koglin's chapter moves us back to a more theoretical approach, grounded in an analysis of the legacy of transport planning in Sweden. He examines the conceptual underpinnings upon which assumptions that drive decisions are grounded. For Koglin, to examine the politics of infrastructure requires us to interrogate the degree to which the concept of reason is embedded within modernity and, conversely, how the presuppositions of modernist regimes are still dominant in transport infrastructure planning. Despite the emergence of new fields of thinking and new modes of design, existing physical mobility spaces express, in very concrete form, a specific, bounded rationalism and a modernist vision. Ultimately, Koglin questions whether that physical legacy is redeemable for more sustainable models of mobility that would break away from the dominance of automobility. More importantly, he poses the question whether breaking from this legacy requires a new thought model less beholden to the rationalist vision. This enables us to move on to two parallel chapters that both explore further dimensions of the entrenched paradigm made visible in Koglin's study. What these two chapters also have in common is their consideration of what a challenge to the current paradigm might require, and how this might be undertaken.

Brezina, Leth and Lemmerer focus their attention on the question of agency. They report on a large-scale study of transport professionals in Austria, to identify how the construction and operation of mental barriers prevents many transport professionals from comprehending or acting upon the scale of change required. Crucially, rather than point the finger at specific groups or practices, they move the question to the processes through which the problems of infrastructure provision are defined. Here the politics is not one of theory but of the circularity of argumentation. To understand the politics of infrastructure, they argue, requires us to go beyond the examination of physical, hard material constructions. The infrastructures they point towards may be as durable and resilient as built environments but are situated in the realm of the cognitive. Through survey, they expose the factors shaping and limiting the social imaginaries brought to bear on infrastructure provisioning. Describing these as mental barriers, they show how planners are able to conceive what might be appropriate interventions only from within a vocabulary provided for them by their training and experience. Whatever guidelines exist, however excellent, and whatever guidance expertise suggests, both are irrelevant if those charged with implementation are not equipped with the appropriate mental infrastructures to utilise them. Guidelines and planning principles do not come alive from the page except when filtered through the social imaginary of the relevant parties. The chapter shows that physical infrastructure development relies on a social infrastructure that, among the cohort studied is limited by mental barriers that mean their anticipation of change is far less than that of advocates who seek to influence and work with them.

Whitelegg's chapter extends this line of argument with a strongly worded call to transform current dominant paradigms in mobility and transport thinking. He moves the debate sideways by examining the concrete examples of Vision Zero and 'Energiewende'. These two policy approaches have both produced fundamental, paradigmatic transformations in road safety thinking and energy policy respectively. They both demonstrate how dramatically different models are needed in order to address the current inequalities faced by cycling. Perhaps even more importantly, they also show that this transformation of policy areas has involved changing the frames of reference for those policy debates. For example, Vision Zero shifts focus for road safety from incident reduction to the ethical questions of road space and endangerment. Whitelegg outlines both critique and concrete proposals for necessary changes, challenging the presumption that greater mobility is socially beneficial and showing how current practices are actually detrimental not just to physical health but also in wider social terms.

Moving on to the second section of the book, subsequent chapters consider a number of specific case studies. Here the more practical considerations of political process are more strongly to the fore. Leyendecker makes a comparative study of policy making in Bremen and Newcastle to show how the issues of urban development, and of cycling as a necessary part of a sustainable urban futures, are tackled in two parallel examples. What emerges is not just policy differences but contrasts in the conceptualisation of change processes. Both cities demonstrate the tensions felt between contradictory policy drivers, and the relative strengths of those contending drivers in broader socio-political contexts. Can demands for city-centre regeneration and a traffic-free city be reconciled within a car-dominated transport setting? Without modal shift, removing motorists from a city removes people from that city. The promotion of modal shift away from private cars requires making other modes more attractive and motoring less attractive, so how can modal shift be managed without risking driving motorists away to other destinations? How can social infrastructures that support physical infrastructural change be provided for and strengthened? What are the relevant priorities in the face of limited budgetary capacity? Systematic comparisons allow insights into these challenging dilemmas.

Feddes, de Lange and Brömmelstroet sketch a history of changing thought and action over transport in Amsterdam since the 1960s. Drawing on a larger body of historical work, they analyse the complex processes and drivers of change in Amsterdam to reveal a number of important points in the practical politics of infrastructure provision. First, there are structural preconditions, historical legacies that have profound impacts on mobility patterns of a city. These arise not only from changing economic fortunes and from obvious influences of topography, but also the social geography of the city is shown as an important factor for the city's development. Second, but perhaps more significantly, the chapter raises important questions concerning citizenship and structures of government. That a city has the authority to govern its transport provisions may be self-evident to those in cities that have this jurisdiction, but it is not always the case. Amsterdam's restructuring into separate city regions suggests that as the structures of governance change, so does the distribution of competencies and therefore the processes of coordination and the equity of provision. Even the simple ability to minimise infrastructure spending by coordinating road maintenance tasks requires levels of government competence that are far from universal. What is also remarkable is the degree of contingency shown by this detailed study of negotiation processes. The overall direction of Amsterdam's urban mobility development could have proceeded in a very different direction to the one with which we have now become familiar. It is easy to consider how development trajectories have become locked in and to highlight our contemporary difficulties in attempting to break path dependencies. The value of this study is that it shows that these path dependencies are created at specific moments through particular courses of decision-making. Thus, it should be possible to address those pivotal decisions and reappraise the ways in which subsequent actions flow form particular developmental prioritisations.

Above all, their study shows the importance of political processes and systems, both historical and contemporary. Governance mechanisms that provide for and respond to citizen voices are at the heart of the capacity for a city to recognise the need for and implement change. In the case of Amsterdam, they are shown to have been vital in the shaping of its mobility: the relative ease of entry for new political actors means that existing parties have to be responsive and flexible in their own policies and approaches. Such openness then encourages the development of civil society expertise. These observations in turn, pose their own questions of whether these (or any other) models of hard infrastructure are transferable without parallel equivalence in the political mechanisms that made them possible.

Through close-grained study of the arguments surrounding the Øresund crossing between Malmoe and Copenhagen, Martin Emanuel alerts us to the dilemmas of cyclists' own processes of advocacy on infrastructure. Over a number of years, different solutions to cross were proposed, and cycling groups had to choose between contending forces of idealism and pragmatism, between principles and 'making the best of it'. Torn between the desire to oppose a motorway bridge on principle and the possibility that the bridge could provide a cycling link, how ought competing factions within the pro-cycling lobby decide? Moreover, the study exposes the degree to which decision-making processes are often contingent upon very fragile moments in time, where individual persons may have a profound impact even within situations that might appear to be determined by more powerful structural forces. Infrastructure delivery, like any other outcome of policy prioritisation, is ultimately political and the product of specific political actors, as also shown by Feddes, de Lange and Brömmelstroet.

Freudendal-Pedersen's chapter proceeds from a situation of high levels of infrastructural provision in Copenhagen and examines how physical infrastructures create social and conceptual infrastructures among their users. Employing a specific version of narrative analysis, she explores how infrastructure users develop their own stories of use, and from these their own expectations of use. Thus, the physical infrastructures are shown to extend beyond their material presence into the expectations of the users and users own understandings of themselves and their capacities. Shove et al's (2012) model of social practices hinges on the entanglement of competencies, materials and meanings, and these interconnections and interdependencies are vividly highlighted by this study. Identity, capacity value and power, in both positive and negative aspects, are all interwoven in the emergent stories of participants in her study, caught up with the physical infrastructure and the performances it enables.

In sharp contrast, the next chapter moves from a city in which cycle-specific infrastructure is ubiquitous and unavoidable to one in which it is a rarity. Plyushteva and Barnfield examine the debates over a specific area of infrastructure provision in the city of Sofia, through the initial planning controversies to eventual construction. The study makes an interesting comparison with the chapter on Amsterdam. Both consider the micro-politics of decision-making but in very different political and temporal contexts. Both studies highlight the contest between competing demands and the desire and necessity of political compromise, but the relation of citizen to state and the openness of the institutions are utterly different. In Sofia, the municipality remains a separate and relatively distant institution, not something open to entry by grassroots groups. Infrastructure interventions appear as an insertion into the city, rather than being integrated in any systemic mobilities framework. The political dimensions remain fragmented, reflecting the analysis made in Cox's discussions in Chapter 1. More importantly, the Sofia study exposes the vital importance of understanding built infrastructures as networked spaces, only comprehensible through a systemic analysis. As was also the case with Emanuel's chapter on the Øresund crossing, the issue at stake is not simply the route itself but its implications within a wider set of mobility processes. Spaces to facilitate cycling may be introduced but the primary mobility imaginary controlling the allocation of space is one of automobility. The primary task of mobility spaces is to facilitate the movement of motorised traffic; other considerations are subsidiary or even decorative. When urban space is a scarce commodity then the primary spatial contradiction must be confronted: it is not possible to keep expanding spaces of mobility within a finite and fixed spatial resource. To increase space for cycling and for walking will necessitate the reduction of space for motor traffic.

The final chapter, by Leticia Lindenberg Lemos, shifts the focus away from Europe to examine the events and peoples behind the creation of cycle-specific infrastructures in São Paulo. The case study illustrates a number of the theoretical arguments presented in the opening chapter, showing how the framing of the image of the cyclists is closely related to the infrastructure and, conversely, how infrastructural provisions reflect the valorisation (or its inverse) of the cyclist in political imaginaries. The chapter focuses on factors behind the implementation of infrastructural; projects in 2013–16. Their subsequent fate also demonstrates how swiftly political fortunes can change and how discursive regimes are subject to rapid reality shifts. While it is a truism that a day is a long time in politics, it is easy to make a similar assumption that built environments are conversely stable, fixed entities. This study shows how both the political and the infrastructural are malleable. What matters are the forms of agency that mobilise the politics of infrastructure and the politics that are mobilised by infrastructures.

While each chapter stands alone as its own study, their juxtaposition is even more valuable. The diversity of experiences and processes pose a number of questions for the provision and development of infrastructures. They do not in any way undermine the need to engage with good practice in the design and engineering of infrastructures (CROW, 2007; Jensen, 2014; Parkin, 2018), but they do suggest that we also need to look beyond the design solutions. Each implementation is preceded by a history of power-games, in which the stakes are not simply gains of social or intellectual prowess. Rather they are about the ways in which the political subject is constructed. The studies reveal the manners in which mobile subjects are (re)produced as citizen subjects and vice versa. Outcomes are rarely predictable and can be extraordinarily contingent.

A note on language

The language used to describe cycling-specific infrastructures, like the forms of those infrastructures, is both diverse and subject to specific local usages. These local uses may be further complicated by the varying legal status of different forms of provisions and designation. In order to provide consistent usage here and to enable comparison to be made between chapters, a set of terms has been adapted from Parkin's (2018: xv–xvii) terminology for international comparison of designs for cycle traffic.

- *Cycle lane* here describes a designated lane within a carriageway (roadway) for use by cycle traffic.
- *Cycle track* here describes a separated lane for cycle traffic along the route of a carriageway. A track may be separated by physical buffering (using various devices such as raised blocks or bollards), by being raised from the level of the carriageway or by full division, running parallel to the roadway.
- *Cycleway* here describes a routeway for cycle traffic only, equivalent to a carriageway (roadway). In some cases, especially in the UK, cycleways are shared with other non-motorised traffic.

These definitions depart in detail from Parkin's original use, but better reflect the situation in this volume, without needing to follow the peculiarities of English legal definitions. In the chapters that follow, use of the definitions cited earlier overwrite the local usages in translation. Such terminological shift is not to deny the importance or legitimacy of local terms and descriptions, but to provide the platform for meaningful comparison.

References

Aldred, R. (2013) 'Incompetent or too competent? Negotiating everyday cycling identities in a motor dominated society', *Mobilities*, 8(2): 252–71.

Banister, D. (2005) *Unsustainable Transport – City Transport in the New Century*, London: Routledge.

Basua, S. and Vasudevan, V. (2013) 'Effect of bicycle friendly roadway infrastructure on bicycling activities in urban India', *Procedia – Social and Behavioral Sciences*, 104: 1139–48.

Béland, D. (2014) 'Developing sustainable urban transportation. Lesson drawing and the framing of Montreal's bikesharing policy', *International Journal of Sociology and Social Policy*, 34(7/8): 545–58.

CROW (2007) *Design Manual for Bicycle Traffic*, Ede, NL: CROW.

Fishman, E. (2016) 'Cycling as transport', *Transport Reviews*, 36(1): 1–8.

Freudendal-Pedersen, M. (2015) 'Cyclists as part of the city's organism: structural stories on cycling in Copenhagen', *City & Society*, 27(1): 30–50.

Furness, Z. (2010) *One Less Car: Bicycling and the Politics of Automobility*, Philadelphia, PA: Temple University Press.

Garrard, J., Rissel, C. and Bauman, A. (2012) 'Health benefits of cycling', in J. Pucher and B. Buehler (eds) *City Cycling*, Cambridge, MA: The MIT Press, pp 31–56.

Götschi, T., Garrard, J. and Giles-Corti, B. (2016) 'Cycling as a part of daily life: a review of health perspectives', *Transport Reviews*, 36(1): 45–71.

Grafl, K., Bunte, H., Dzeikan, K. and Haubold, H. (2019) *Framing the Third Cycling Century: Bridging the Gap between Research and Practice*, Dessau-Roßlau: German Environment Agency.

Handy, S., Van Wee, B. and Kroesen, M. (2014) 'Promoting cycling for transport: research needs and challenges', *Transport Reviews*, 34(1): 4–24.

Jensen, O.B. (2014) *Designing Mobilities*, Aalborg: Aalborg University Press.

Koglin, T. (2015a) 'Vélomobility and the politics of transport planning', *GeoJournal*, 80(4): 569–86.

Koglin, T. (2015b) 'Organisation does matter – planning for cycling in Stockholm and Copenhagen', *Transport Policy*, 39: 55–62.

Lanzendorf, M. and Busch-Geertsema, A. (2014) 'The cycling boom in large German cities – empirical evidence for successful cycling campaigns', *Transport Policy*, 36: 26–33.

Mrkajić, V. and Anguelovski, I. (2016) 'Planning for sustainable mobility in transition cities: cycling losses and hopes of revival in Novi Sad, Serbia', *Cities*, 52: 66–78.

Nuhn, H. and Hesse, M. (2006) *Verkehrsgeographie – Reihe: Grundriss Allgemeine Geographie*, Paderborn: Verlag Ferdinand Schöningh.

Oldenziel, R., Emanuel, M., Albert de la Bruheze, A. and Veraart, F. (eds) (2016) *Cycling Cities: The European Experience: Hundred Years of Policy and Practice*, Eindhoven: Foundation for the History of Technology.

Parkin, J. (2018) *Designing for Cycle Traffic: International Principles and Practice*, London: ICE Publishing.

Pojani, D., Bakija, D., Shkreli, E., Corcoran, J. and Mateo-Babiano, I. (2017) 'Do northwestern and southeastern Europe share a common "cycling mindset"? Comparative analysis of beliefs toward cycling in the Netherlands and the Balkans', *EJTIR*, 17(1): 25–45.

Pooley, C., Jones, T., Tight, M., Horton, D., Scheldeman, G., Jopson, A. and Strano, E. (2013) *Promoting Walking and Cycling: New Perspectives on Sustainable Travel*, Bristol: Policy Press.

Pucher, J. and Buehler, R. (2008) 'Making cycling irresistible', *Transport Reviews*, 28(4): 495–528.

Pucher, J. and Buehler, R. (2017) 'Cycling towards a more sustainable transport future', *Transport Reviews*, 37(6): 689–94.

Pucher, J., Dill, J. and Handy, S. (2010) 'Infrastructure, programs, and policies to increase bicycling: an international review', *Preventive Medicine*, 50: 106–25.

Shove, E., Pantzar, M. and Watson, M. (2012) *The Dynamics of Social Practice, Everyday Life and How It Changes*, London: Sage.

Smith, M. (2016) 'Cycling on the verge: the discursive marginalisation of cycling in contemporary New Zealand transport policy', *Energy Research & Social Science*, 18: 151–61.

te Brömmelstroet, M., Koglin, T. and van Wee, B. (forthcoming) 'Cycling in Copenhagen and Amsterdam', in J. Pucher and R. Buehler (eds) *Future of City Cycling*, Cambridge, MA: The MIT Press.

van Goeverden, K., Sick Nielsen, T., Harder, H. and van Nes, R. (2015) 'Interventions in bicycle infrastructure, lessons from Dutch and Danish cases', *Transportation Research Procedia*, 10: 403–12.

van Wee, B. (2007) 'Environmental effects of urban traffic', in T. Gärling and L. Steg (eds) *Threats from Car Traffic to the Quality of Urban Life – Problems, Causes and Solutions*, Amsterdam: Elsevier, pp 9–32.

1

Theorising infrastructure: a politics of spaces and edges

Peter Cox

Introduction

As an increasing number of authors demonstrate, 'infrastructure is never neutral and always inherently political' (compare McFarlane and Rutherford, 2008; Young and Keil, 2014; Nolte, 2016: 441). Moreover, as Sheller (2018: 97) argues, 'The politics of infrastructure concerns the politics of mobility'. Infrastructures of all types, whether hard (as in material structures) or soft (as in skills and knowledge), are those systems that support action. Infrastructures for cycling are not limited to dedicated or designated cycleways but are inseparable from wider mobility infrastructures. Building cycling infrastructures is not just a matter of providing physical spaces, but also of building the skills, competencies and confidences required for moving in public spaces.

If infrastructure is inherently political, then the ways in which different infrastructures permit some courses of action and deny others, how they route and re-route mobile practices, and how and what any given infrastructure makes possible, are matters of justice and injustice (Sheller, 2018). This chapter seeks to engage with a selected range of current theorisations of the politics of infrastructure, and to apply them to specific cases of cycle-specific infrastructures. It subsequently relates the ideas of social and spatial justice arising from these perspectives to bell hooks' (1990) consideration of marginalisation, to consider how the patterns of marginalisation and mainstreaming revealed in the contributions to this volume might be understood through a lens of a critical and radical politics.

What does infrastructure do?

Infrastructures both provide the potential for social actions and processes and are produced by social actions and processes. In creating potential, however, infrastructures inevitably also order and govern the actions they make possible (Koglin, 2017). Infrastructures organise and shape potentials, providing for some courses of action and not for others. As infrastructure opens up some paths of action, it also closes down other possibilities. This increase and decrease of possibilities affects people differentially, which is why it must be considered in terms of justice.

The mechanism of ordering and governing action is one of facilitation: infrastructural provision being the provision of material facilities (hard) or the facilitation of actions through social development (soft). While certain actions are facilitated by both kinds of infrastructure (hard and soft), actions and practices that fall outside of its desired outcomes are simultaneously rendered unruly, ungoverned; perhaps even ungovernable and deviant. Consequently, material infrastructures are not only comprised of their material dimension but also operate on discursive levels. Actor Network Theory (ANT) provides a lens through which we can understand how infrastructure's political and physical agency is dispersed both through people and through physical objects (Cox, 2019). Infrastructure's multiple dimensions and impacts can be traced, according to Picon (2018: 263), as 'the result of the interactions between a material basis, professional organisations and stabilised sociotechnical practices, and social imagination'. These interactions, and the constitution of those actants, are ably traced in individual chapters elsewhere in this volume.

Theorising infrastructure

Ash Amin (2014) brings together a range of recent discussions on cities and infrastructure observing the multiple ways in which thinking about infrastructures allows us to rethink the social life of city. Clearly echoing Jane Bennett's (2010) concern with *Vibrant Matter*, he introduces the phrase *Lively Infrastructure* to highlight the agentic qualities it has in the formation of urban life. In line with both ANT and New Materialist approaches, it is not only humans that have social agency (see Fox and Alldred, 2017 for an introduction). Not only is infrastructure political, but it also has to be seen as more than an inert material product of human design. Amin highlights three areas of discussion in relation to cities and infrastructure that, between them, provide a framework for discussion of the politics of cycle infrastructure.

First, the city emerges as 'a provisioning machine'. Yet, simultaneously, its capacity to provision is limited: cities' supply and distribution of goods are often unequal. Importantly, Amin (2014: 138), points out, 'failed, incomplete or mismanaged infrastructures' affect the poor and the marginalised most. The expectation that a city can and will act for its populace as a supply source of the requisite necessities defining the good life is part of the social contract that distinguishes a citizen from a denizen. However, the reality is that unequal and asymmetric provision and distribution of physical and social infrastructures ensures the continuation and exacerbation of inequalities. Thus, citizenship is unequally distributed. Though envisaged as a provisioning machine, the city (or other relevant unit of governance) does not produce and provision all its citizens to the same degree.

Second, and developing this argument further, Amin observes how infrastructures both embody and enact symbolic power and social selectiveness, privileging certain groups above others, raising their status as well as providing material support. These inequalities are not simply due to failings or mismanagement but are specifically built into the system. They do not just concern the distribution of infrastructure provisioning, but inequalities are further produced through the design and form of implementation. Koglin's chapter (Chapter 3, this volume) demonstrates both of these qualities in relation to recent provisioning of physical cycle infrastructure in Sweden. Not only has motorised transport been prioritised in the volume of provision, but also the practical design relegates other mobilities to marginal and 'leftover' spaces. Amin's concerns for the symbolic power and social selectiveness embodied in infrastructure can be extended by explicitly connecting them with Soja's (2010) insistent concern for spatial justice. Integrating a stronger understanding of and concern for the spatiality of infrastructure allows us better to consider how the spaces of mobility and the topography of provision serve to promote or hide questions of social justice and injustice. Through this combination, infrastructure is revealed as having a moral political dimension.

Amin's third interpretive lens focuses on how infrastructures 'are implicated in the human experience of the city and in shaping social identities' (Amin, 2014: 139). He highlights how infrastructure has important aesthetic dimensions: sensory landscapes contribute to shaping human capacities to move through and to dwell in the spaces of the city. Recent work on sensory ethnographies of cycling (Cox, 2018; Popan, 2019) reveal the ways in which cycling infrastructures shape behaviours. These shaping influences operate at collective rather than individual levels, reinforcing Shove's (2010) argument that collective practices needs to be seen as more than choices or the aggregate of individual behaviours (Southerton, 2013). The aesthetic and sensory dimensions of cycling infrastructure shape users' perceptions. They have the discursive power to celebrate or to denigrate their users depending on the qualities of the mobility spaces and practices produced. These powers are reinforced by the physical qualities of built environments and their impact on the types and styles of performances that their designs permit (or constrain). Put another way, mobility infrastructures organise and discipline mobility practices, and in so doing, create specific mobile political subjectivities.

Infrastructure as the exercise of power

To understand the politics of infrastructure we need to attend to the interactions that Amin outlines and understand how they express and perform a variety of distributions of power. Power as discussed here should be read through Lukes' (2004) analysis, modified with perspectives arising from activist perspectives (see especially Starhawk, 1988). That is, it moves away from a classical Weberian understanding of power defined simply as the capacity to determine the actions of another. More complex views of power extend this conceptualisation. Power is not just an object or state to be attained, but a quality of all relationships. It is not just framed in terms of domination but also as capacity (power-to-act or power from within) and also power-with (the power not to act but to bind together). This multi-dimensional analysis of power has been important in the development of feminist reflections on power as relational (compare Hartsock, 1983; Da Costa et al, 2015). So how might these other forms of power be realised in practice in relation to the governance of cycling?

First, we can consider how capacity or power-with can be built through infrastructuring. Community Development practice perspectives (www.iacdglobal.org), draw on the ideas of Paulo Freire in their exploration of the practical problems of empowerment and disempowerment and consequently stress that structural relations of privilege and subordination cannot be overcome by grant or favour. Empowerment cannot be given or delivered as a gift from spaces of privilege. It can only arise through endogenous development. However, that does not mean one cannot create space for its growth or the appropriate conditions for its nurture. If empowerment needs conceptual space and time for growth, we must also acknowledge that material spaces created by infrastructure provision may be vital to provide opportunities for the growth of social imaginaries. Infrastructure in itself cannot deliver empowerment, but it may provide the spaces – physical and/or social – in which these dimensions of power (as capacities) can more easily develop.

As a traveller, the cyclist is not only created as a subject by the infrastructure, but infrastructures, and the spaces of travel they provide, are essential elements of cycling as a sociotechnical assemblage, constituted by the interweaving of rider, machine and environments of travel (Cox, 2019). Physical infrastructures of cycling are not just spaces in which the rider as agent performs the action of riding; they are part of a whole performance that involves rider, machine and space. Thus the spaces of travel are more than simply agentic objects, since, as Amin (2014) points out, infrastructure can also be conceptualised as a sociotechnical assemblage. It hybridises both human and nonhuman elements, inextricably linking the material to the politics of its formation, through the agencies of all those involved in conceptualisation, planning and delivery, as contributors to this volume consistently make clear. The spaces of travel are agentic in producing the travelling subject and part of that subjectivity. The design and implementation of spaces of travel enable empowerment or produce disempowerment to the extent that they enable or dis-able autonomous and self-determined travel (Sheller, 2018). To illustrate her argument, Sheller uses the example of routing and re-routing to illustrate the subtle mechanisms through which these power relations are enacted. Volition and compulsion in movement produce different effects on the person, moving either of their own will or being moved by external agency. The former line of action locates control in the one moving, the latter, re-routed or diverted, moves at the will of another, unseen agent. Infrastructures that re-route from the desired line subtract from the agency of the traveller, disempowering them.

Infrastructure and justice

Notwithstanding Sheller's (2018) pertinent critique of the limits of his conceptualisation of spatial justice, Soja (2010) impels us to consider space. It is not just a contributory element to inform the political and ideas of social justice but space is a causative agent, creating both new forms of the political and of justice. Thinking in terms of spatial justice reprioritises our consideration of the ways that space is ordered and governed. Not only does a spatial justice perspective reveal that infrastructure is inherently and inescapably political, it also highlights, as Nolte (2016) demonstrates, how the infrastructures that order those spaces express the politics of the regimes that construct them. This linkage is ably demonstrated by Morgan in Chapter 2, this volume. We can illustrate these concerns and processes by relating them to discussions around the value put on the appropriate provision of infrastructure in order to encourage (or at the very least, not to discourage) cycling.

Infrastructures not only reflect the regimes that produce them, but also reproduce the power inequalities inherent (or unexamined) by those regimes. 'Build it and they will come', has provided a powerful slogan for academic advocacy for cycling, especially in the US (see, for example, Cervero et al, 2013), but following the analysis presented here, this simple catchphrase would have to be rewritten. If one builds infrastructure without addressing the fundamental imbalances of power that make cycling unpleasant or unsafe, those who have to use it will see their world shaped by other forces. The contemporary power reality for most cyclists globally is that they ride within the context of mobility regimes dominated by automobility, as Whitelegg (Chapter 5, this volume) demonstrates. The shape of segregated physical cycling infrastructure is all too often determined by its allocation from surplus or redundant space once the needs of motor traffic have been prioritised (Koglin, Chapter 3, this volume). Even when justified and proposed as separate but equal provision, we need to be aware of the political power relations which that phrase has been employed to justify. 'Build it and they will be confirmed to a certain image bound up in the design conceptualisation of that infrastructure'. Perhaps the phrase is not as snappy, and incapable of acting as a recruiting slogan, but it does designate a counter to the over-simplification and erasure of deep-seated structural inequalities of class, race and gender that much infrastructural provision overlooks. However strongly worded is the insistence (from whatever quarter) that only high-quality infrastructure should be built, and that failures are due to the inadequacy of some specific part of the design implementation and construction process, a reading of the politics of infrastructure suggests that the situation is more complex. This is especially true when implementation is made with disregard for existing inequalities of class, race and gender (Golub et al, 2016; Lugo, 2018). Good, quality cycle infrastructure may privilege certain sectors of the population at the expense of others, or contribute to processes for gentrification which exacerbate further exclusionary trends in urban development (let alone the increasing gap between urban and non-urban provision and investment in mobilities).

A purely anti-reformist, one might almost say Leninist, rejection of infrastructure development and provision is not the necessary corollary of this critique. Absolutist rejection, for example, in Forester's (1993 [1984]) dismissal of cycle infrastructure, (in favour of 'vehicular cycling') does not help with the everyday realities of fear on the roads. Consequently, while comprehending that infrastructural provision is not the total answer, it may very well be a necessary part of the answer and a vital redress in the context of the world as it is at present. Indeed, such is the importance of infrastructural identification that it is even embraced by activists who have create their own painted cycle lanes when authorities refuse to act (See, for example, Doolittle, 2007; Moynihan, 2013; O'Sullivan, 2017).

Even when it originates in guerrilla actions subsequently embraced by government, the official provision of infrastructure produces new forms of political subjectivity. How these are perceived by those subjects created crucially depends on the existing relations of subject to state: infrastructures become the interface between governance and citizen. To a third party, infrastructure indicates the value of the subjects governed by it. Hence, the quality of infrastructure is vital, not merely in terms of design adequacy, but also in discursive terms because of the statements it makes about those who are defined by it. Divergent trajectories of infrastructure development, from above and from below, are the starting point for Gartner's (2016) work on the politics of infrastructure development discussed later in this chapter. However, before we consider her contributions, we need to examine existing conflicts over types of provision.

Insurgent infrastructure, such as activist guerrilla painting of white lines to create bike lanes, demonstrates the value of infrastructure in specific locations and also points to the need to consider how multiple forms of infrastructure development can co-exist. We need a more sophisticated model here than one which assumes that all infrastructure is imposed on a passive, malleable populace. In trying to resolve the dilemmas this applies to infrastructure, Kistner (2014) revisits and revises a Lockean form of social contract. She does this to link Chatterjee's (2004) postcolonial subaltern politics with both the materiality of infrastructure and the ambiguities of counter-politics and politics from below in their capacity to frame alternative worlds. Using similar assumptions about infrastructure and governance as developed in this chapter, she spotlights Mitropoulos' (2012) observations on infra-political actions as a way of articulating insurgent infrastructural provision from below: 'the infra-political, in other words, revisions activism not as representation but as the provisioning of infrastructure for movement, generating nomadic inventiveness rather than royal expertise.' (Mitropoulos, 2012: 117, cited in Kistner, 2014: 6). The guerrilla actions of painting bike lanes precisely fit this model, proceeding from below rather than imposed from above. Kistner's point, however, is that while these are to be recognised and celebrated, they are also problematic inasmuch as their actions alleviate problems but do not provide means through which to tackle the structural inequalities at work. Advocacy for cycle infrastructure is poised between two worlds: that which is and that which could be. Solutions can never be pure or perfect. The more effectively they address existing problems the more they may hinder deeper structural changes.

Tensions between defensive and future-oriented actions are manageable within activist and advocacy communities as long as these communities remain the agents of change. While infrastructure users remain the drivers of change, they retain a sense of ownership of the physical infrastructure, since they are an integral part of the social infrastructures of which the physical is a manifestation. When users and advocacy communities are separated from processes of planning, implementation and governance, and when there is no sense of ownership by users (see Freudendal-Pedersen, Chapter 9, this volume), then problems become significant. Infrastructures appear as imposed.

Chatterjee's (2004) arguments within the context of subaltern politics exposed the modern figure of the governed as one that lies between sovereignty and government. The promise of investment and infrastructure always comes with a price: of being governed. In terms of mobilities, the protection of the rights of the mobile subject is necessarily linked to the constraint of the subject. Thus, the history of infrastructure provision can also be read as one that shifts the mobile subject from citizen to the subject of administrative policy. Far from being merely a semantic problem of changing linguistic description, this shift is one that carries the inherent danger of homogenisation of its subject. The subject of administrative policy is not defined in its diversity and multi-layered complexity, but only in terms of where it exists within the structures of governance and of administration. The multiplicity and diversity of cycle-using travellers becomes a single, undifferentiated subject, 'the cyclist'.

Following Soja consistently in his attention to spatial justice, we must also consider space not just *as* a construction, but also *how* it is constructed and, thus, how space acquires different meanings in different locations. Locality matters. Similar physical conditions can produce utterly different experiences depending on their governance and social context. To provide an example, fast cycle routes (*Snelfietsroutes*) are being promoted across the Netherlands, Belgium and Germany as an important provision to extend cycle use to longer distance and/or higher speed cycle traffic than hitherto (see, for example, Province of Gelderland, 2017). These encourage use of a wider diversity of cycle styles that the typical upright Dutch bicycle, particularly e-bikes and more aerodynamically efficient cycle designs such as velomobiles (achieving higher speeds for the same human power). The physical characteristics of high-speed cycle routes are directness and longer distances of uninterrupted travel, sufficient width, wide turn radii and minimal gradient change. These are physical characteristics also provided by the repurposing of rail lines built expressly for a higher speed transport mode. These physical characteristics not only permit higher speed riding but also positively script it (Akrich, 1992). That is, the sensory scape itself suggests a style of riding.

Against a background of high numbers of everyday cyclists, but relatively low speeds of travel, higher speed cycle travel is understood to be critical for further increase in cycle use. Consequently, the new form of infrastructure attracts investment, and users discover a consonance between the infrastructure provision and the development of faster riding styles. In the UK, where cyclist numbers are small, repurposed rail lines form significant parts of the national cycle network. In this very different context the scarcity of segregated spaces means that they are 'aimed at attracting people who do not currently cycle, [and who] are not likely to ride as fast as the experienced urban cyclist. Route designs are not, therefore, based on a high cycling speed' (Sustrans, n.d). The physical characteristics of the spaces, however, are the same as the *snelfietsroutes*. A considerable degree of dissonance therefore exists between the infrastructure and the functions that it scripts. The political dynamics created by the infrastructures set up tension within an already numerically small number of cyclists. Novice cyclists are constituted as a needy group, experienced cyclists are encouraged to revert to riding in among road traffic or denied the capacity to ride in the way that the physical infrastructure encourages.

A further dimension to the politics of infrastructure in this particular case arises from the relation of the infrastructure provision to the state itself. The sole strategic cycle infrastructure in the UK is the National Cycle Network (NCN), initiated and undertaken by a charitable body, Sustrans (Sustrans, n.d.). While the NCN covers 16,575 miles, 68 per cent is on existing public highway. Sustrans only owns or has access rights to 3 per cent of the total; 97 per cent is run in negotiation with a wide variety of landholders. Upkeep and maintenance are therefore subject to a wide range of agreements and arrangements, and much local maintenance work is undertaken through local volunteer labour. Consequently, cycleways frequently fall outside any consideration of transport provision, and although provision for cycling should be included in local transport plans these are necessarily disconnected from any strategic consideration. In a context of hostile road environments, those riding for everyday transport and those giving of their time to ensure the maintenance of Sustrans routes can feel aggrieved at a lack of any sense of reciprocity from the state, whose investment in support for roads is clear.

The nonphysical infrastructures 'formed by people and their social networks' that support urban mobility are as important as the physical infrastructures, according to Mains and Kinfu (2017: 265), especially in situations where direct state investment in these infrastructures is limited. From the combination of failure to nurture these networks and the cognitive dissonance induced by the gap between the ideals of the management of the network and the scripted discourses arising from the physical infrastructure we should not be surprised by a resultant deep ambivalence towards aspects of cycling infrastructure voiced by many of its regular users. This ambivalence is reflected in wider discourses concerning the relevance of cycling-specific infrastructure, even among riders themselves. Consequently, hard cycling infrastructure then becomes even more politicised as an object of direct contention.

The politics of infrastructure development

Thinking through the politics of infrastructure development, Gartner (2016) starts by distinguishing between two directions of infrastructure development, as described in the examples earlier. The first arises from local perspectives, expressive of and sensitive to existing conditions; the second, imposed from afar, serves to consolidate inequitable power relations. While the gaps between these may be overcome by processes labelled participation or consultation, frequently the mechanisms employed are little more than surface redress or conciliation, rather than a serious attempt to bridge the gulf. Emphasising pragmatic processes as a means to overcome disparities, creating spaces for contending parties to discuss their different perspective may be insufficient. Cornell West's (1993) powerful critique points out that the noble, pragmatic, liberal emphasis on the pedagogical and the dialogical errs in assuming that vast disparities in resources can be overcome by offering dominated subjects a voice at the table or in the negotiations. Even the most ambitious transition management process, designed to include and give voice to all stakeholders in a process of change, (see, for example, van de Kerkhof and Wieczorek, 2005) is problematic. The language of stakeholder erases differences in the resources and capacities of participants. Invitations to participate presuppose and emphasise the existing conditions and marginality of those who have to be invited to participate in a process not of their own devising and action.

Gartner (2016) provides a general analytical framework to understand infrastructure development, particularly appropriate for the politics of cycling infrastructure. First, reflecting on the kind of concerns highlighted earlier, she argues in a general sense that the exclusion of particular and critical perspectives in planning and development is indicative of the operation of a greater politics of inclusions and exclusions. In order to address this lacuna, there is a vital need for 'a more representative and inclusive knowledge of infrastructure development' (Gartner, 2016: 378). The processes through which infrastructure is planned and negotiated must become transparent: the academic task is clear for investigation and mapping of the processes.

Gartner identifies a threefold typology of approaches to the implicit politics of infrastructure development: the technocratic, the interventionist and the critical. Based on a much broader theorisation of infrastructure development in the context of critical (post-) development studies, these observations are equally applicable as we explore the contestations over infrastructure development described in other contributions to this volume.

Technocratic approaches to infrastructure primarily focus on the material value and provision of physical systems: necessary as part of the modernisation process. Most frequently, justification is premised on cost-benefit analysis and the calculation of likely systemic benefits according to the value measures adopted. Applied to cycling infrastructure, the problem of the lack of cycling for transport is simply a technical one to be remedied by the provision of infrastructure. Both advocates and institutional planners can be seen to treat cycling infrastructures as a technocratic problem, Solutions, by definition are to be found in infrastructural implementation. For example, provision of cycling infrastructure is a necessary part of the redefining of transport infrastructures for a low carbon economy.

The problems of technocratic approaches are, according to Gartner, twofold. First, the approach tends to homogenise those at whom the infrastructure is aimed. Social agents in their own right, capable of participation and self-determination are transformed into passive recipients through their assumed willingness to use the facilities. While good design might create desire among some, the second dimension of difficulty created is that, by referring solely to the users of infrastructure, it overlooks those who are rendered as non-users. Rather than considering why provision might not match desire and considering reasons for this disjuncture, non-use is rendered as deviant behaviour. Both of these problems are linked, in the case of cycling infrastructures, to systemic disregard to the physicality and material effective realities of the infrastructure. Focusing solely on the importance of provision, technocratic modelling rarely considers the actuality of delivery; who it serves, how it constructs its users and who it therefore includes and excludes (even when fit for purpose). In designing for cycle traffic, Parkin (2018) highlights the danger of the automatic assumptions of best practice as universally applicable. While there may be physical and material realities that should always be taken into account when planning spaces for cycle use, the diversity of designs of uses and of expectations requires careful consideration and understanding of the local conditions and the heterogeneity of users.

A further powerful effect of approaching infrastructure development and implementation as a purely technological challenge, to be solved through technocratic lens, is that of de-politicisation. As Zhang (2016) argues, structural tensions are redefined as technical issues of supply and shortage. Thus, social conflicts that may be at the heart of mobility problems are rendered invisible, and infrastructure becomes a means by which to divert the gaze or to disguise more fundamental socio-economic and socio-ecological problems. Or, in Picon's more provocative but succinct phrasing, 'engineers do politics while pretending only to be serving objective purposes' (Picon, 2018: 269).

Gartner's second category of approaches is the *interventionist*, an approach dominant in cycle advocacy. As with the purely technocratic approach, infrastructure is considered as instrumentally valuable, but its value derives more broadly from the degree to which it facilitates other developmental objectives. For example, health, environment and economic gains might all be considered as justifications for intervention, rather than for cycling itself. Interventionist approaches usefully (for planning and for cost-benefit dominated approaches) provide numerous opportunities to produce indicators and metrics through which the success or otherwise of interventions can be measured.

A problem that Gartner identifies with interventionist approaches is that like technocratic approaches to infrastructure development they reproduce a curious circular logic, unable to deal with issues of exclusion. Because interventionist approaches consider that exclusion exists because of a lack of intervention, then intervention by definition should end exclusion. Continued exclusion after intervention is not therefore the fault of the intervention, but of the excluded who are unwilling to take advantage of the interventions. Interventions, designed according to best practice, it is implicitly claimed, must automatically offer the ideal solutions to the problems they address. This circular logic lacks a deep understanding of the 'diverse complexity of place-specific environments and, like technocratic perspectives, underestimate the heterogeneity of societies. In other words, the interventionist perspective is premised on the assumption that infrastructure is inherently good, valuable, and has a benefit to society – no matter what that society' (Gartner, 2016: 382). When applied to the design of cycling infrastructure, including the soft infrastructures of training and skilling, interventionist logics also curiously downplay actual cycling practices. By constantly stressing its value in terms of other goals, inherent qualities of cycling are disvalued. Cycle travel is rendered as a necessary but potentially undesirable action, justified only by its contribution to greater goods. Only through its contribution to other, external goals does it become worthwhile.

The lack of criticality in both technocratic and interventionist approaches also hints at an underlying and unexamined positivism. In a discussion of New Urbanism, Wang (2009) employs Ellul's critique of technique to highlight a series of assumptions about the influence of built environment on behaviour. Perceptively he observes that 'today's technical consciousness simply cannot see the logical contradiction that, while its own zeitgeist rejects positivism, nevertheless it embraces [a] cause and effect mechanism' (Wang, 2009: 462) assuming that the provision of certain environments and facilities will automatically engender specific behaviours. While it is argued here that spaces do have measurable effects and affect, these should not be considered in a positivist, predictable and linear causal relationship.

In contrast to these two interlinked (and dominant) perspectives, Gartner proposes a third, *critical* way of thinking about infrastructure, more sensitive to its political dimensions and implications. A critical perspective does not refute the utility and the practicality of technocratic and interventionist approaches, nor would it undermine the necessity of their deployment as a means to unlock technocratic bureaucracies or to ensure funding or planning from bodies based on interventionist logics. Nevertheless, a critical approach demands that these not be used without conscious reflection. Rather, Gartner argues 'the value of infrastructure cannot be pre-assigned without careful consideration of the socio-political environment' (Gartner, 2016: 382). Because infrastructure is 'fundamentally a relational concept' (Star, 1999: 380 cited in Gartner, 2016: 382), its impact and the values it embodies and propagates depend on the actors engaged and their prior power relations.

Gartner's critical perspective argues perceptively that 'infrastructure can be simultaneously beneficial and harmful for populations … infrastructure objects are not apolitical instalments but can symbolise existing power struggles and can be understood as the material outcomes of social-political relationships that exist within fragmented and inequitable societies' (Gartner, 2016: 382). This provides a lens through which to reinterpret Warrington Cycle Campaign's nearly 20-year online photographic chronicle of poorly designed and implemented cycle infrastructure (http://wcc.crankfoot.xyz/facility-of-the-month/index.htm; see also Warrington Cycle Campaign, 2007; Warrington Cycle Campaign, 2016). Implementation that ignores the safety or the basic requirements of users is not simply a problem of adequacy but is an outworking of power structures: visible implementation of the disregard of its (potential) users by providers. McFarlane and Rutherford (2008) use Latour's description of technology as 'politics pursued by other means' (Latour, 1988: 38 in McFarlane and Rutherford 2008: 370) as a way to emphasise how the technical dimensions of infrastructure manifest the balance of power. In similar vein, Gartner (2016) notes that lack of infrastructure provision, or the withholding of infrastructure, is also an assertion of power over potential user groups and a statement on their social value.

Parts of this ambiguous contribution, simultaneously both positive and negative, arise from the manner in which infrastructures, including cycling infrastructures, necessarily discipline and govern (Bonham and Cox, 2010). The benefits of route provision are the constraints that the route imposes on the traveller. Within a comprehensive system of mobility provision (such as a road network), these constraints are not experienced as restrictive. When networks are limited to few nodes, and connections and adequate routes are in short supply, constraint is felt much more strongly. The traveller loses agency in themselves, and their movement is governed and directed by the scarce supply of infrastructure. The agency of technocratic governance emerges once more as the strongest power. Provision is governed by scarcity, and potential beneficiaries must compete for access.

As previously noted, a peculiarity of the provision of dedicated cycling infrastructure in northern European nations, especially in Belgium and in the UK, is the opportunistic repurposing of redundant rail lines. Providing direct interurban routings, these routes also highlight the disjuncture between different transport modes and their characteristics in terms of spatial service provision. Roads provide a fine-grained network connecting every point within a community through multiple junctions and branchings, each of which increases access. The necessary linearity of railways often creates local disconnection. While operational, rail lines bisect the landscape, uncrossable except at specific points. They are designed around a much coarser granularity, with stations (not junctions) as nodes. In their repurposing as cycleways, these same lines, while providing inter-communal communication, are frequently problematically disconnected and cannot function as intra-communal facilitators of travel. They inherit infrequent access from their former identity and, as cycleways, may continue to bypass the communities through which they travel. Exclusions remain built in to the infrastructure through the spatial reality.

Observing from the margins

One corollary of spatial governance and constraint is the way in which cycle infrastructure in particular has come to inhabit a spatial marginality. At the edge of the road, or segregated by verges from traffic, cycleway design separates cycle traffic from other modes for good reason (Parkin, 2018). Whether or not cycle-specific infrastructure following existing mixed mode use is located on the road, or separated and parallel to the roadway, the rider always travels at the physical edge of larger traffic flow. Numerically, motor vehicle traffic may not be as large but the sheer physical mass of motorised vehicles, often (but not always) travelling more rapidly, highlights the comparative fragility of the cyclist. Mass and physical volume dominate space. As travellers, cyclists necessarily perceive their progress in comparison with other modes. The metaphor of flow and traffic streams locates the cyclist at the margin of that flow. Continuing the metaphor, the edges of the main flow is the space of turbulence, of eddies. Indeed, airflow patterns in mixed mode traffic move this experience from metaphor to physical reality as anyone who has felt the buffeting from passing vehicles while riding will be aware. Following Soja's emphasis on spatiality, we can focus this at micro-level to interrogate the implications of the spatial location of cycleways at the edges of other traffic provision in terms of their access to power.

For bell hooks, marginality occupies a special position in both the politics of space and feminist theory: 'to be in the margins is to be part of the whole but outside the main body' (hooks, 1990: 341). Her analysis is of the exclusions attached to race, class and gender and the physical separations that enact and enforce them, a far more powerful place of exclusion than the edges of mobility spaces discussed here. Yet her insights provide a valuable means to articulate the politics of cyclists' spaces. She continues exploring how the margin 'is also the space of radical possibility, a space of resistance, … a central location for the production of a counter-hegemonic discourse that is not just found in words but in habits of being and the way one lives' (hooks, 1990: 341). This same theme is taken up by Rob Shields (1991: 277): 'Margins, then, while a position of exclusion, can also be a position of power and critique. They expose the relations of the entrenched, universalising values of the centre'. From the edge of the road, contrasts between travel modes are highlighted. The physical and discursive power asymmetries are made visible. The distance from the centres of power and the concentrations of value is that which lends perspective. But to place this perspective into a constructive critique, this marginalisation needs to be harnessed to more than a feeling of isolation or ressentiment. To continue using hooks' insights: 'Many of us are motivated to move against domination solely when we feel our self-interest directly threatened. Often, then, the longing is not for a collective transformation of society, and end to the politics of dominations, but rather simply for an end to what we feel is hurting us' (hooks 1994: 244). To be a cyclist, re-routed to the margins of mobility spaces, is also to be allowed an insight into the distributions of mobility power. Such a view is largely invisible to those in the mainstream of travel.

The political challenge of cycling infrastructure provision is to balance between a series of contending needs. Provision is required that provides protection from the very real fears and dangers produced by the dominance of automobility. Simultaneously, this needs to be both inclusive and to send a message that all users are valuable. Yet both of these also need to recognise and communicate that the ultimate goal of cycle infrastructure provision should not be to provide a safe and comfortable means to ride while maintaining a world dominated by automobility. Instead, in the context of the paradigm shift needed in transport thinking, cycling mobility and its infrastructures need to present a radical challenge to automobility. The cycle track at the road margin looks forward to the day when auto-traffic no longer dominates – a transformation of the mobility scape. Perhaps the ultimate goal is for the day when car traffic might have to be diverted and re-routed on separate, minimal infrastructure in favour of the direct mobility of the cyclist reclaiming the roads that connect the locations in which we live and work. For the time being, riding at the margins constantly reminds us of the scales of change required for a profound mobility transformation. To understand and theorise the politics of infrastructure is to engage in a process of both analysis and to engage a prospectus. A common theme among the writers examined here is that their commitment to understanding a politics of space echoes a parallel commitment to a politics of transformation, of which infrastructure is but one aspect.

References

Akrich, M. (1992) 'The de-scription of technical objects', in W. Bijker and J. Law (eds) *Shaping Technology/Building Society: Studies in Sociotechnical Change*, Cambridge, MA: The MIT Press, pp 205–24.

Amin, A. (2014) 'Lively infrastructure', *Theory, Culture & Society*, 31(7/8): 137–61.

Bennett, J. (2010) *Vibrant Matter: A Political Ecology of Things*, Durham: Duke University Press.

Bonham, J. and Cox, P. (2010) 'The disruptive traveller? A foucauldian analysis of cycleways', *Road and Transport Research*, 19(2): 42–53.

Cervero, R., Cadwell B. and Cuellar, J. (2013) 'Bike-and-ride: build it and they will come', *Journal of Public Transportation*, 16(4): 83–105.

Chatterjee, P. (2004) *The Politics of the Governed. Reflections on Popular Politics in Most of the World*, New York: Columbia University Press.

Cox, P. (2018) 'Senses matter: a sensory ethnography of urban velomobility', in M. Freudendal-Pedersen, K. Hartmann-Petersen and E.L.P. Fjalland (eds) *Experiencing Networked Urban Mobilities: Practices, Flows, Methods*, Abingdon: Routledge, pp 101–5.

Cox, P. (2019) *Cycling: A Sociology of Velomobility*, Abingdon: Routledge.

Da Costa, L.B., Icaza, R. and Ocampo Talero A.M. (2015) 'Knowledge about, knowledge with; dilemmas of researching lives, nature and genders otherwise', in W. Harcourt and I.L. Nelson (eds) *Practicing Feminist Political Ecologies*, London: Zed, pp 260–85.

Doolittle, R. (2007) 'Bike activists going guerrilla', *The Star* [Toronto], Monday, 18 June 2007, www.thestar.com/news/2007/06/18/bike_activists_going_guerrilla.html

Forester, J. (1993 [1984]) *Effective Cycling* [6th edn], Cambridge, MA: The MIT Press.

Fox, N.J. and Alldred, P. (2017) *Sociology and the New Materialism. Theory, Research, Action*, London: Sage.

Gartner, C. (2016) 'The science and politics of infrastructure research: asserting power, place and agency in infrastructure knowledge', *Journal of Human Development and Capabilities*, 17(3): 377–96.

Golub, A., Hoffmann, M.L., Lugo. A.E. and Sandoval G.F. (eds) (2016) *Bicycle Justice and Urban Transformation: Biking for All?*, Abingdon: Routledge.

Hartsock, N. (1983) *Money, Sex and Power: Toward a Feminist Historical Materialism*, Boston: Northeast University Press.

hooks, b. (1990) 'Marginality as a site of resistance', in R. Ferguson, M. Gever, T.T. Minh-ha and C. West (eds) *Out There: Marginalization and Contemporary Cultures*, Cambridge, MA: The MIT Press, pp 341–4.

hooks, b. (1994) *Outlaw Culture: Resisting Representation*, London: Routledge.

Kistner, U. (2014) 'The "political society" of the governed? Marginalia beyond "marginalisation"', *HTS Teologiese Studies/Theological Studies*, 70(1) Art. #2618, https://hts.org.za/index.php/HTS/article/view/2618

Koglin, T. (2017) 'Urban mobilities and materialities – a critical reflection of "sustainable" urban development', *Applied Mobilities*, 2(1): 32–49.

Lugo, A. (2018) *Bicycle/Race: Transportation, Culture, and Resistance*, Portland, OR: Microcosm.

Lukes, S. (2004) *Power: A Radical View* [2nd edn], London: Palgrave Macmillan.

Mains, D. and Kinfu, E. (2017) 'Governing three-wheeled motorcycle taxis in urban Ethiopia: States, markets, and moral discourses of infrastructure', *American Ethnologist*, 44(2): 263–74.

McFarlane, C. and Rutherford, J. (2008) 'Political infrastructures: governing and experiencing the fabric of the city', *International Journal of Urban and Regional Research*, 32(2): 363–74.

Moynihan, C. (2013) 'Unauthorized Bike Lanes Created in Midtown', *New York Times*, 22 September 2013, https://cityroom.blogs.nytimes.com/2013/09/22/unauthorized-bike-lanes-created-in-midtown/

Nolte, A. (2016) 'Political infrastructure and the politics of infrastructure', *City*, 20(3): 441–54.

O'Sullivan, F. (2017) '*Guerrilla Bike Lanes' Prove a Reluctant City Wrong*, Citylab online, www.citylab.com/transportation/2017/05/guerrilla-bike-lanes-spring-up-overnight-in-riga/527568/

Parkin, J. (2018) *Designing for Cycle Traffic: International Principles and Practice*, London: ICE Publishing.

Picon, A. (2018) 'Urban infrastructure, imagination and politics: from the networked metropolis to the smart city', *International Journal of Urban and Regional Research*, 42(2): 263–75.

Popan, C. (2019) *Bicycle Utopias: Imagining Fast and Slow Cycling Futures*, Abingdon: Routledge.

Province of Gelderland (2017) *Snelfietsroutes: Fast cycling between home and work*, Province of Gelderland.

Sheller, M. (2018) *Mobility Justice: The Politics of Movement in an Age of Extremes*, London: Verso.

Shields, R. (1991) *Places on the Margin. Alternative Geographies of Modernity*, London: Routledge.

Shove, E. (2010) 'Beyond the ABC: climate change policies and theories of social change', *Environment and Planning A: Economy and Space*, 42(6): 1273–85.

Soja, E. (2010) *Seeking Spatial Justice*, Minneapolis: University of Minnesota Press.

Southerton, D. (2013) 'Habits, routines and temporalities of consumption: from individual behaviours to the reproduction of everyday practices', *Time & Society*, 22(3): 335–55.

Starhawk (1988) *Truth or Dare: Encounters with Power, Authority and Mystery*, San Francisco: HarperSanFrancisco.

Sustrans (n.d.) *Route Planning Criteria for the National Cycle Network.* http://www.sustrans.org.uk/sites/default/files/documents/criteria.pdf (Accessed: 21 November 2018).

van de Kerkhof, M. and Wieczorek, A. (2005) 'Learning and stakeholder participation in transition processes toward sustainability: methodological considerations', *Technological Forecasting & Social Change*, 72: 733–47.

Wang, D. (2009) 'Ellul on New Urbanism', *Christian Scholars Review*, 38(4): 457–70.

Warrington Cycle Campaign (2007) *Crap Cycles Lanes: 50 Worst Cycle Lanes in Britain*, Amersham UK: Eye Books.

Warrington Cycle Campaign (2016) *Crapper Cycle Lanes: 50 More of the Worst Cycle Lanes in Britain*, Amersham: Eye Books.

West, C. (1993) 'The limits of neopragmatism', in C. West *Keeping Faith Philosophy and Race in America*, London: Routledge, pp 135–42.

Young, D. and Keil, R. (2014) 'Locating the urban in-between: Tracking the urban politics of infrastructure in Toronto', *International Journal of Urban and Regional Research*, 38(5): 1589–1608, https://doi.org/10.1111/1468-2427.12146

Zhang, J. (2016) 'Taxis, traffic and thoroughfares: the politics of transportation infrastructure in China's rapid urbanization in the Reform era', *City & Society*, 28(3): 411–36.

2

The cultural politics of infrastructure: the case of Louis Botha Avenue in Johannesburg, South Africa

Njogu Morgan

Introduction

Cycle infrastructure, especially cycle tracks and cycleways, have commanded significant attention in cycle planning. They have, for some, been seen as a 'silver bullet' to promote utility cycling since, when separated from vehicle flows, they can shield cyclists from motor traffic thereby improving road safety. For this reason, the maxim that 'build it and they will come' (Cervero et al, 2013) has developed to refer to the potential for mode shift associated with infrastructure development. It is not surprising that cycle tracks and cycleways are held in such high regard since studies have found that concerns over road safety are a major barrier against utility cycling (Winters et al, 2011; Lee et al, 2015). Buehler and Dill (2015: 1) surveying a broad literature on 'bikeway infrastructure and cycling levels … [conclude that] Most studies suggest a positive relationship between bikeway networks or aspects of the network and cycling levels.'

While some studies exhibit confidence in the role of infrastructure in stimulating cycling, others urge caution. Handy et al, (2014) point to a range of methodological challenges in establishing cause and effect relationships. For example, 'communities where cycling is seen as normal are more likely to invest in cycling infrastructure which in turn tends to reinforce the cycling norm' (Handy et al, 2014: 10). In this instance the direction of causality is unclear: is it culture or infrastructure (Dill and Carr, 2003; Emanuel, 2012)? Rather than this binary approach, Aldred (2017) has sought out a more nuanced understanding of the determinants of everyday cycling in which infrastructure, culture and contexts of cycling interact in complex ways.

Other scholarship suggests that infrastructure could have a 'darker side' in spite of the road safety benefits, as illustrated by Koglin in relation to rationality and planning (Chapter 3, this volume) or Whitelegg on safety and risk (Chapter 5, this volume). For example, various studies conducted in the United States have shown how cycle infrastructure development projects have been associated with processes of neighbourhood gentrification (Hoffman and Lugo, 2014; Stehlin, 2014; Flanagan et al, 2016; Lubitow, 2016). Not only have poorer communities been displaced, but also cycling infrastructure has been allocated to more affluent populations. A number of cycling historians show how cycling infrastructure could in fact be used to strengthen alternatives such as the system of automobility. By the same token, cycle tracks could be a tool to maintain the subaltern status of cycling. For example, Oldenziel and De la Bruhèze (2011: 37) argue 'In Germany … in the interwar period … Traffic engineers designed separate bike paths not to create riding comfort for cyclists, but to take them off the road through segregation.'

This chapter follows these critical lines of inquiry about cycle infrastructure to examine an historical case of cycle lane provision in Johannesburg, South Africa. In 1935, a cycle lane was allocated on Louis Botha Avenue. While the road remained an important cycling corridor well into the 1960s, and there were policy recommendations for such high volume corridors to have barrier protected cycle tracks, the cycle infrastructure was never upgraded and was eventually abandoned. How do we make sense of the appearance of the cycle lane as well as the failure to upgrade the facility? This chapter draws on insights from science and technology studies, and in particular the notion of co-evolution between society and technology as advanced in the social construction of technology (SCOT) theory for the analysis. The chapter argues that the cycle lane and the subsequent road 'improvement' patterns should be read as a materialisation of the parallel political and social changes through which the rights of cycle users on Louis Botha Avenue were in question, as were also their rights of residence in an area called Alexandra Township adjacent to the road. The design evolution of Louis Botha Avenue, as read through the historic cycle lane, was a manifestation or materialisation of the politics of difference within colonial and apartheid systems. As such, this chapter strongly echoes the arguments made by Cox (Chapter 1, this volume) concerning the political nature of infrastructure.

The analysis of this chapter is based on information on the changing design of Louis Botha Avenue, perspectives of different social groups on the road, and changing user and use practices, drawn from a variety of sources including newspaper records, archives, secondary material and historical street level photography. To make sense of these multiple sources and perspectives, the first part of the chapter gives a background of the cycle lanes in terms of their ostensible rationales, design and users. The theoretical framework is then introduced, followed by analysis of the empirical material. The chapter concludes with a call for more critical analysis of the work that contemporary cycle infrastructure conducts and suggestions for further research.

Background

On 21 August 1935, a cycle lane was opened on Louis Botha Avenue (*Rand Daily Mail*, 1935b; *The Star*, 1938b). It was described 'as the city's first experimental cycle track, a white line a few feet from, and parallel to, the left hand kerb, cutting of a strip of the road for the use of pedal cyclists' (*Rand Daily Mail*, 1935b: 12). A picture in a newspaper of the cycle lane features a man on a bicycle. Written inside the cycle lane are the words: 'Cycle-Way' (*The Star*, 1935). The cycle lane had been constructed ostensibly for the safety of numerous workers on bicycles travelling along Louis Botha Avenue (*Rand Daily Mail*, 1935a). The safety dimension of the lane was glowingly reported on by a newspaper in the United States: 'A white line marks off the safety zone, and within its boundaries cyclists may scoot along without worrying about death-dealing motor traffic' (*The Washington Post*, 1935). Another newspaper article headline capturing this theme read: 'Safer Streets for Cyclists' (*Rand Daily Mail*, 1935b: 12).

The cycle users of Louis Botha Avenue primarily resided in an urban settlement called Alexandra Township. Located about 10 miles from the central business district of Johannesburg, the township was established in 1912 'as a freehold township for Africans and coloureds' (Bonner and Nieftagodien, 2008: 17). In the context of colonialism and later, apartheid, it was a place where 'native' populations could own land (Bonner and Nieftagodien, 2008). In addition to the land-owning possibility, it was also popular for the 'native' population since 'it was not subject to the controls of the Johannesburg municipality' (Callinicos, 1987: 186). From Alexandra, the workers would travel to places of work, sometimes to the surrounding suburbs but mainly to the business centre, directly along Louis Botha Avenue.

From the perspective of cycling comfort and road safety, the cycle lane had its limitations. Descriptions suggest that the cycle lane was located on one side of the avenue and it did not travel along the entire length of the road (*Rand Daily Mail*, 1935b). One report described

Figure 2.1: Men cycling along Louis Botha Avenue, 1946

Source: Museum Africa Picture Archives

it as being '40-inch' (Motor Editor, 1946a: 9) in width. This width was recognised as being insufficient to accommodate the volumes of cycle users, as one person noted in a letter to a newspaper: '[the] … weight of numbers destroys the Traffic Department's fond hope that the 40-inch cycle track at the kerbside will contain the two-wheeled horde' (Motor Editor, 1946a: 9). The 'horde' was separated from motor traffic by white paint. This prompted a sympathetic letter to the editor of a newspaper with the author beseeching 'those responsible for the layout of Louis Botha Avenue … to get on bicycles and ride through Orange Grove just to get the horrible feeling of being run over any moment that the poor unfortunates have to tolerate week in week out' (Not for Yesterday, 1940). There were grounds for such concern. In 1941 a council committee investigating traffic conditions on Louis Botha Avenue found that the leading cause of accidents on the road was cars parked on the cycle lane which 'forced cyclists to swing out of the special cycle lane' (*The Star*, 1941).

In 1938, the chief traffic officer of the municipality expressed regret at having to repaint the cycle lanes every few years because they were being worn away by motor vehicles driving on them. What he actually preferred were cycle tracks separated by barriers, or physically separate from the road, as had been implemented in a nearby municipality (*The Star*, 1938b). Road engineers also had formal recommendations for how to provide safer cycle lanes. In 1937, the Main Reef Road Commission, a deliberation on road safety involving Johannesburg and other adjacent municipalities, recommended that cycle tracks separated by a verge be constructed on major arterial routes carrying high cycle traffic (Main Reef Road Commission, 1937). These findings were echoed in 1947 by a national road safety inquiry, which also recommended cycle tracks (Motor Editor, 1947). Despite this, the road was not redesigned. Eventually, the cycle lane was abandoned (Vorster, 1963). By 1973, that there once had been a cycle lane on Louis Botha Avenue would but be a memory (Hughes, 1973). How do we understand this evolution?

Openness and emerging conflicts

According to SCOT models of technological change, in the first phase of technological development there is great variation, with respect to not only designs but also its conceptualisations, for example by those pertaining to use by different social groups. This phenomenon is known as interpretive flexibility. Usually, interpretive flexibility tends to be most abundant while the technology is new, but it can be re-introduced later on (Norton, 2011; Pinch and Bijker, 2012).

Figure 2.2: Louis Botha Avenue, 1888, then known as Pretoria Road. It was renamed in 1917 (Burgess, 2016)

Source: Museum Africa Picture Archives

The variety of use of Louis Botha Avenue is evident in its early history. One function was transport for residents of a range of suburbs that emerged along its spine from the turn of the 20th century, and then later Alexandra Township. It connected these residential areas with the central business district and also became a key pathway between Johannesburg and the capital of the then Transvaal Republic, Pretoria (Applebaum, 2016). While the transportation function was important, it was not dominant. It was also a site of interactions as is evident in a series of historical street level images as depicted in Figures 2.3 and 2.4 (Museum Africa, 2016). Mirroring this openness, in this phase, there were no design features such as lines, curbs and traffic islands as would later emerge for the purpose of governing different uses.

Scholars argue that interpretative flexibility becomes more evident during controversies or problems pertaining to a technology (Bijker et al, 2012). In such moments, underlying relations between society and technology are thrown into sharper relief (Pinch, 2015). Along Louis Botha Avenue and other streets in Johannesburg, conflicts unfolded increasingly from the 1920s onwards. This was generally associated with rising motorisation and population growth linked to economic expansion across the city (Morgan, 2017; 2018). These macro developments became manifest in and around Louis Botha Avenue. One consequence was that '… the white northern suburbs grew steadily in the direction of Alexandra' (Callinicos, 1987: 187). At the same time, the population of Alexandra Township increased due to

Figure 2.3: Street scene, 1907, on Louis Botha Avenue

Source: Museum Africa Picture Archives

Figure 2.4: Louis Botha Avenue, 1909

Source: Museum Africa Picture Archives

the economic dynamism. Significantly, there was a wave of migration into the township as black people sought a home after having been evicted from residential areas close to the central business district due to racist segregation policies in the context of colonialism (Callinicos, 1987). These developments would lead to more people crowding into Louis Botha Avenue.

The pronounced pressure on Louis Botha Avenue elicited a variety of proposals from different social groups. Some of these materialised on the road. One solution advocated by the traffic department and traffic police officials was a white line system '… to serve the dual purpose of showing traffic where to stop when held up by pointsmen, and suggesting to pedestrians where to cross' (*Rand Daily Mail*, 1922: 10). While white lines were to be used to govern conduct at intersections, they were also to separate traffic streams according to speed. In advocating for the adoption of the white line system, police officials cited its successful use in the United Kingdom and elsewhere in Europe as grounds for implementation (*Rand Daily Mail*, 1927a; 1927b; 1927c). By 1929, a municipal by-law had been introduced regulating the use of white lines to control traffic (*Rand Daily Mail*, 1929). One variation of the use of the white lanes was the concept of 'threeways.' It was described as 'a system of two white lines running along a roadway dividing into three traffic lanes … on each side is for the traffic proceeding along the left-hand side of the road, and the middle lane is reserved exclusively for a faster vehicle to overtake a slower one' (*Rand Daily Mail*, 1936). The 1935 cycle lane on Louis Botha Avenue can be considered part of the white line heritage.

Following Norton (2011) in his study of American streets, the cycle lane can also be understood as an expression of early traffic management principles adopted by engineers based on their experiences in managing other municipal services such as waste and water. Norton argues that engineers drew upon such experiences because there was a lack of formalised knowledge on traffic management. For these engineers, the most important principle derived from managing other municipal services was the need to maximise efficiencies of existing utilities, rather than to undertake expensive building or reconstruction. In this line of deliberation, the road should have been able to accommodate different users in harmony. For E.J. Hamlin, city engineer from 1932 to 1958 (Grant and Flinn, 1992), who inaugurated the cycle lane as a space demarcated by white paint, this perspective would have resonated with his prior experience in municipal waste management (Plug, 2014). This view of maximising the use of existing assets by engineers probably also informed the introduction of traffic islands, which were used both to slow down vehicles and to offer pedestrians spaces where they could await gaps in vehicle flows before crossing (City Engineer, 1935: 2). Figure 2.5 shows one of these wide central islands with vegetation growing in the middle. Hamlin, however, faced considerable pressure against the islands from automotive interests. A principal concern pertained to what was perceived as their excessive width, which was seen to slow down cars (*Rand Daily Mail*, 1935c; Not for Yesterday, 1940).

Louis Botha Avenue as a motoring corridor

According to SCOT, following initial proliferation of views about and designs of a technology, further processes unfold that limit variation. This diversity of interpretations and uses dissipates over time, leaving a dominant one (Norton, 2011; Bijker, 2015). Much like this account, Louis Botha Avenue would develop from its early open character (with respect to diversity of uses and design approaches) to a thoroughfare for automobiles. Some solutions that had been experimented with would give way, while others would survive. For example, while the white line system would persist, the 'three-way' variation would 'die'. The wide traffic islands would be narrowed down to enable faster flows. Figure 2.6 shows workers removing plants from a central island on Louis Botha Avenue as they prepare to narrow the island in order to increase road width. What were the processes through which

Figure 2.5: A section of Louis Botha Avenue, 1935

Source: Museum Africa Picture Archives

Louis Botha Avenue became transformed in this way? Scholars have theorised that processes of closure can be achieved through various mechanisms (Rosen, 1993).

One such mechanism was the cycle lane itself. The Chief Traffic Inspector at the time, describing the design of the cycle lane, argued that 'the line placed about a yard from the kerb is designed to stop cyclists riding abreast, which is a common cause of accidents' (*Rand Daily Mail*, 1935b). In 1939 a newspaper reported that residents of one of the suburbs adjacent to Louis Botha Avenue and motorists were very pleased with the work that the special 'native' police were doing ensuring that 'native' cyclists kept inside the cycle lane (*Rand Daily Mail*, 1939a; Two Hoots, 1939). Underlining their role in enabling automobility, one pleased motorist said, 'These tracks have proved a boon and a blessing to motorists' (Two Hoots, 1939). In other words, from a police officer's perspective the cycle lane had been introduced as a solution to problems of order, and from an engineer's perspective to enable efficient flows of traffic on the limited resource of the road: both foregrounded rights of motor cars.

An oft-cited social mechanism in the SCOT literature for creating closure is known as rhetorical closure. This involves the making of claims or assertions about problems associated with a technology

Figure 2.6: Narrowing down islands on Louis Botha Avenue, 1948

Source: Museum Africa Picture Archives

regardless of their veracity. Rather than factuality, what is crucial is that the social groups involved in the controversy believe the claims. In this way, the claims help to settle a controversy (Pinch and Bijker, 2012). Regarding the problem of who the rightful users of Louis Botha Avenue were, rhetoric was a key device to assert the preferences of the automobile using public, who, as noted earlier, were primarily white. In narratives in media, people cycling were characterised as a prime reason for congestion, accidents and other woes on the road (compare *Rand Daily Mail*, 1938; 1947). In this line of thought, the different modes of transport simply could not co-exist along the road (Motor Editor, 1946b). The avalanche of hostile rhetoric against bicycles on Louis Botha Avenue rarely, if ever, examined the conduct of motorists. Recall, for instance, the reports of cars parked on the cycle lane or the cycle lane being used to overtake other cars.

As is evident in the foregoing discussion, the various closure mechanisms were interwoven. This interrelationship was evident in another closure mechanism: a 1937 municipal law prohibited people cycling side by side (City of Johannesburg, 1936; 1938). The rationale for the law was based on the rhetorical claim that people cycling were creating congestion. Furthermore, by impeding 'traffic' they themselves were not a form of traffic. The law then provided the legal basis for police officials to discipline cycles to the margins of the road, as can be seen in newsreel footage from 1940 (Pathé, 1940).

Finally, turning to the wider social context to explain the transformation of Louis Botha Avenue, the cycle lane remained as a painted white line and eventually disappeared because bicycle users on Louis Botha held a precarious citizenship in Johannesburg. About 20 years after the foundation of Alexandra Township, some white residents who lived in adjacent suburbs begun to agitate for its abolition. This coincided with the growth of white suburbs ever closer to Alexandra. In July 1938, the white residents organised themselves into an association called the North-Eastern Districts Protection Association. The purpose of the group was to lobby for the removal of Alexandra Township. The association also intended to ensure that no other 'native' townships would be established to the north of the central business district. Its members constituted residents of suburbs to the north of the central business district of Johannesburg (*The Star*, 1938a).

At its founding meeting the reasons expressed for the removal of the township was that the township 'was a grave menace to … public health and safety, and that it could not be adequately controlled' (*Rand Daily Mail*, 1939b). Furthermore, 'the existence of the township on an arterial road constituted a serious danger to traffic' (*Rand Daily Mail*, 1939b). The chairman of the North-Eastern Districts Protection Association was clear that danger to 'traffic' was caused by buses and cycles used by Alexandra residents (Thomas, 1939). The claims that Alexandra residents generated traffic congestion and endangered other road users on Louis Botha Avenue as they travelled by bus and on cycles were ongoing arguments for the township's removal (see Lawrence, 1942). There were some objections to the proposed removal of the township by private citizens (Commonsense, 1939; *The Star*, 1939b), a pastor (*The Star*, 1939a), an organisation in charge of the welfare of the township (the Alexandra Township Health Committee) and groups seeking cordial relations between white and 'native' populations (Hoernle et al, 1943). Yet the distribution of power was arrayed against these voices. Instead, the agenda for removal remained in public narratives and policy discussions for many decades (Bonner and Nieftagodien, 2008).

When the country turned to official national government ideology of racial segregation in 1948 (Apartheid), the political commitment towards separation heightened (Beavon, 2004). Thus, by 1963 the fate of the township was under threat when a decision was taken to remove all the houses and replace them with hostels. The township was to cease being a residential area in which families could live. Instead, it 'was to become a hostel city for the black working population needed to service the needs of industrial Johannesburg' (Webster, 1984: 4). This decision precipitated an intensive programme of forced relocations in the 1960s and 1970s as some families were evicted to other townships in Johannesburg and others to rural areas (Webster, 1984).

Throughout this tumultuous time, municipal officials in charge of Louis Botha Avenue were also influenced by proposals to evict township residents. E.J. Hamlin was directly involved in eviction talks. For example, on 27 June 1938 he participated in a conference whose sole purpose was 'to discuss ways and means of dealing with Alexandra Township' (Unknown, 1938). This meeting took place at the same time that the Main Reef Road Commission was meeting. Hamlin was one of the appointed commissioners of the Main Reef Road Commission and was therefore aware of the emerging proposed solutions to the safety problems, including the creation of barrier protected cycle tracks on corridors such as Louis Botha Avenue (Main Reef Road Commission, 1937). Ongoing uncertainty about Alexandra undermined the merits of investing resources to maintain the painted lane or build protected cycle tracks for Hamlin and other municipal officials. Indeed, in 1963, the Secretary of the Johannesburg Road Safety Organisation in a report on the feasibility of constructing cycle tracks to serve 'native' population made this explicit: 'It is the stated Government policy to reduce the population of this Township [Alexandra] gradually, until the people living here have been resettled elsewhere, so no useful purpose would be served to conduct a traffic count or press for a Cycle track in the area at this time' (Vorster, 1963).

Under different circumstances, for example where Alexandra residents had a more secure place, other solutions might have emerged. One was a proposal from the municipality that the national government build a railway service (*Rand Daily Mail*, 1944). The municipal council, like their counterparts in the nearby town of Springs (Editors, 1939), may have created safer cycling infrastructure, albeit also as a means of controlling the lives of black people as Maylam (1995) notes, was a key feature of South African colonial and apartheid systems. Indeed, in the 1960s, the Johannesburg municipal council considered erecting protected cycle tracks in other residential areas where 'native' populations were segregated but whose existence was less in doubt (Vorster, 1963).

By the time a final decision against the Alexandra Township's removal was announced in 1979 in Parliament (Bonner and Nieftagodien, 2008), it would have been too late to make the case for cycleways on the grounds of volumes of cycle traffic. Cycling along Louis Botha Avenue was in decline as some cycle users were relocated in the

1960s and 1970s. Moreover, seeking respite from an arduous (and increasingly perilous) journey, some cycle users had resorted either to state subsidised buses serving Louis Botha Avenue or to flexible, affordable minibus services. Johannesburg also increasingly acquired a poly-centric form with new commercial, residential, retail and industrial nodes emerging. This eroded the centrality of the central business district as a place of work, minimising the southwards flow of traffic from Alexandra along Louis Botha Avenue (Beavon, 2001; 2004).

Conclusions

In charting the changing fortunes of the cycle lane on a single road, Louis Botha Avenue in Johannesburg, South Africa, this chapter has shown how the cycle lane was constructed (and deconstructed) by different social and political forces. The original conception was as a solution for road safety prevalent within then road engineering practices. However, the chapter also shows that the cycle lane was one of the mechanisms through which the road was transformed into a corridor primarily for the movement of automobiles. Other road uses and users were marginalised. That the cycle lane was not improved for road safety lent weight to a darker reading of developments on Louis Botha Avenue. Here we saw that the plight of cycle users on the road was as precarious as it was in their place of residence, Alexandra Township. That is, the cycle lane was neglected in wake of plans to forcibly relocate residents of Alexandra Township elsewhere in Johannesburg. The neglect of the cycle infrastructure was inextricably linked to the wider neglect of social infrastructure of the township: city engineers, police officers and road safety organisation eventually saw no reason to maintain the cycle lane as eviction momentum gathered.

These historical findings underline the co-evolutionary relationship between technology and society. Cycle infrastructure cannot be considered in isolation from other social and political considerations. The broad argument was that as Johannesburg, and wider South African society, became more racially polarised, so those struggles were reproduced on Louis Botha Avenue, manifested in a road design that marginalised the oppressed. Reading other cases cited in the Introduction, together with results of this chapter, if the 'work' that cycle lanes, cycle tracks and cycleways do is also a function of societal characteristics and developments, then there is need for such critical analysis to uncover other 'intentions' beyond road safety. For instance, to what extent might suggesting a harmonious outcome in which all road users co-exist do cycle tracks obscure more radical solutions? For instance, to what extent do they facilitate the ongoing legitimacy of automobility even in the face of ever-evident negative social and environmental impacts?

This chapter also raises broader questions about the possibilities of inclusive embedding of cycling given prevailing societal arrangements. It has, reading the history in the opposite direction, suggested that a more inclusive society could have produced a more inclusive road design. That is, by understanding the physical infrastructure as a manifestation and materialisation of the discursive politics of exclusion, the study argues that a different politics would have produced very different infrastructural arrangements. Observing policy interest in utility cycling across South Africa, Jennings (2015: 486) wondered if a cycling renaissance was underway. If the controversy on Louis Botha Avenue unfolded as it did due to wider social malaise in Johannesburg and South Africa, could the turn to democratisation and rediscovery of the cycle produce more inclusive cycling cultures? Further research in this line could be fruitful.

Acknowledgements

The production of this chapter was supported by a grant from the Life in the City project at the Wits School of Governance and institutional hosting at the South African Research Chair in Spatial Planning and City Analysis, both at the University of the Witwatersrand. I would also like to thank Dr Lisa Kane and Alexandra Applebaum for their useful comments on the first draft of this chapter.

References

Aldred, R. (2017) 'The culture behind infrastructure: reflections on nearly a decade of research into cycling culture and policy in the UK', *International Eco-Cities Initiative Reflections Series*, (21). Available at: www.westminster.ac.uk/eco-cities/reflections (Accessed: 8 February 2018).

Applebaum, A. (2016) *Contestation, Transformation and Competing Visions: a study of Orange Grove and Norwood*. 7. Johannesburg, South Africa: South African Research Chair in Spatial Analysis and City Planning: University of the Witwatersrand. Available at: www.wits. ac.za/sacp/spatial-transformation-through-tod-in-jhb/

Beavon, K. (2001) *The role of transport in the rise and decline of the Johannesburg CBD, 1886–2001*. SATC. Available at: http://repository. up.ac.za/handle/2263/8191 (Accessed: 4 September 2014).

Beavon, K. (2004) *Johannesburg: The Making and Shaping of the City*, (1st edn), Pretoria: Unisa Press.

Bijker, W.E. (2015) 'Technology, social construction of', in J.D. Wright (ed) *International Encyclopedia of the Social & Behavioral Sciences* (2nd edn), Oxford: Elsevier, pp 135–40.

Bijker, W.E., Hughes, T.P., Pinch, T. and Douglas, D.G. (2012) *The Social Construction of Technological Systems: New Directions in the Sociology and History of Technology* (Anniversary edition), Cambridge, MA: The MIT Press.

Bonner, P. and Nieftagodien, N. (2008) *Alexandra: A History*, Johannesburg: Wits University Press.

Buehler, R. and Dill, J. (2015) 'Bikeway networks: a review of effects on cycling', *Transport Reviews*, 36(1): 9–27.

Burgess, J. (compiler) (2016) *The Road Through the Grove: Friendship and Adventure along Louis Botha Avenue, Johannesburg, in the 1950s, '60s and '70s*, Johannesburg: Redsky Publishing.

Callinicos, L. (1987) *Working Life, 1886–1940: Factories, Townships, and Popular Culture on the Rand*, Johannesburg: Ravan Press.

Cervero, R., Caldwell, B. and Cuellar, J. (2013) 'Bike-and-ride: build it and they will come', *Journal of Public Transportation*, 16(4): 83–105.

City Engineer (1935) *Annual Report of the City Engineer: For the Year Ended 30 June, 1934*, Johannesburg, South Africa: City of Johannesburg.

City of Johannesburg (1936) *Council Minutes*, Johannesburg, South Africa: City of Johannesburg.

City of Johannesburg (1938) *Minutes of the Mayor for period 6 November 1936 to 4 November 1937*, Johannesburg, South Africa: Radford, Adlington, Ltd.

Commonsense (1939) 'If Alexandra is abolished suburbs will not get servants: Present Plan has many weaknesses', *Rand Daily Mail*, 21 March.

Dill, J. and Carr, T. (2003) 'Bicycle commuting and facilities in major US cities: if you build them, commuters will use them', *Transportation Research Record: Journal of the Transportation Research Board*, 1828(1): 116–23.

Editors (1939) 'Safety first propaganda: Grant made by council', *The Springs & Brakpan Advertiser*, 15 September.

Emanuel, M. (2012) 'Constructing the cyclist: ideology and representations in urban traffic planning in Stockholm, 1930–70', *The Journal of Transport History*, 33(1): 67–91.

Flanagan, E., Lachapelle, U. and El-Geneidy, A. (2016) 'Riding tandem: does cycling infrastructure investment mirror gentrification and privilege in Portland, OR and Chicago, IL?', *Research in Transportation Economics*, (Transportation and Land Development: A Global View), 60: 14–24.

Grant, G. and Flinn, T. (1992) *Watershed Town: The History of the Johannesburg City Engineer's Department*, Johannesburg: Johannesburg City Council.

Handy, S., van Wee, B. and Kroesen, M. (2014) 'Promoting cycling for transport: research needs and challenges', *Transport Reviews*, 34(1): 4–24.

Hoernle, R.F.A. et al. (1943) 'An open letter to the citizens of Johannesburg on the future of Alexandra Township by the Alexandra Township Health Committee'.

Hoffman, L.M. and Lugo, A.E. (2014) 'Who is "world class"? Transportation justice and bicycle policy', *Urbanities – Journal of Urban Ethnography*, 4(1): 45–61.

Hughes, A.B. (1973) 'How to empty the buses', *Rand Daily Mail*, 6 September.

Jennings, G. (2015) 'A Bicycling Renaissance in South Africa? Policies, Programmes & Trends in Cape Town', in Proceedings of the 34th Southern African Transport Conference (SATC 2015), Pretoria, South Africa.

Lawrence, H.G. (1942) 'Minutes (Abridged) of Conference Held in Conference Room, Union Buildings, Pretoria on 23rd October 1942'.

Lee, A.E., Underwood, S. and Handy, S. (2015) 'Crashes and other safety-related incidents in the formation of attitudes toward bicycling', *Transportation Research Part F: Traffic Psychology and Behaviour*, 28: 14–24.

Lubitow, A. (2016) 'Mediating the "white lanes of gentrification" in Humboldt Park: community-led economic development and the struggle over public space', in A. Golub, M.L. Hoffmann, A.E. Lugo and G.F. Sandoval (eds) *Bicycle Justice and Urban Transformation: Biking for All?* New York, NY: Routledge, pp 249–59.

Main Reef Road Commission (1937) *Report of the Main Reef Road Commission*. Transvaal Province.

Maylam, P. (1995) 'Explaining the apartheid city: 20 years of South African urban historiography', *Journal of Southern African Studies*, 21(1): 19–38.

Morgan, N. (2017) 'An inquiry into changes in everyday bicycling cultures: the case of Johannesburg in conversation with Amsterdam, Beijing and Chicago', University of the Witwatersrand.

Morgan, N. (2018) 'Context and utility cycling culture development: the case of Springs in comparison to Johannesburg, late 19th century to mid-1930s', in J. Harber, G. Maree, A. Parker and K. Joseph (eds) *Taking Streets Seriously*, Johannesburg, South Africa: Gauteng City-Region Observatory, pp 97–114. Available at: www.gcro.ac.za/outputs/research-reports/ (Accessed: 3 February 2018).

Motor Editor (1946a) 'Alexandra cyclists may be diverted from arterial highway', *Rand Daily Mail*, 1 November.

Motor Editor (1946b) 'Native cyclists offer ready accident harvest', *Rand Daily Mail*, 15 July.

Motor Editor (1947) 'Highest death rate is from rural accidents', *Rand Daily Mail*, 17 October.

Museum Africa (2016) 'Museum Africa Picture Archives', Johannesburg, South Africa.

Norton, P.D. (2011) *Fighting Traffic: The Dawn of the Motor Age in the American City* (2nd edn), Cambridge, MA: The MIT Press.

Not for Yesterday (1940) 'Louis Botha Avenue: Those Bottlenecks', *The Star*, 5 November.

Oldenziel, R. and De la Bruhèze, A.A. (2011) 'Contested spaces: bicycle lanes in urban Europe, 1900–1995', *Transfers*, 1(2): 29–49.

Pathé, B. (1940) *Black Police Aka Native Traffic Cops Issue Title Is Believe It Or Not*. Available at: www.britishpathe.com/video/black-police-aka-native-traffic-cops-issue-title/query/Johannesburg (Accessed: 17 January 2018).

Pinch, T. (2015) 'Scientific controversies', in J. D. Wright (ed) *International Encyclopedia of the Social & Behavioral Sciences* (2nd edn), Oxford: Elsevier, pp 281–6.

Pinch, T.J. and Bijker, W.E. (2012) 'The social construction of facts and artifacts: or how the sociology of science and the sociology of technology might benefit each other', in W.E. Bijker, T.P. Hughes and T.J. Pinch (eds) *The Social Construction of Technological Systems: New Directions in the Sociology and History of Technology*, Cambridge, MA: The MIT Press.

Plug, C. (2014) S2A3 Biographical Database of Southern African Science, Southern Africa Association for the Advancement of Science (S2A3). Available at: www.s2a3.org.za/bio/Biograph_final.php?serial=1206 (Accessed: 3 October 2018).

Rand Daily Mail (1922) 'The new traffic regulations', *Rand Daily Mail*, 4 October.

Rand Daily Mail (1927a) 'Solving Johannesburg's traffic problem', *Rand Daily Mail*, 24 February.

Rand Daily Mail (1927b) 'The white line system: Colonel Godley wants it in Johannesburg', *Rand Daily Mail*, 30 December.

Rand Daily Mail (1927c) '"White lines" for the city', *Rand Daily Mail*, 8 February.

Rand Daily Mail (1929) 'What is the future off our city traffic', *Rand Daily Mail*, 5 June.

Rand Daily Mail (1935a) 'A better traffic policy', *Rand Daily Mail*, 23 August.

Rand Daily Mail (1935b) 'Safer streets for cyclists', *Rand Daily Mail*, 22 August.

Rand Daily Mail (1935c) 'Ten-Foot islands', *Rand Daily Mail*, 7 August.

Rand Daily Mail (1936) '"Threeways" to get a real test in Johannesburg', *Rand Daily Mail*, 4 March.

Rand Daily Mail (1938) 'Accidents: Reader's views wanted', *Rand Daily Mail*, 18 August.

Rand Daily Mail (1939a) 'Native cyclists are controlled by Men of their own colour; Experiment promises good results', *The Rand Daily Mail*, 5 July.

Rand Daily Mail (1939b) 'North-Eastern city suburbs urge abolition of Alexandra', *Rand Daily Mail*, 29 June.

Rand Daily Mail (1939c) 'Unknown', *Rand Daily Mail*, 5 July.

Rand Daily Mail (1944) 'Council may buy Alexandra bus service', *Rand Daily Mail*, 20 December.

Rand Daily Mail (1947) 'Cyclists who are a danger', *Rand Daily Mail*, 22 July.

Rosen, P. (1993) 'The social construction of mountain bikes: technology and postmodernity in the cycle industry', *Social Studies of Science*, 23(3): 479–513.

Stehlin, J. (2014) 'Regulating inclusion: spatial form, social process, and the normalization of cycling practice in the USA', *Mobilities*, 9(1): 21–41.

The Star (1935) 'Reserved for cyclists', *The Star*, 23 August.

The Star (1938a) 'Alexandra Township: Ratepayers want removal', *The Star (South Africa)*, 11 July.

The Star (1938b) 'Traffic problem of the cyclist', *The Star*, 14 January.

The Star (1939a) 'Alexandra Township: No case for demolition', *The Star (South Africa)*, 1 April.

The Star (1939b) 'The humane point of view', *The Star (South Africa)*, 3 November.

The Star (1941) 'Road traffic statement: Louis Botha Avenue, improvements suggested', *The Star*, 3 October.

The Washington Post (1935) 'Cycle highway', *The Washington Post*, 24 November.

Thomas, L.S. (1939) 'Alexandra Township: Protection League activities', *The Star (South Africa)*, 25 March.

Two Hoots (1939) 'Appreciated by motorists: Work of Native Traffic Inspectors', *Rand Daily Mail*, 5 July.

Unknown (1938) *Notes of Proceedings of Conference Held at the Raadsaal, Pretoria on 27 June 1938 to Discuss Ways and Means of Dealing with Alexandra Township*. Pretoria, South Africa.

Vorster, J.C. (1963) *Memorandum on Cycle Tracks Along Roads and Specially Designed Roads with Cycle Tracks to Link up Urban Bantu Townships with Urban Highways*. Johannesburg Road Safety Association.

Webster, G. (1984) '*Its History*'. The Black Sash.

Winters, M., Davidson, G., Kao, D. and Teschke, K. (2011) 'Motivators and deterrents of bicycling: comparing influences on decisions to ride', *Transportation*, 38(1): 153–68.

3

Spatial dimensions of the marginalisation of cycling – marginalisation through rationalisation?

Till Koglin

Introduction

Transport and urban planning are very complex issues in general (Koglin and Pettersson, 2017). Moreover, urban cycling is closely connected to urban space and urban and transport planning (Koglin, 2011; 2013). With 12 per cent of all trips made by cycle, a level similar to that of Germany, Sweden is often regarded as a country where cycling is a regular part of everyday mobility. Compared with countries such as the United States or Great Britain, the argument is even stronger. However, the proportion of work journeys using cycles as a mode of travel has declined from 16 per cent in the period 1995–98 to 12 per cent in the period 2011–14. For school trips, cycling has fallen even further: from 23 per cent between 1995 and 1998 to 14 per cent between 2011 and 2014 (Trafikanalys, 2015). Moreover, research has shown that cycling remains a marginalised mode of transport, especially in Sweden's capital city Stockholm (Emanuel, 2012; Koglin, 2013; 2015). Seeking explanation, Koglin and Rye (2014) have identified space as a vital element in the marginalisation of cycling. This chapter further analyses the impact of the spatial dimension and connects it to a very influential form of rationalisation of transport planning in Sweden.

The theoretical starting point for this chapter is threefold. First, it builds on Lefebvre's (1991 [1974]) discussion of the production of space. This theoretical framework offers a deeper understanding of how space is produced and what effects such production might have on people's everyday lives. The second argument is broader, connecting the rationalisation of the social sciences (see Marcuse,

1999 [1941]; 2002 [1964]) to the development of transport planning as a scientifically valid(ated), rational profession. The third strand of discussion uses Bauman's (1998; 1999) idea of urban space wars to understand the effects of this kind of rationalisation.

This connected framework is used to analyse the Swedish transport and urban planning system through an interrogation of published planning documents, policies and visions for transport and cycling in Sweden. Reading the documentation through the theoretical lens reveals how Swedish transport and urban planning operate to marginalise cycling through a process of rationalisation. Moreover, the analysis in this chapter will show that this 'rational' planning has created urban spaces and infrastructures that marginalise cycling as a mode of transport in several ways, making it hard to use the cycle as a mode of transport in everyday urban life.

Exploring the production of space and urban space wars

Since transport and mobility are embedded into space (often urban space), a spatial dimension is important in analysing cycling issues. By focusing on social relationships in terms of preconditioning and rationalisation, we can critically understand the structures that affect both materiality and mobility (Koglin, 2017). Here, Lefebvre's theory of the production of space can offer an analytical tool. Lefebvre (1991 [1974]) argued that space should be seen as both socially produced and as re-produced through social relations. Space is thus a complex construction that can be seen as absolute, relative, or relational.

In each case, there are three ways of thinking about space (Lefebvre, 1991 [1974]: 33):

- Spatial practice. Practices embrace production and reproduction, and the particular locations and spatial sets characteristic of each social formation. Spatial practices ensure continuity and some degree of cohesion. In terms of social space, and of each member of a given society's relationship to that space, this cohesion implies a guaranteed level of competence and a specific level of performance.
- Representations of space. Representations are tied to the relations of production and to the 'order' which those relations impose, and hence to knowledge, to signs, to codes and to 'frontal' relations.
- Representational spaces. These embody complex symbolisms, sometimes coded, sometimes not, linked to the clandestine or underground side of social life, as also to art (which may come

eventually to be defined less as a code of space than as a code of representational spaces).

This spatial triad emphasises that space is created or newly produced through social relations. It does not pre-exist them. The way in which space is practised and presented is important because it defines how the space should or could be viewed and used. In addition, the triad provides a tool to analyse the spatial impact on social relationships and the use of space. In addition, the third aspect allows for another dimension of theoretical space dealing with the embedding of symbols in space, thus providing an opportunity to analyse both spatial practice and social life (Lefebvre, 1991 [1974]; Koglin, 2017). It is important to consider *how* space is represented and practised because this outlines the means for how space *can* and should be used and seen, as norms are also produced through the performance of space. For example, if the space is full of symbols of the automobile society and only a small amount of space is dedicated to cycling, people might use the car instead of the bicycle (see also Koglin, 2017). In this way, space has an impact on peoples' mobility and can influence peoples' mobility choices even if they are unaware of that influence. Furthermore, the spatial triad offers a way of analysing what impact space has on social relations and the use of space and vice versa. Additionally, the third aspect of the spatial triad proposes one more dimension about how space and spatial use can be theorised. Here, Lefebvre sees symbols as embedded in space, which affects both social life and spatial practise (Lefebvre, 1991 [1974]).

Overall, Lefebvre's understanding of space is important because he views it not as incidental or contributory to questions of justice and of norms in social relations, but as causative. This distinguishes him from other theorists of urban space as Harvey (2006), similarly rooted in reflections on urban activism in the 1970s, who, while emphasising the importance of urban spaces in their contribution to (in)justice and to oppression, remains sceptical of their causative agency (see Soja, 2010). Through transport and urban planning spaces materialities are created that influence peoples' behaviour and can marginalise, for example cycling in urban space. As a theoretical underpinning, Lefebvre offers an understanding of how space is produced and re-produced and how that might affect one's choice of transport mode (Koglin, 2017).

To this discussion one can add Zygmunt Bauman's (1998; 1999) work on urban space wars. Bauman sees that urban 'space wars' erupt as space is forced into measurable facts (Bauman, 1998; Koglin, 2013). According to Bauman, social space does not evolve from measurable and objective space. Rather, it is objective space that is created from social space. It is in the social relations in spaces, most often urban spaces, where Bauman sees the fight over space occurring (Bauman, 1998). He sees those struggles as connected to how space is measured or as he puts it: 'Not just the question of measuring the space "objectively" presented a problem, however. Before it may come to measuring, one needs first to have a clear notion of what is there to be measured' (Bauman, 1998: 28).

Elsewhere, Bauman (1999) states: '… most power is exercised by the unit closest to the source of other units' uncertainty. The manipulation of uncertainty is essential; it is the primary stake in the struggle for power and influence inside every structured totality – first and foremost in its radical form of modern bureaucratic organization' (Bauman, 1999: 177). Connecting the measurement of space to the struggle for power, Bauman explains that cities try to incorporate space into objectively measurable units in order to avoid local subjectivities because cities see that these local subjectivities might have different interpretations of the meaning of space. 'Space wars', the conflicts over urban space, are engendered by attempts to measure space objectively. Further, the fight over urban public space is a battle over daily spatial interpretations and practices. In Bauman's terms, 'Urban territory becomes the battlefield of continuous space war, sometimes erupting into public spectacle of inner-city riots, ritual skirmishes with the police, the occasional forays of soccer crowds, but waged daily just beneath the surface of the public (publicised), official version of the routine urban order' (Bauman, 1998: 22).

Because the interpretation of space can change and will change over time, space has to be seen as produced through subjective social relations. Urban conflicts over space occur when those subjective interpretations do not fit into the objectively measurable units. Those units are, according to Bauman (1998), global actors, and cities attempt to suppress other interpretations of space, which are not neo-liberal views. Thus, it can be said that space wars emerge from the tension between the objective and subjective interpretation of space (Bauman, 1999).

The concept of urban space wars has previously been used in research about gentrification (see, for example, Lund Hansen, 2006). Such space wars also become obvious within transport planning and urban traffic spaces when considering urban spaces of mobility and cycling. The author has previously used this concept to explore struggles over urban street space between cyclists and other road users (see Koglin, 2013; Koglin, 2018). However, the connection between the production of space, space wars and mobility is seldom part of research on cycling and has not been theorised to a significant degree. In order to develop such theorisation further, production of space, developing space wars, and cycling as transport all need to be seen through the lens of rationalisation of transport planning. The next section applies this analysis with specific reference to the Swedish context.

The rationalisation of transport planning

The combination of spatial practice, urban space wars and the interpretation of the production of space provides a means to think about planning in general, and transport planning in particular. Traffic space is produced through transport and urban planning and, since the 1950s, transport planning especially has gone through a period of rationalisation (Brown, 2006; Brown et al., 2009; Lindelöw et al, 2016; Koglin, 2017). The issue of rationality has been a research interest in the planning field for many years (Flyvbjerg, 1993; 1998; Alexander, 2000). This chapter is mainly concerned with exploring how views on different transport modes as rational or measurable play out in planning practice and how that affects the production of space and urban space wars. Rationality in transport planning should be seen in the light of changes within the research world overall.

Herbert Marcuse (2002 [1964]) argued that a shift towards positivistic and seemingly rational research emerged in the social sciences. Lundin (2008) argues the fact that much focus within transport planning, which has been on measures and models linked to motorised modes of transport, has to be seen in light of the shift from metaphysical and theoretical social research to empiricism and measurable research as noted by Marcuse. Transport and urban planners' rationalities can influence decision makers at a political level, and thus it is also important to mention that transport planning through quantification has generally been seen as apolitical and neutral. Nevertheless, transport planning also has a political dimension, (Brown, 2006; Koglin, 2013; Koglin and Rye, 2014). Marcuse explains that, through the influence of Hegel, Kant and Fichte, 'the world was to be an order of reason' (Marcuse, 1999 [1941]: 4). This led to a shift within the social sciences and humanities towards quantification and rationalities. In this new paradigm, research into social phenomena is no longer supposed to theorise, but rather should deal with generalisations. Hence, reason and rationality have also become two very important aspects that have affected transport planning in the 20th century in the Western world; rationalities in transport planning should be seen in the light of a shift towards positivistic and rational research, especially in the social sciences.

Rationality plays an important role here because issues that are measurable and quantifiable are more reasonable to analyse and to deal with than issues that are harder to measure. Marcuse (2002 [1964]) explained what this shift has meant.

> Made into a methodological principle, this suspension has a twofold consequence: (a) it strengthens the shift of the theoretical emphasis from the metaphysical 'What is ...?' ... to the functional 'How...?', and (b) it establishes a practical (though by no means absolute) certainty which, in its operations with matter, is with good conscience free from commitment to any substance outside the operational context. (Marcuse, 2002 [1964]: 155)

Thus, Marcuse argues that theoretical research has become less important in relation to data driven empirical research, because it has meant that research should deal only with measurable facts. This has also meant a shift from 'what' to 'how'. Through this, the focus has moved towards questions of how things are and not why things are the way they are. Here the work of Marcuse can provide an insight into the rationalities and structures of transport planning (Marcuse, 1999 [1941]; 2002 [1964]). What Marcuse means here is that certain aspects of reason and theoretical thoughts no longer have a priority within the development of societies. This is because only measurable aspects have a bearing on such development. Therefore, the fact that much focus within transport planning has been on measures and models linked to motorised modes of transport has to be seen in light of the shift from metaphysical and theoretical social research to empiricism and measureable research. Here Marcuse's work can be connected to important issues of today's mobile societies, particularly to the fact that modes of transport that are seen as difficult to measure are not prioritised in transport planning. This is especially true for walking and cycling (Marcuse, 2002 [1964]; Koglin and Rye, 2014; Lindelöw et al, 2016).

Such thinking can also, to a certain degree, be traced in urban and transport planning, although this stretches over slightly different time periods. Rational and quantified transport planning started more or less in the 1920s and remains dominant, despite recent signs of a shift towards other forms of planning. Consequently, questions of justice or of making changes towards sustainable modes of transport are reduced to mechanical or technical problems. They thus miss the normative dimension. Further, quantitative research and numbers in transport planning are assumed to be neutral while in fact being deeply political (see Cox, Chapter 1, this volume). This gives those aspects more traction in transport planning. Social aspects can be omitted from the planning process and cycling marginalised. The broader issues of what planning seeks to address and to change are rendered non-pertinent. This leads to a marginalisation of certain modes of transport and issues connected, for example, to justice (compare Sheller, 2018).

Knowledge produced after this shift of thinking was, and often still is, seen as apolitical, generalisable and objective, whereas theoretical knowledge and knowledge produced in a qualitative way is often seen as political, subjective and non-generalisable (Lundin, 2008). Habermas wrote in 1968 that this view needs to be questioned. He saw technology as a carrier of certain technological rules, but also as a carrier of certain meanings and values and, thus, as ideological. This means that the shift in research and knowledge production Marcuse talked about (1999 [1941]; 2002 [1964]) should not be seen as apolitical, but as equally value-laden as qualitative research (Habermas, 1968).

One important aspect of this quantification has been to approach transport planning in a quantitative manner, which makes it into a question of models, mathematics and forecasts. This process of quantification justifies itself by appealing to values such as objectivity, formality and generalisability (Lundin, 2008). Transport planning has historically been keener on using quantitative techniques and methods compared to other parts of the planning field (te Brömmelstroet and Bertolini, 2010; Brown et al, 2009). This quantitative approach has been particularly present in car-based transport planning and has, whether implicitly or explicitly, proven successful in its ability to give justification to policies that are beneficial for car use (Lundin, 2008). Through this quantification of transport planning, influenced by the scientific shift within research, soft modes of transport such as walking and cycling have been marginalised. Due to the focus on measurements, cycling is not usually seen as a mode of transport that can be planned for. Here, the technocratic and political incentive and motivation to measure different modes of mobility play an important role. This has to do with traditional ways of seeing, understanding and monitoring transport. Those decisions determine what is built or not in the transport system.

Within transport and urban planning, reason and rationality are often seen as central aspects. However, what defines rational decisions can be debated. Flyvbjerg (1993) uses the argument that when some societal groups gain power, the rationality of their decisions loses its importance. Additionally, Flyvbjerg elaborates that rationality has to be seen in its context and that rationality is bound to a specific context. In transport and urban politics, as well as in transport and urban planning, power is frequently characterised by stable power relations. Open confrontations are often absent, and power relations are produced and re-produced throughout the planning processes (Flyvbjerg, 1993; 1998). This means that a change in power relations might occur if and when transport planning ideals are developed from theories, models, and so on, that are not used for motorised traffic in the first place, but come from a different rationality, namely that of the soft modes of transport.

By developing new theories and models for cycling, power relations in transport planning could be shifted towards cyclists, and cycling might then be viewed as a viable mode of transport within transport and urban planning. Koglin and Rye (2014) expanded Cresswell's (2010) work on the politics of mobility into a specific focus on 'the politics of vélomobility'. Starting in social theory, Koglin and Rye (2014) conclude that planning for cycling should observe the following four points:

- Physical movement from A to B – infrastructure for cycling without obstacles and the creation of free and safe flow for cyclists.
- Power relations in urban traffic space – consideration of power relations between the different groups that share urban traffic space, to create spaces where cycling is not marginalised.
- Positive representations of cycling – adapted and targeted to different groups of people and which create shared meanings of cycling that go beyond class, gender, ethnic and other boundaries.
- Everyday practice and the experience of cycling – cycling should make the everyday and social lives of people easier, thus infrastructure and cycle planning must involve aspects of everyday life in order to make the cycling experience more pleasant. (Koglin and Rye, 2014: 220)

Focusing on 'the politics of vélomobility' necessitates a broader view on what is important in terms of cycling, planning for cycling and also increasing cycling. Koglin and Rye (2014) argue that it is vital to consider social aspects such as class, gender and ethnicity in order to create different representations of cycling that can be viewed positively by a large variety of people and not just, for example, white middle-class men. Taking all this into account requires cycle planning and cycle infrastructure to go beyond classical transport rationalities because it is through such rationalities that certain groups are marginalised in public space, leading to conflict over urban space, as Bauman suggests (Bauman, 1999).

Cycling infrastructure and transport planning in Sweden – influences and 'neutral rationalities'

At the beginning of the 20th century, the focus in urban and transport planning was on street life, aesthetics and a mix of functions. However, during the 1920s, and increasingly after the Second World War, the focus shifted more and more towards separation of functions and to primary facilitation of motorised modes of transport (Brown, 2006). In this modernistic style of planning, the focus was on replacing streets with roads, because streets were seen as unable to satisfy the needs of modern modes of transport. Streets were old-fashioned places and meeting spaces for people where obsolete forms of transport mixed. On the other hand, roads were regarded as modern arteries of motorised traffic flows in urban areas and cities, uninterrupted by other modes of transport. The idea was to develop highway systems in cities and urban areas (Holston, 2002). Modernity influenced planning, which led to modernistic planning in the spirit of Le Corbusier, and the focus on modern traffic, which became synonymous with car traffic, was a common idea in modernistic planning (Hall, 2002).

In the Swedish case, modernism had a powerful impact as seen in Figure 3.1. Car domination abounded in urban areas.

The influence of modernistic thinking in transport planning also led to a scientification of the profession of transport planners. Through theoretical foundations within, for example, modelling and through quantification, the rationality of transport planning was thus founded in a neutral and apolitical 'science' (Paterson, 2007; Koglin and Rye, 2014). This thinking then shaped the urban transport systems. Through emphasis on, and construction of, mode-segregated transport infrastructure, planned to maximise traffic flow, the focus on the motor vehicle practically excluded cycles from urban spaces.

In a circular, self-justificatory argument, the conception of a modern city and modern traffic fostered a rational ideology within transport planning, and led to an increased focus on motorised traffic. This also triggered an increase in motorised traffic through methods like 'predict and provide'. Through this rational planning approach within modernistic planning, power relations were built into the urban

Figure 3.1: Car domination in urban spaces in Sweden. Picture to the left, inner-city highway, Stockholm; picture to the right, car-parking in the Western Harbour in Malmö

Source: Author

infrastructure, and this infrastructure has often marginalised cycle traffic. Visible effects of transport planning affected by modernistic thinking are noticeable in urban areas that were built in the 1960s, 1970s and 1980s in many cities throughout Europe and North America. While modified, such modernism in practice continues to influence policy and planning today, and these ideas are still at work in urban and transport planning (see Brezina et al, Chapter 4, this volume). Through technological development, which modernistic planning and thinking draws on, non-motorised modes such as cycling have been marginalised in transport planning and urban spaces. This marginalisation has been legitimised through technological developments, which today becomes clear, for example, in the discussions about self-driving or autonomous cars, which supposedly will, at least according to Google and other major actors from the car industry, be the solution to the problems caused by motorised traffic (Koglin and Rye, 2014).

After the Second World War, Sweden developed a deeply rationalised planning ideal. Through influences from the US, Sweden's urban and transport planning focused on modernistic planning paradigms and rational decision–making within planning. From the work of a research group at the Technical University, Chalmers, in Gothenburg, a planning guide called SCAFT was developed, epitomising this way of thinking. SCAFT was originally developed as a set of traffic safety guidelines to decrease accidents between cars, and between cars and cyclists and pedestrians. The traffic safety problem in Sweden was linked to an increase in car ownership, which led to more collisions between motorists and cyclists and pedestrians and thus became a problem in many Swedish cities from the 1950s onwards (Koglin, 2013). Comparable issues could already be seen in the UK before the Second World War (Cox, 2012). The ideas put forward in the SCAFT guidelines included separation of modes of transport and differentiation of speeds within cities (Statens planverk, 1967; Gunnarsson and Lindström, 1970). The guidelines were illustrated by Gunnarsson and Lindström in 1970 in order to make the implementation easier (see Figures 3.2 and 3.3).

These ideas about planning triggered investments in transport infrastructure for motorised modes of traffic, which simultaneously resulted in further development of theoretical knowledge and models for such modes of transport (Taylor, 2004; Brown et al, 2009; Cars et al, 2009; Koglin and Rye, 2014). Belief in the power of technology was very strong in the post-war period (and remains so). This affected the development of so-called modern traffic, synonymous with car traffic. Technological developments also affected transport

Figure 3.2: Principles of separations

Source: Gunnarsson and Lindström, 1970

Figure 3.3: Principles of differentiation

Source: Gunnarsson and Lindström, 1970

planning with a conviction that transport planning, transport models and theoretical development in this field are neutral (Gray, 2004; Koglin and Rye, 2014). Researchers and planners with an interest in creating less congestion, better traffic flows and faster and better travel possibilities for the private car user primarily introduced new theoretical developments within transport planning. This did not happen for cycle traffic (Hall, 2002; Holston, 2002). Although many cities in Sweden today want to see an increase in cycling, theoretical thinking does not accommodate this wish because cycling is seen as irrational in general transport planning models. In Sweden after the Second World War, the wish to become a truly modern society was quite strong. The embrace of modernism was seen as the way forward and had a substantial impact on transport and urban planning (Koglin, 2013). Technocratic views on infrastructure, influenced by modernism, further dominated the provision of infrastructure, which often sees cycling infrastructure as a problem (Cox, Chapter 1, this volume).

Sweden today is of course stuck with the infrastructure that was built during the 1960s and 1970s, as illustrated in Figures 3.4 and 3.5.

Figure 3.4 shows highways in Uppsala and Figure 3.5 shows a modernistic/SCAFT area in Malmö with car parking close to the housing and an inner-city highway as an arterial road. Spaces for cars are produced in Sweden through a rationalistic planning regime. Street spaces, therefore, can provoke conflict over space between different modes of transport.

Koglin (2018) demonstrates that Stockholm cyclists feel that most of their problems are created by motorised traffic, which in turn is linked to the lack of space for cyclists in the city. Furthermore,

Figure 3.4: Transport infrastructure in Uppsala, Sweden

Source: Holger Ellgaard, 2010

Figure 3.5: Transport infrastructure in Malmö, Sweden

Source: Author

transport planning today in Sweden is still influenced by modernistic rationalities. Newly built areas in Malmö, for example, still marginalise cyclists, as exemplified by the case of the Western Harbour in Malmö (Koglin, 2017. See also Koglin, 2013; Koglin and Rye, 2014 for further examples of this marginalisation in other areas in Sweden). Through the rationalisation of planning, a development of 'rational' spaces has taken place that has led to conflicts over space because the cycle as a mode of transport has been marginalised. This marginalisation has also led to violence in urban spaces, although not necessarily physical, again illustrating Bauman's description of urban space wars (Balkmar, 2014; Koglin, 2018).

In a further twist, because space in Swedish cities is created primarily for motorised traffic, cyclists frequently have to share space with pedestrians. The Western Harbour in Malmö, a new brownfield development project with a focus on sustainability, illustrates how this provokes further conflict and marginalisation in practice (see Figure 3.6; Koglin, 2017).

Such spaces have led to conflicts between road users, and are often hostile spaces for cyclists (Balkmar, 2018; Koglin, 2018). Where road space in Sweden is normalised for motorised traffic, cyclists are exposed to violence and are verbally attacked because their presence has been delegitimised (Balkmar, 2018). The connection between a rationalisation of planning (Marcuse, 1999 [1941]), the production of space (Lefebvre, 1991 [1974]) and space wars (Bauman, 1999) becomes clear. Inclusion is not possible within the existing modernistic planning paradigm. In order not to exclude cycling and pedestrian traffic, visionary thinking and paradigmatic change are required to transform urban spaces and planning in favour of cycling, as indicated by Whitelegg (Chapter 5, this volume).

Figure 3.6: Cycling infrastructure in the Western Harbour, Malmö, Sweden

Source: Author

Conclusions

This chapter has dealt with the theoretical implications of space, rationality and cycling. Planning, and especially transport planning, has been rationalised in Sweden through a focus on quantification, 'rational' transport models, and 'neutral' analyses in the form of 'predict and provide' models. The intense development of transport planning after the Second World War focused on motorised traffic. Through this, space for motorised traffic has been created, which affects the social relations (confirming Lefebvre's argument). In terms of cycling, the rationalisation of planning has created infrastructures that marginalise cycling as a mode of transport and lead to cycle-unfriendly environments in many cities in Sweden. The logic and rationality within transport planning has made it difficult to develop good bicycle infrastructure in Sweden because, among other things, cycling is not considered a rational mode of transport in models and calculations. Thus, one of the major issues today in transport planning in Sweden is how planning traditions can be changed and how urban spaces can be transformed into cycle-friendly spaces. This also has a theoretical dimension because theoretical development in the field of cycle planning is needed in order to strengthen the cycle as a mode of transport.

This rationalisation of planning and thus of space also has a theoretical bearing on Bauman's concept of urban space wars. Because space is created predominantly for motorised traffic, conflicts in urban space are built into the infrastructures, and urban mobility space wars can easily erupt in Swedish cities. Furthermore, such rational planning forces cyclists into measurable space: that is, the cyclist becomes a quantified and quantifiable object. However, the object created and represented might not actually correspond with the actualities of the mobile subject, creating tensions between different cyclists, and between cyclists and pedestrians. Through such rationalisation of planning and of space, conflicts are created and the weaker road user, often the cyclist, loses. Because urban space often marginalises cyclists in Sweden this tends to lead to a decrease in cycling.

In the end, one has to ask if rational spatial planning by rational transport planners fulfils the needs for cyclists and leads the way for a transition to sustainable forms of mobility. When planners only seek to make rational decisions, it is easy to think that figures, models and numbers are rational and thus neutral. However, as seen in this chapter, this is not always the case. Transport planning is highly politicised and not neutral, regardless of the method used for developing traffic spaces. Therefore, in order to create urban spaces that do not marginalise cyclists, a change in the way people think is required.

References

Alexander, E.R. (2000) 'Rationality revisited: planning paradigms in a post-postmodernist perspective', *Journal of Planning Education and Research*, 19(3): 242–56.

Balkmar, D. (2014) 'Våld i trafiken – Om cyklisters utsatthet för kränkningar, hot och våld i massbilismens tidevarv', *Tidskrift för Genusvetenskap*, 2–3: 33–54.

Balkmar, D. (2018) 'Violent mobilities: men, masculinities and road conflicts in Sweden', *Mobilities*, 13(5): 717–32.

Bauman, Z. (1998) *Globalization – The Human Consequences*, Cambridge: Polity Press.

Bauman, Z. (1999) 'Urban space wars: on destructive order and creative chaos', *Citizenship Studies*, 3(2): 173–85.

Brown, J. (2006) 'From traffic regulation to limited ways: the effort to build a science of transportation planning', *Journal of Planning History*, 5: 3–34.

Brown, J., Morris, E. and Taylor, B. (2009) 'Planning for cars in cities: planners, engineers, and freeways in the 20th century', *Journal of the American Planning Association*, 75: 161–77.

Cars, G., Malmsten, B. and Tornberg, P. (2009) *Bana väg för infrastruktur*, TRITA SoM 2009–02 Forskningsrapport Kungliga Tekniska Högskola, Stockholm.

Cox, P. (2012) '"A denial of our boasted civilisation": cyclists' views on conflicts over road use in Britain, 1926-1935', *Transfers*, 2(3): 4-30.

Cresswell, T. (2010) 'Towards a politics of mobility', *Environment and Planning D: Society and Space*, 28: 17–31.

Ellgaard, H. (2010) *Uppsalavägen från Frösundatoppen mot norr.* Available at: https://sv.wikipedia.org/wiki/Uppsalav%C3%A4gen#/media/Fil:Uppsalav%C3%A4gen_2010.jpg (Accessed: 1 June 2019).

Emanuel, M. (2012) *Trafikslag på undantag – Cykeltrafiken i Stockholm 1930–1980*, Stockholm: Stockholmia Förlag.

Flyvbjerg, B. (1993) *Rationalitet og magt – Et Case–baseret Studie af planlægning, Politik og Modernitet*, København: Akademisk Forlag.

Flyvbjerg, B. (1998) *Rationality and Power – Democracy in Practice*, Chicago: University of Chicago Press.

Gray, J. (2004) *Heresies – Against Progress and Other Illusions*, London: Granta Books.

Gunnarsson, S.O. and Lindström, S. (1970) *Vägen till trafiksäkerhet*, Stockholm: Rabén & Sjögren.

Habermas, J. (1968) 'Technik und Wissenschaft als "Ideologie"?' , *Continental Philosophy Review*, 1(4): 483–523.

Hall, P. (2002) *Cities of Tomorrow*, Oxford: Blackwell Publishing.

Harvey, D. (2006) *Spaces of Global Capitalism*, London: Verso.

Holston, J. (2002) 'The modernist city and the death of the street', in S.M. Low (ed) *Theorizing the City – The New Urban Anthropology Reader*, London: Rutgers University Press, pp 245–76.

Koglin, T. (2011) 'Planning for cycling = planning for equity – a response to the Cupples and Ridley article "Towards a heterogeneous environmental responsibility: sustainability and cycling fundamentalism" (2008)', *Area*, 43(2): 225–7.

Koglin, T. (2013) *Vélomobility – A critical analysis of planning and space.* Doctoral Dissertation, Lund University, Department of Technology and society, Transport and roads, 2013, Bulletin 284.

Koglin, T. (2015) 'Vélomobility and the politics of transport planning', *GeoJournal*, 80(4): 569–86.

Koglin, T. (2017) 'Urban mobilities and materialities – a critical reflection of "sustainable" urban development', *Applied Mobilities*, 2(1): 32–49.

Koglin, T. (2018) 'Urban velomobility and the spatial problems of cycling', in M. Freudendal-Pedersen, K. Hartmann-Petersen and E. Perez Fjalland (eds) *Experiencing Networked Urban Mobilities*, New York: Routledge, pp 112–18.

Koglin, T. and Rye, T. (2014) 'The marginalisation of bicycling in Modernist urban transport planning', *Journal of Transport and Health*, 1(4): 214–22.

Koglin, T. and Pettersson, F. (2017) 'Changes, problems and challenges in Swedish spatial planning', *Sustainability*, 9(10): 1836.

Lefebvre, H. (1991 [1974]) *The Production of Space*, Oxford: Blackwell Publishing.

Lindelöw, D., Koglin, T. and Svensson, Å. (2016) 'Pedestrian planning and the challenges of instrumental rationality in transport planning: emerging strategies in three Swedish municipalities', *Planning Theory & Practice*, 17(3): 405–20.

Lund Hansen, A. (2006) *Space wars and the new urban imperialism*. Doctoral Dissertation, Department of Social and Economic Geography, Lund University.

Lundin, P. (2008) *Bilsamhället: ideologi, expertis och regelskapande i efterkrigstidens Sverige*, Stockholm: Stockholmia förlag.

Marcuse, H. (1999 [1941]) *Reason and Revolution – Hegel and the Rise of Social Theory*, New York: Humanity Books.

Marcuse, H. (2002 [1964]) *One-Dimensional Man – Studies in the Ideology of Advanced Industrial Society*, New York: Routledge Classics.

Paterson, M. (2007) *Automobile Politics – Ecology and Cultural Political Economy*, Cambridge: University Press.

Sheller, M. (2018) *Mobility Justice: The Politics of Movement in an Age of Extremes*, London: Verso.

Soja, E. (2010) *Seeking Spatial Justice*, Minneapolis: University of Minnesota Press.

Statens planverk (1967) *SCAFT 1968: Riktlinjer för stadsplanering med hänsyn till trafiksäkerhet*. Publikation nr 5, Stockholm.

Taylor, B.D. (2004) 'The geography of urban transportation finance', in S. Hanson and G. Giuliano (eds) *The Geography of Urban Transportation*, New York: The Guilford Press, pp 294–331.

te Brömmelstroet, M. and Bertolini, L. (2010) 'Integrating land use and transport knowledge in strategy-making', *Transportation*, 37: 85–104.

Trafikanalys (2015) *Cyklandets utveckling i Sverige 1995–2014 – en analys av de nationella resvaneundersökningarna*. Rapport 2015: 14, Trafikanalys, Stockholm.

4

Mental barriers in planning for cycling

Tadej Brezina, Ulrich Leth and Helmut Lemmerer

Introduction

Globally identified demand to stabilise anthropogenic greenhouse gas emissions (Steffen et al, 2018) also urgently demands research on implementation and for action to be taken locally (geographically and sectorally) in transport. The EU roadmap 2050 calls for a 54 to 67 per cent reduction in transport emissions compared to the base year 1990. Only very ambitious policies and interventions can meet or undercut these reduction goals given by the roadmap (Müller et al, 2012). The only feasible climate mitigation strategy is to thoroughly re-structure urban mobility organisation (Massink et al, 2011). However, unfortunately the transport sector has been lagging behind other sectors in the need to meet its share of emission reduction (Anderl et al, 2018). Facing these big challenges in transportation, legislators and policy makers have recently begun to consider cycling as their bearer of hope, due to the positive climate value of cycling (Massink et al, 2011). Nevertheless, climate change mitigation and adoption are by no means the only reasons for demanding a re-structuring of urban transport regimes; liveable cities (Gehl, 2011), fair space allocation (Knoflacher, 2015), improved health (Douglas et al, 2011; Goodman et al, 2012) are also among the specific goals being considered, (see also Whitelegg, Chapter 5, this volume).

This rising awareness has led, and continues to lead, to cycling receiving an increasingly prominent role in urban (for example, Telepak et al, 2015), regional (for example, Rosinak & Partner and Besch + Partner, 2006) and national transport master plans (for example, Heinfellner et al, 2015). But quite often, as already highlighted by Brezina and Castro (2017), there is a considerably large gap between ambitious policy drafting and effective on-site realisation (Pilko et al, 2015).

In the second half of the 20th century, planning, constructive and organisational solutions for transport and urban space revolved mostly

73

around cars; other modes were left marginalised (Koglin and Rye, 2014). Ample strategies for sustainable transport have been developed in recent decades, but these plans have been insufficiently detailed for infrastructural implementation (Bell and Ferretti, 2015). This finding also resonates with Davies et al (2000) and Daley and Rissel (2011), who survey misinterpretations of transport user needs by decision makers. Strategic plans articulate reasons for encouraging cycling in urban environments, but fail to challenge the dominance of motorised vehicles (Bell and Ferretti, 2015) that discourage cycling, either in the field or in projects. Sagaris (2015) appraises this increasing orientation towards sustainable transport modes as mostly just a paper tactic.

In order to understand the barriers to engagement with cycling in transport planning, we apply a wider definition (including investment) and pursue a purely quantitative approach, in contrast to Aldred et al (2017) who applied a hybrid quantitative (n=413) and qualitative (n=7) approach to understand investment. While Aldred et al (2017) also talk about a virtuous cycle, Brezina and Castro (2017) have sketched one based on Horton (2007) to identify the element which appears most likely to bear fruit to initiate system change: decision makers. Barriers to cycling use that arise from the built environment originate from human hands and can therefore be changed by human hands. Decision makers are responsible for shaping the built environment and the (quality of the) implementation of transport policies and therefore can act as either driving or restraining forces to the implementation of progressive policies and infrastructure (Brezina and Castro, 2017). We therefore focus our research on a survey of decision makers (administrators and planners) and cycling advocates who may pressure decision makers on cycling planning issues.

The following section reviews literature on general barriers to implementation of sustainable transport regimes and cycling, a field which has not been studied in great depth, before we proceed to elaborate our survey methods and the data gained from them. After presenting the survey analysis, the last two sections discuss the results and draw conclusions.

Literature review

In contrast to a large body of research on barriers to cycling for individuals (for example, Hagemeister et al, 2004; Parkin et al, 2007; Sener et al, 2009; Piatkowski and Marshall, 2015), studies on systematic or institutional barriers to sustainable transport policies are more limited (Banister, 1996; Vigar, 2000; Low et al, 2003; Cole et al, 2010). Surveys of public authority managers, associations and private companies identified that public apathy towards alternative transport forms operates in combination with transport planners' lack of perception of active modes as legitimate. This combination leads to inappropriate planning and resource provision (Cole et al, 2010). At decision-maker level, this apathy may be conceptualised as a mental barrier (Brezina and Castro, 2017). Mental barriers are the unexamined presuppositions that prevent full consideration of the options available or exclude some potential actions. One may also interpret mental barriers in decision makers as 'withholding forces' that reduce the potential of implementation or even prevent it (Banister, 2014).

In his seminal work on planning barriers, Banister (2014) defines six types of barrier and five framework conditions. Most pertinently for this study, the barriers include unqualified personnel, reducing implementation capacity and reproducing institutional and policy barriers. The framework conditions are those factors that permit or prevent successful and consistent policy implementation. A close link exists between institutional and resource barriers: institutions of political power allocate funding to policies according to their preferences. The barrier most commonly found among decision makers is a lack of real political commitment to implement measures that address key issues comprehensively and consistently (Banister, 2014). Vigar (2000) points out that the shift towards alternative transport regimes has been observed to be much stronger in transport planning rhetoric than in actual actions for promotion or implementation. It appears that a considerable number of 'best practice' collections on good design and planning methods have been published as a reaction to this trend of barriers towards qualitative infrastructure planning and implementation (for example, Gerike and Parkin, 2015; Becker et al, 2018; Berney, 2018; Parkin, 2018). While Bell and Ferretti (2015) question the requirements needed to understand the transition from strategy to infrastructure delivery, the automobility paradigm is still ubiquitous and taken for granted in planning (see Whitelegg, Chapter 5, this volume). In order to change city systems, planning systems need to change and invoke relevant key actions or dynamics to make cities more cycle inclusive, rather than hoping for single 'magic bullets', according to Sagaris (2015): a finding strongly consonant with Frey's (2014) conceptualisation of planning progress.

An essential core of the problem is the large share (47 per cent) within transport planning authorities that lack a professional transport planning culture (Envall, 2009). Others have already shown examples of how a possible change in design procedures towards higher quality implementation can be initialised within urban planning processes and hierarchies (Lokar, 2014) by, for example, implementing visual communication of planning alternatives impacts to decision makers. While implementation failure is easily identified, overcoming barriers that prevent even conceptualisation of appropriate interventions is not that easy and requires interactive and participatory processes to ensure intentions and outcomes coincide (Banister, 2014).

Most people act on their beliefs, and beliefs have origins (Low et al, 2003). Planners' education is both traditionally understood and socio-institutionally embedded as the source of their ideas about change (Frey, 2014). Rose (2015) and Dill and Weigland, (2008) give an insight into how little Civil Engineering students learn about cycling at Australian and American universities of technology. But, even making a change in this trend conceivable requires prior change in decision makers' minds (Knoflacher, 2001). Thus we have a central conundrum. There is a need to change the emphasis in education, but to achieve such a change requires a change in its outcomes. The question is therefore what strategies might be used in order to break this circularity. Ways proposed to change the existing planning and engineering paradigm (Knoflacher, 2016) include breaking up entrenched cycles of old-school thoughts and actions by means of education (Brezina et al, 2014), rejecting traditional expectations in transport planning (Frey, 2014) or applying non-standard solutions (Leth et al, 2014).

Methods and data

Brezina and Castro (2017) identified three categories of barriers: legal, planning and infrastructure, and the survey questions reflect this categorisation. As the questionnaires were sent to local/regional administrators, planners and cycling advocates but not to national or provincial legislators, the law-making perspective was mostly omitted. We developed a set of questions and made three versions of online questionnaires, slightly deviating in formulation depending on the three stakeholder groups. The questionnaires, after identifying the participants (location, field of action, age, experience, gender), inquire about the frequency of bicycle use and the appraisal of cycling as a means of transport, types of barriers, instances where participants have experienced such barriers and their personal experiences with breaking up such barriers. Not only did we ask for an appraisal of the point in time when cycling is considered within urban projects, we also asked for perceived priorities in cases of space scarcity. The appraisal of quality and quantity of bicycle parking was scrutinised, as was the assessment of past and future development paths. In the end, not only reasons for lack of priority setting were surveyed but also types of measures implemented, with or without strategic documents preceding them. The following nomenclature is used for (sub) sample sizes: N_0 population, N, n number of people, N_R, n_R number of responses.

Questionnaire hyperlinks for administrators were distributed via email to all 2,100 municipalities and 79 districts and statutory cities. Planners and advocates had been addressed over various info channels, for example: newsletters of the regional branches of the Austrian chamber of chartered engineers and the cycling advocacy group Radlobby Österreich. For both, the authors do not know the number of addressees and therefore, a response rate is only available for administrations (municipalities and districts). Responses were accepted between 6 April and 29 May 2018. The sample includes 290 (N) survey responses in total and Table 4.1 shows the size of sub samples.

Figures 4.1 and 4.2 show the distribution of survey participants (where names or ID numbers of territorial units were given) on the district (Figure 4.1) and municipal (Figure 4.2) level. With the exemption of Tirol and Kärnten provinces at least one district per province responded, either from a single stakeholder group or various combinations thereof. The municipal granularity map (Figure 4.2) shows a quite even distribution over Austria, where just the central region of the main alpine range from East-Southeast to Northwest (Vienna) is less present.

Figures 4.3, 4.4 and 4.5 illustrate the demographic composition of our sub samples by age (in comparison to the Austrian population), gender and experience respectively. Note that most of the population falls into the older age categories and that the sample contains more males (76.6 per cent) than females (22.1 per cent) averaged across respondents.

Table 4.1: Different sizes of sub samples and response rate

	Sub sample			
	Administration		Advocates	Planners
	Districts	Municipalities		
Respondents (N)	16	224	31	19
Population (N_0)	79	2,100	N.A.	N.A.
Response rate N/N_0 [%]		11.0	N.A.	N.A.

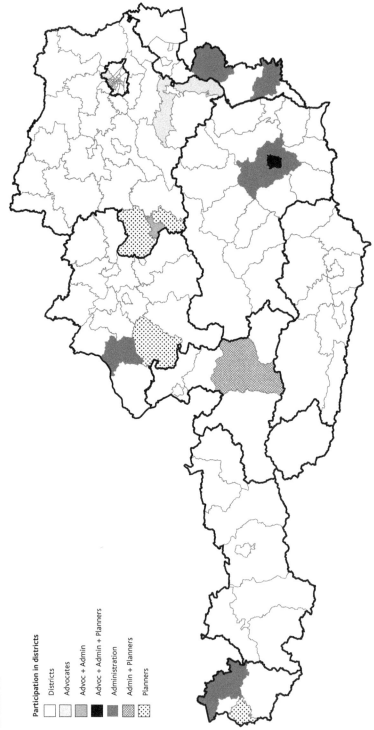

Figure 4.1: Geographical distribution of survey participants (where territorial IDs were provided) based on administrations, advocacies and planners in districts

Participation in districts

Districts
Advocates
Advoc + Admin
Advoc + Admin + Planners
Administration
Admin + Planners
Planners

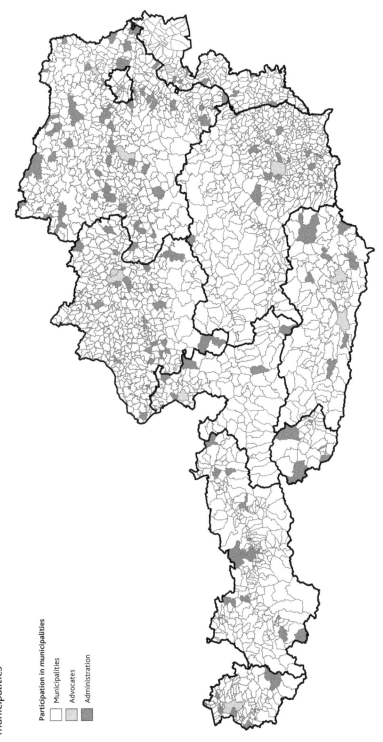

Figure 4.2: Geographical distribution of survey participants (where territorial IDs were provided) based on administrations and advocacies in municipalities

Participation in municipalities

Municipalities
Advocates
Administration

Figure 4.3: Age distribution by sub samples

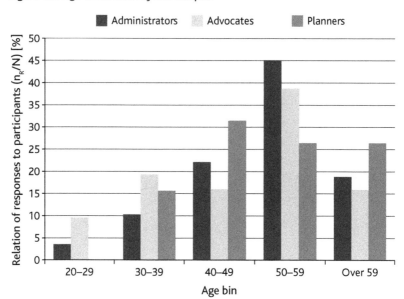

Figure 4.4: Gender distribution [%] by sub samples

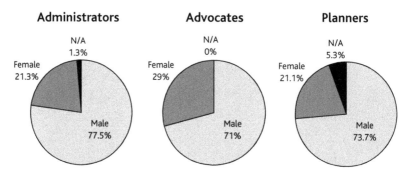

A significant number of administrators (30.8 per cent) and planners (64.2 per cent) have spent over 15 years in position indicating established careers and potentially settled work habits, while advocates have mostly (29.0 per cent) only been active for 3 to 5 years. When it comes to frequency of bicycle usage, planners show higher cycling affinity than administrators: 42.1 per cent versus 9.2 per cent cycle on a day-to-day basis, and 47.4 per cent versus 27.9 per cent do it 'several times a week'.

Figure 4.5: Years of experience in field of action by sub samples

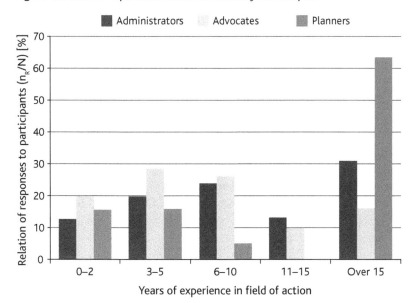

Survey analysis

The first two core items of the questionnaire asked the respondents of all three sub samples: (Q1) which occurrences of barriers in planning and implementation of cycling measures they have already experienced and (Q2) with whom they have experienced these barriers. Question (Q2) included answering options for naming other people (by institutions) as well as themselves. Table 4.2 shows that administrators are appraised to be the biggest group of stakeholders bearing barriers (34.9 to 35.7 per cent), by advocates and planners conjointly and even judge themselves and their administration peers strongly (28.1 and 24.6 per cent). This first result demonstrates the need to consider

Table 4.2: Whom did you identify as bearers of barriers? Institutional cross-appraisal in percent of multiple responses possible (sums of n_R add up to >100%)

		Those who appraise:		
		Advocates	Administrators	Planners
Those who were appraised:	Advocates	4.8	8.9	14.3
	Administrators	34.9	28.1 + 24.6[a]	35.7
	Planners	25.8	12.8	7.1

Note: [a] 28.1% of administrators admitted to have noticed barriers with themselves, while 24.6% noticed these barriers with other representatives of administrative bodies.

carefully the roles and place of administrators in order to understand the barriers.

It appears necessary to check possible discrepancies in perceptions: administrators of themselves versus advocates and planners of administrators. We selected administrators who answered 'unfortunately also with myself' in question Q2 and planners and advocates who answered 'administrators', and then ran a frequency analysis of question Q1, their perception of barrier manifestation. Table 4.3 shows this cross-perception of barriers. While self-accusing administrators consider the lack of budget (72.7 per cent) to be the biggest barrier (ahead of an incomplete network – 64.8 per cent), advocates appraise the incomplete network higher (95.2 per cent), together with lack of practicability and lack of budget (90.5 per cent). Advocates consider insufficient road surfaces to be the smallest among the problems (66.7 per cent), a view not shared by administrators and planners. While administrators and advocates consider lack of budget as a major problem (72.7–90.5 per cent), this is not an issue to planners. Planners have a strong focus in barrier perception on design parameters such as curve radii, insufficient lines of sight and detours. The comparison of total values suggests that advocates observe more barriers than administrators.

Question Q3 asked participants from all three sub samples what kinds of experiences they had in the past to overcome barriers in

Table 4.3: Manifestations of barriers split by perceptions of participants of administrators being bearers of barriers: self-perception of administrators and perceptions by advocates and planners

Barrier manifestation	Self-perception of administrators		Perception by advocates		Perception by planners	
	n_R	Share [%] [a]	n_R	Share [%] [a]	n_R	Share [%] [a]
Narrow curve radii	21	24.9	15	71.4	4	80.0
Lack of practicability	32	36.4	19	90.5	3	60.0
Insufficient lines of sight	32	36.4	17	81.0	3	60.0
Lack of parking spaces	36	40.9	18	85.7	2	40.0
Insufficient road surface	40	45.5	14	66.7	3	60.0
Detours	28	31.8	15	71.4	3	60.0
Incomplete network	57	64.8	20	95.2	4	80.0
Inconsistent signage	22	25.0	18	85.7	0	0.0
Lack of budget	64	72.7	19	90.5	1	20.0
None	1	1.1	0	0.0	0	0.0
Other	10	11.4	7	34.3	1	20.0

Note: [a] Relation of responses to participants (n_R/N).

planning and implementation. Response options were: 'I think this is impossible'; 'I didn't even try'; 'I tried, but failed'; 'I tried and succeeded'; 'This didn't even come to my mind'; 'Other'. As the share of those who have tried and failed and those who succeeded was equal (34.2 per cent) in administrators, we examined all those who claimed to have had success concerning their appraisal of development over time in Question Q4. Q4 asked all three sub samples to give a view on the development of cycling solutions over time in their field of action: How was it ten years ago? How will it be ten years from now? As the number of planners claiming to have had success in overcoming barriers proved to be very low (n=2), their results are not shown. However, Table 4.4 does show that self-perception by administrators and perception of advocates differs quite strongly. While 92.2 per cent of administrator responses state that today's planning and approaches are more innovative than they were ten years ago, this view is not shared by advocates (30.0 per cent). On the other hand, less than half of administrators (45.1 per cent) think that the decade to come will provide an increase of innovation, but 70.0 per cent of advocates share this view of the future. It appears that the advocates' more positive appraisal of the planning of the future may be considered as expedient optimism in contrast to a more reserved notion held by the administrators in charge.

As 34.2 per cent of administrators concede having been unsuccessful, the follow-up question on the reasons for failure appears inescapable. Question Q5 asked for the perceived reasons: 'What prevents you from giving cycling higher infrastructural priority or being more innovative than before in your field of action?'. Multiple responses were possible. In all sub samples, the answer 'Nothing, cycling has highest possible priority' was most frequent: advocates 76.2 per cent, administrators 35.0 per cent and planners 50.0 per cent (Table 4.5). In the category 'Other' (25.7 per cent), this sub sample highlights budgetary resources,

Table 4.4: Appraisal of development over time by administrators and advocates who have claimed to have been successful in overcoming planning barriers

	Administrators		Advocates	
	n_R	Share [%] [a]	n_R	Share [%] [a]
Today innovation is higher than ten years ago	47	92.2	3	30.0
In ten years innovation will be higher	23	45.1	7	70.0
Nothing has changed	1	2.0	2	20.0
I don't know	0	0.0	1	10.0
Other	2	4.9	1	10.0

Note: [a] Relation of responses to participants (n_R/N).

Table 4.5: What prevents you from giving cycling higher infrastructural priority?

	Administrators		Advocates		Planners	
	n_R	Share [%] [a]	n_R	Share [%] [a]	n_R	Share [%] [a]
Nothing, cycling has highest possible priority	49	35.0	16	76.2	3	50.0
No strategic decisions	32	22.9	3	14.3	1	16.7
Political pressure	5	4.6	0	0.0	1	16.7
Expectation of political pressure	2	1.4	2	9.5	0	0.0
Pressure by public	10	7.1	3	14.3	2	34.3
Expectation of pressure by public	7	5.0	2	9.5	1	16.7
Pressure by print media	2	1.4	2	9.5	1	16.7
Expectation of pressure by print media	1	0.7	3	14.3	0	0.0
Guidelines do not allow	10	7.1	1	4.8	1	16.7
Laws do not allow	10	7.1	0	0.0	0	0.0
Cyclists will find their way around	14	10.0	2	9.5	0	0.0
I don't care about cycling	1	0.7	0	0.0	0	0.0
Cyclists need no special measures	9	6.4	0	0.0	0	0.0
Cycling is not important enough	16	11.4	2	9.5	0	0.0
Cycling is too dangerous	5	4.6	0	0.0	1	16.7
Other	36	25.7	3	14.3	0	0.0

Note: [a] Relation of responses to participants (n_R/N).

prioritisation of other infrastructure projects and topographical situations as obstacles. Administrative perspectives diverge in relation to budgetary resources (Table 4.6). Since the majority of advocates and planners (54.4–66.7 per cent) did not know the cycling budget's

Table 4.6: How big is the share of the cycling infrastructure budget within the road construction budget?

	Municipalities		Districts	
Share of cycling budget [%]	n	Share [%]	n	Share [%]
0–2.5	70	51.5		
2.5–5	17	12.5		
5–7.5	7	5.1	1	8.3
7.5–10	9	6.6		
10–12.5	7	5.1		
12.5–15	1	0.7		
>15	5	4.7		
I don't know	20	14.7	11	91.7

share in their field of action, only the values given by administrators (separated by districts and municipalities) are considered. While municipalities could account for precise ranges of budgetary shares – 51.5 per cent reported 2.5 per cent or smaller budgets – the majority of districts could not.

Furthermore, we asked all sub samples (Q6) if there are any strategic planning documents that favour cycling and (Q7) what kinds of measures are being implemented in their field of action. We split respondents by answers to Q6: yes versus no, and examined measures implemented in both situations: with or without strategic planning documents (Table 4.7). Two decisive observations can be made. Firstly, from the larger total share values it can be concluded that almost twice as many measures can be implemented when a strategic document exists. Secondly, shared spaces and 30 km/h restriction zones are implemented with almost equal frequency regardless of whether or not strategic documents are available for municipalities or districts.

The open answers ('Other') given by the administrators revealed other barriers that were not just conceptual. Difficulties with property purchase or property owners were mentioned as impediments by several respondents. Road space availability, pointing either at non-municipality property or at car-centred priority, and costs also appeared in the answers as barriers to better solutions for cycling. However, both

Table 4.7: Which measures are being implemented in relation to the existence of strategic planning documents?

Measure installed	Existing strategic planning documents			
	Yes		No	
	n_R	Share [%] [a]	n_R	Share [%] [a]
Contraflow cycling	24	44.4	5	8.8
Speed limit 30km/h	28	51.9	27	47.4
Shared space	19	35.2	16	28.1
Cycling priority street	14	25.9	5	8.8
Separated cycle path	35	64.8	25	44.9
Cycling and walking path without separation	31	57.4	15	26.3
Mandatory cycling lane	24	44.4	7	12.3
Advisory cycling lane	19	35.2	7	12.3
Bicycle parking on roadside	26	48.1	17	29.8
Bicycle parking on sidewalks	17	31.5	6	10.5
Other	9	16.7	7	12.3

Note: [a] Relation of responses to participants (n_R/N).

might only be a pretext. Some administrators also expressed that the lack of political will is a major barrier.

And finally we asked (Q8) how have barriers been overcome in the past in their respective fields of action? (Figure 4.6) Consistently, administrators, advocates and planners rank the following three options as most promising: 1) 'By means of essential decision makers making own experiences where there is a need for change' (31.1 per cent, 45.8 per cent, 34.3 per cent), 2) 'By means of population groups building up social pressure' (26.7 per cent, 66.7 per cent, 66.7 per cent) and 3) 'We attempted overcoming it actively' (36.7 per cent, 50.0 per cent, 50.0 per cent). Planners conceded (34.3 per cent) that all attempts to do so may have been in vain.

Figure 4.6: How have barriers been overcome in the past in your field of action?

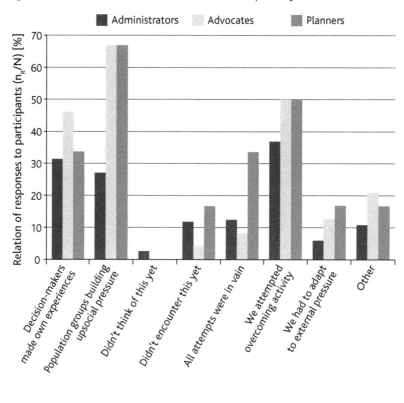

Discussion

The demographical scope of our respondents shows a clear picture: stakeholders are overwhelmingly comprised of older men (> 50). This is especially true for administrators – and does not seem to be a solely Austrian phenomenon (see Leyendecker, Chapter 6, this volume). Administrators and planners report a large share of respondents having 15 or more years of experience: for planners this is an absolute majority (64.2 per cent). These demographics paint a picture of mature decision makers, who may have adopted grounded transport notions from their car-centred socialisation and education a long time ago and the work experience of many years, and may therefore not be open for innovation adoption. This assertion is easily supported by the findings from Table 4.4: 47.1 per cent (92.2–45.1 per cent) of administrative responses claim to have reached peak innovation today. This 47.1 per cent being in accordance with Envall's 47 per cent may be a coincidence, but it confirms not only his findings but also Banister's (2014) notion of inertia. The necessary paradigm shift (see Whitelegg, Chapter 5, this volume) is stuck. The forces restraining stakeholders from giving cycling a higher priority are mostly neglected, as 35 per cent of responses with administrators claim to already provide cycling with the highest possible priority. A notion that remains un-surveyed in our work is the meaning of 'highest probability' in this context. Interestingly, a non-negligible amount of administrative responses (10.0 and 11.4 per cent respectively) share a view that cyclists can be left on their own, as they will find their way around, and that cycling is simply not relevant enough to be given higher attention. No direct evidence for lack of personnel qualification could be obtained, although individual administrators expressed a lack of concern towards cyclists and their needs.

While Horton (2007) identified cycling often to be considered not only as generally inferior but also as dangerous, this notion reflects just partly in the general responses of administrators. Only 4.9 per cent of multiple-choice responses consider it as too dangerous and 2.8 per cent as an obstruction of all other road users. While 9.7 per cent think it is unpractical, 15.3 per cent as suitable just for sports and spare time. Hence, in our investigation the notion of cycling fear and the societal marginalisation do not appear to be as strong as with Horton (2007). It is surprising to learn that advocates perceive the category 'Pressure by print media' (14.3 per cent) more strongly than administrators do with just 0.7 per cent responses. It can therefore be assumed that the advocates give more attention to daily cycling coverage in print media than do administrators. The budge-related results leave some room for debate. Firstly, we consider it quite obvious that advocates and planners know so little about actual budget allocation and therefore may not have an overview of financial barriers. The municipalities split shows that cycling infrastructure budget shares are in general very small and only a few will reach double digits. The minimal knowledge of budgets on the district level may be explained through district administrations being mainly executive branches of regional governments, and their budgets, therefore explicit cycling budgets on a district level may not exist at all.

In our survey, the availability of land for infrastructure was named often in the category 'Other'. Making privately owned land accessible for public use is a funding per se. Lack of funding was previously identified to be a major barrier (Aldred et al, 2017).

While general traffic calming measures such as speed limits and shared spaces are reported to be implemented almost irrespective of the existence of strategic planning documents, higher levels of bicycle-centred measures are reported to be achieved more easily when strategic documents exist. However, we did not check the quality and stringency of the existing documents. A lack of strategic documents could be also viewed as systematic lack of leadership, a barrier also identified elsewhere (Aldred et al, 2017). The figures in Table 7 could possibly be explained by the notion that smaller/rural municipalities/ districts in general do not have such strategic planning documents, as these appear to be more a matter of larger/urban areas.

We have highlighted the notion that planning takes place based on individual beliefs and education. But it is not beliefs of individuals alone; a wider perspective on the implementation gap – the difference between what can be implemented or achieved and what the actual actions taken are – can be adopted. Koglin and Rye (2014) emphasise the need for the development of positive representation of cycling to make cyclists' needs thoroughly understood by planners. Deffner and Hefter (2015) argue in a similar direction, as they put on record that sustainable mobility culture is not yet part of decision makers' daily tasks. Our findings suggest that the establishment of bicycling culture is on its way, although still in its infancy, as 'Cyclists will find their way around' is not among the most prominent answers of Table 4.5. Feddes et al (Chapter 7, this volume) show that continuous policy, planning and stakeholder involvement led to Amsterdam becoming a cycling city.

Conclusion

We quantitatively identified mental barriers to manifest in different stakeholder groups, but administrators proved to be the most important group. Observed barrier manifestation showed that administrators in general see about 50 per cent less barriers than advocates and planners do. This is combined with a strongly opposing view as to whether the most innovative planning decade lies in the past or in the future. Administrators lean towards the idea that the biggest innovation in planning has already taken place in the past.

Feedback received from the respondents and the analysis point towards further research. Decision makers (in all three stakeholder groups involved) need to be asked where they think their own and other stakeholder's presuppositions come from and how much did they have to adapt their mental models and planning procedures from education to fine-tune them with real-world necessities.

Only limited literature (for example, Curtis, 2008; Hull, 2008; Dill and Weigland, 2010; Deegan and Parkin, 2011; Deffner and Hefter, 2015) was found to offer a (somewhat limited) perspective on the cycling and sustainable transport policy implementation training of planners and the so-called 'implementation gap' (Duffhues and Bertolini, 2015; Silva et al, 2017), but none exercises an evaluation of such efforts. We consider issues of reduction of mental barriers and reduction of friction losses during implementation to be a yielding field of future research.

We have surveyed a limited scope of 'the hows' when it comes to tackling barriers. An essence of future, implementation-based research from our point of view needs to be: How did respondents overcome barriers (in themselves and/or among others) in between two extreme positions: incremental change (evolution) versus radical policies (revolution). Nevertheless, the analytical identification of decision makers (Brezina and Castro, 2017) as key elements to tackle planning barrier manifestation is quantitatively backed by our findings.

Completing the mental-barriers perspective are the final findings on what appear to be the most promising approaches in overcoming mental barriers in decision makers: social pressure upon and self-experience by decision makers.

Acknowledgements

The authors wish to thank and acknowledge The Austrian Regional Chambers of Chartered Engineers for helping us to distribute the questionnaire among their members; all the planners and chartered engineers, representatives of municipalities and district administrations as well as bicycle advocates for participating in our survey; Manuela Winder for sharing her experience with social survey design and Kyle Johnston for proofreading.

References

Aldred, R., Watson, T., Lovelace, R. and Woodcock, J. (2017) 'Barriers to investing in cycling: stakeholder views from England', *Transportation Research Part A: Policy and Practice*, 128: 149–59.

Anderl, M., Burgstaller, J., Gugele, B., Gössl, M., Haider, S., Heller, C., Ibesich, N., Kampel, E., Köther, T., Kuschel, V., Lampert, C., Neier, H., Pazdernik, K., Poupa, S., Purzner, M., Rigler, E., Schieder, W., Schmidt, G., Schneider, J., Schodl, B., Svehla-Stix, S., Storch, A., Stranner, G., Vogel, J., Wiesenberger, H. and Zechmeister, A. (2018) '*Klimaschutzbericht 2018*', Wien: Umweltbundesamt.

Banister, D. (1996) 'Barriers to implementation of urban sustainability', European Regional Science Association – 36th European Congress, 26–30 August, ETH Zürich, Switzerland: ERSA.

Banister, D. (2014) 'Overcoming barriers to the implementation of sustainable transport', in P. Rietveld and R.R. Stough (eds) *Barriers to Sustainable Transport: Institutions, Regulation and Sustainability*, London and New York: Routledge.

Becker, A., Lampe, S., Negussie, L. and Cachola Schmal, P. (eds) (2018) *Fahr Rad! Die Rückeroberung der Stadt*, Basel: Birkhäuser Verlag.

Bell, W. and Ferretti, D. (2015) 'What should planners know about cycling?', in J. Bonham and M. Johnson (eds) *Cycling futures*, Adelaide: University of Adelaide Press, pp 321–56.

Berney, R. (ed) (2018) *Bicycle Urbanism – Reimagining Bicycle Friendly Cities*, London, New York: Routledge.

Brezina, T. and Castro Fernandez, A. (2017) 'Cycling related mental barriers in decision makers: the Austrian context', in H. Knoflacher and E.V. Öcalir-Akünal (eds) *Engineering Tools and Solutions for Sustainable Transportation Planning*, IGI Global, www.igi-global.com/book/engineering-tools-solutions-sustainable-transportation/172014

Brezina, T., Frey, H., Emberger, G. and Leth, U. (2014) 'Teaching ethics to transport engineers – The rationale behind and practice at Vienna Univ. of Technology', in S. Lakusic (ed) *3rd International Conference on Road and Rail Infrastructure CETRA 2014*: Split, HR: Department of Transportation, University of Zagreb, 867–74.

Cole, R., Burke, M., Leslie, E., Donald, M. and Owen, N. (2010) 'Perceptions of representatives of public, private, and community sector institutions of the barriers and enablers for physically active transport', *Transport Policy*, 17(6): 496–504.

Curtis, C. (2008) 'Planning for sustainable accessibility: the implementation challenge', *Transport Policy*, 15: 104–12.

Daley, M. and Rissel, C. (2011) 'Perspectives and images of cycling as a barrier or facilitator of cycling', *Transport Policy*, 18(1): 211–16.

Davies, D., Brook-Carter, N. and Gardner, G. (2000) *Institutional and organisational attitudes to cycling*', Crowthorne, Berkshire: Transport Research Laboratory (TRL).

Deegan, B. and Parkin, J. (2011) 'Planning cycling networks: human factors and design processes', *Proceedings of the Institution of Civil Engineers – Engineering Sustainability*, 164(1): 85–94.

Deffner, J. and Hefter, T. (2015) *Sustainable mobility cultures and the role of cycling planning professionals*, Frankfurt/Main, Deutschland: Institute of Social-Ecological Research (ISOE).

Dill, J. and Weigand, L. (2010) 'Incorporating bicycle and pedestrian topics in university transportation courses: a national scan', *Transportation Research Record*, 2198: 1–7.

Douglas, M.J., Watkins, S.J., Gorman, D.R. and Higgins, M. (2011) 'Are cars the new tobacco?', *Journal of Public Health*, 33(2): 160–9.

Duffhues, J. and Bertolini, L. (2015) 'From integrated aims to fragmented outcomes: urban intensification and transportation planning in the Netherlands', *Journal of Transport and Land Use*, 9(3): 15–34.

Envall, P. (2009) 'What is hindering good cycle planning: how do city planners think?', *Velo-city 2009 – Re-cycling cities*, 12–15 May, Bruxelles, Belgium.

Frey, H. (2014) 'Wer plant die Planung? – Widersprüche in Theorie und Praxis', in M. Schrenk, V.V. Popovich P. Zeile and P. Elisei (eds) *Proceedings of CORP 2014*: Wien, 783–91.

Gehl, J. (2011) *Life Between Buildings: Using Public Space*, Washington, DC: Island Press.

Gerike, R. and Parkin, J. (eds) (2015) *Cycling Futures: From Research into Practice*, London: Routledge.

Goodman, A., Brand, C. and Ogilvie, D. (2012) 'Associations of health, physical activity and weight status with motorised travel and transport carbon dioxide emissions: a cross-sectional, observational study', *Environmental Health*, 52(10).

Hagemeister, C., Schmidt, A., Seidel, T. and Schlag, B. (2004) 'Criteria for cyclists' everyday route choice', *3rd International Conference on Traffic and Transport Psychology*: Nottingham.

Heinfellner, H., Ibesich, N. and Kurzweil, A. (2015) *Masterplan Radfahren 2015–2015*, Wien: BM für Land- und Forstwirtschaft, Umwelt und Wasserwirtschaft.

Horton, D. (2007) 'Fear of cycling', in D. Horton, P. Rosen and P. Cox (eds) *Cycling and Society*, Aldershot: Ashgate Publishing, pp 133–52.

Hull, A. (2008) 'Policy integration: what will it take to achieve more sustainable transport solutions in cities?', *Transport Policy*, 15: 94–104.

Knoflacher, H. (2001) 'Wie die Trendumkehr der Verkehrsentwicklung denkbar machen? ', ÖIAZ – *Österreichische Ingenieur- und Architekten-Zeitschrift*, 146: 190–4.

Knoflacher, H. (2015) 'Wer hat Vorfahrt im urbanen Raum? Wissenschaftliche Bewertung der Verkehrsträger in der Stadt', *Der Nahverkehr*, 33: 11–15.

Knoflacher, H. (2016) 'Paradigmenwechsel im Verkehrswesen', in H. Knoflacher and H. Frey (eds) *Paradigmenwechsel im Verkehrswesen*, Wien: ÖVG.

Koglin, T. and Rye, T. (2014) 'The marginalisation of bicycling in Modernist urban transport planning', *Journal of Transport & Health*, 1: 214–22.

Leth, U., Frey, H. and Brezina, T. (2014) 'Innovative approaches of promoting non-motorized transport in cities', in S. Lakusic (ed) *3rd International Conference on Road and Rail Infrastructure CETRA 2014*: Split, HR: Department of Transportation, University of Zagreb, 875–81.

Lokar, B. (2014) 'Making cycling again part of Ljubljana's DNA', in H.J. Zukal and T. Brezina (eds) *Ringvorlesung SS 2014: Radfahren in der Stadt – Ausgewählte Vorträge*, Wien: Institut für Verkehrswissenschaften, TU Wien.

Low, N., Gleeson, B. and Rush, E. (2003) 'Making believe: institutional and discursive barriers to sustainable transport in two Australian cites', *International Planning Studies*, 8: 93–114.

Massink, R., Zuidgeest, M., Rijnsburger, J., Sarmiento, O.L. and van Maarseveen, M. (2011) 'The climate value of cycling', *Natural Resources Forum*, 35(2): 100–11.

Müller, A., Redl, C., Haas, R., Türk, A., Liebmann, L., Steininger, K., Brezina, T., Mayerthaler, A., Schopf, J.M., Werner, A., Kreuzer, D., Steiner, A., Mollay, U. and Neugebauer, W. (2012) 'EISERN – Energy Investment Strategies And Long Term Emission Reduction Needs (Strategien für Energie-Technologie-Investitionen und langfristige Anforderung zur Emissionsreduktion) – Projektendbericht', Wien: Klima- und Energiefonds.

Parkin, J. (2018) *Designing for Cycle Traffic: International Principles and Practice*, London: ICE Publishing.

Parkin, J., Ryley, T. and Jones, T. (2007) 'Barriers to cycling: an exploration of quantitative analyses', in D. Horton, P. Rosen and P. Cox (eds) *Cycling and Society*, Aldershot: Ashgate Publishing, pp 67–82.

Piatkowski, D.P. and Marshall, W.E. (2015) 'Not all prospective bicyclists are created equal: the role of attitudes, socio-demographics, and the built environment in bicycle commuting', *Travel Behaviour and Society*, 2: 166–74.

Pilko, H., Tepes, K. and Brezina, T. (2015) 'Policy and programs for cycling in the City of Zagreb – a critical review', *Promet – Traffic & Transportation*, 27(5): 405–15.

Rose, G. (2015) 'Teaching Australian civil engineers about cycling', in J. Bonham and M. Johnson (eds) *Cycling futures*, Adelaide: University of Adelaide Press, pp 303–20.

Rosinak & Partner and Besch + Partner (2006) *Mobil im Ländle – Verkehrskonzept Vorarlberg 2006*, Bregenz.

Sagaris, L. (2015) 'Lessons from 40 years of planning for cycle-inclusion: reflections from Santiago, Chile', *Natural Resources Forum*, 39: 64–81.

Sener, I.N., Eluru, N. and Bhat, C.R. (2009) 'An analysis of bicycle route choice preferences in Texas, US', *Transportation*, 36(5): 511–39.

Silva, C., Bertolini, L., te Brömmelstroet, M., Milakis, D. and Papa, E. (2017) 'Accessibility instruments in planning practice: bridging the implementation gap', *Transport Policy*, 53: 135–45.

Steffen, W., Rockström, J., Richardson, K., Lenton, T.M., Folke, C., Liverman, D., Summerhayes, C.P., Barnosky, A.D., Cornell, S.E., Crucifix, M., Donges, J.F., Fetzer, I., Lade, S.J., Scheffer, M., Winkelmann, R. and Schellnhuber, H.J. (2018) 'Trajectories of the Earth System in the Anthropocene', *Proceedings of the National Academy of Sciences of the United States of America*, 115(33): 8252–9.

Telepak, G., Winkler, A., Stratil-Sauer, G., Käfer, A., Posch, H., Gerlich, W., Trisko, A., Rischer, M., Fürst, B., Klimmer-Pölleritzer, A., Semela, H., Frank, J., Rauscher, B. and Keller, T. (2015) *STEP 2025 – Fachkonzept Mobilität*, Wien: Magistratsabteilung 18.

Vigar, G. (2000) 'Local "barriers" to environmentally sustainable transport planning', *Local Environment*, 5(1): 19–32.

5

Safety, risk and road traffic danger: towards a transformational approach to the dominant ideology

John Whitelegg

Introduction

There are very few subject areas in public policy that can lay claim to as many co-benefits as an increase in cycling. And few embrace as many beneficial social, economic and health outcomes as an increase. The gains that flow from increases in cycling have a proven, positive impact on ten major policy areas (Table 5.1). All these policy areas are characterised by strategies and speeches declaring the commitment of elected politicians and professional groups to improve matters at national, regional or city-region levels. In the vast majority of cases, deeds do not follow words, and policies that deter cycling are given a higher priority than those policies that would result in increases. This is the case in the majority of UK city and regional councils who pursue policies that increase the quantity of motorised traffic and do very little to implement the list of 17 pro-cycling initiatives identified by Pucher and Buehler (2012a: 350).

One of the 17 items on this list is 'Combine incentives for cyclists with disincentives for car use' and this is very rarely pursued as part of a package of measures to increase levels of cycling. In the case of climate change, cycling has the capacity to improve matters on a global scale. Cycling as a policy issue is characterised by a vast amount of evidence and data in support of its ability to deliver public policy objectives and a remarkable paucity of real change 'on the ground'. There are, of course, examples of excellent outcomes that exploit this ability, and Copenhagen is frequently mentioned in the literature (Koglin, 2013; Koglin and Rye, 2014; Koglin, 2015a; Koglin, 2015b). Every year, international cycling conferences add to this list of best practice, and the scientific literature on the benefits of cycling grows at a faster rate than in many other public policy areas (World Health Organization

Table 5.1: How cycling contributes to the delivery of policy areas

- Improving individual health and community-wide public health
- Reducing air pollution caused by passenger vehicles
- Reducing community exposure to noise caused by traffic
- Reducing Greenhouse Gases and contributing to achieving climate change policy objectives
- Reducing congestion
- Reducing death and injury in the road traffic environment
- Improving local economic performance
- Reducing the cost of transport to individuals and to public expenditure
- Transforming public space in cities and making more efficient use of highway space
- Contributing to the reduction of inequalities and a fair distribution of taxation revenue

(WHO), 2018). The uniqueness of cycling lies in the enormous gap between what we know about its exceptional ability to deliver desirable outcomes and the very low level of acceptance, development, funding and delivery on the ground in the vast majority of administrations globally. This gap points to a fundamental ideological and cultural problem. Every country remains committed to a paradigm that puts the car, motorised mobility and large amounts of expenditure on infrastructure to support that paradigm first. The paradigm firmly establishes the street as a space for motorised vehicles and emphasises the importance of unimpeded motorised trips. For example, in the UK 'increasing journey time reliability' and 'reducing the time needed for a car trip' are key policy objectives, with no recognition of the time spent by pedestrians attempting to cross a street and no recognition of the impact of speed and volume of motorised traffic on the likelihood that children or women will take up cycling. The failure here is not just of the lack of physical infrastructure but also a failure of the political infrastructures necessary to translate the rhetorical commitment into meaningful policy. Change requires not just policy adaptation but a paradigmatic shift. The strength of the paradigm and its supportive ideology is well understood and described in the writings of Bailey (1987), Sachs (1992), Whitelegg (2016) and Cross (2018).

There is published evidence on all ten delivery areas but this chapter concentrates on health, road traffic danger and the urgent need to create a totally safe walking and cycling environment as the bedrock of pro-cycling interventions. It explores the barriers to wide adoption of pro-cycling policies and links this to the urgent need to focus on system-wide paradigm shift. A paradigm shift in transport, based on the work of Goepel and the Wuppertal Institute in Germany (Goepel, 2016) is achievable and will liberate the potential of cycling to make its maximum contribution to the ten policy areas listed in Table 5.1.

The central argument is that cycling is not part of the current transport paradigm. It is excluded. The current paradigm is based on the flawed argument that higher levels of motorised transport are inevitable, are the result of desirable increases in GDP and personal disposable income, and deliver increases in quality of life, freedoms and choice. This is a powerful cocktail of assumptions and fits the definition of a paradigm (Kuhn, 1962). A paradigm is a worldview and during its hegemony, rebuffs challenges. Over time the dominant paradigm weakens, the challenges become stronger and the paradigm is overturned and replaced.

As Koglin (Chapter 3, this volume) demonstrates, cycling cannot prosper within the current transport paradigm. If we wish to promote cycling we have to go further than talking about cycling itself and challenge the paradigm so that it becomes untenable and is replaced by a new paradigm. This chapter attempts to do three things:

- demonstrate that the current paradigm obstructs the promotion of cycling;
- show that there are examples of paradigm shift that we can learn from; and
- explore two examples of paradigm shift that provide us with evidence and support with which we can overthrow the transport paradigm. Specifically, we can learn from the Swedish 'Vision Zero' road safety policy and the German 'Energiewende' transformation to inform how we go about achieving paradigm shift in transport.

While Banister (2005) has identified the unsustainability of the current transport paradigm and its associated policies, this chapter proposes a further move beyond the critique and thus addresses the policy and the cognitive infrastructure required for paradigm transformation. It argues that to achieve paradigm shift in transport we need to learn from the historical record of similar shifts. For example, the 'Energiewende' in Germany (Lechtenboehmer and Samadi, 2013) and the insights in Goepel (2016). This in turn requires large-scale, system-wide, transformative thinking: the Swedish 'Vision Zero' road safety policy is discussed as a model for this wider transformational agenda (Whitelegg and Haq, 2006; Whitelegg, 2016).

The chapter also argues that public health has a huge potential to contribute to paradigm shift. Currently, politicians and powerful lobby groups argue persuasively for more roads, more car parking, more subsidies for vehicles that will undoubtedly produce more traffic and outcomes that are bicycle-unfriendly and deter cycling. This creates an unequal struggle in the competition for priorities in transport policy. Cycling lobby groups do not have the 'clout' to out-perform the road-building lobby and the latter's reliance on rejecting the evidence that shows that additional road building generates extra traffic (Whitelegg, 2017). The explicit reliance on 'fake truth' and the strong bias towards growth in car traffic is a clear example of a dominant ideology at work. A key message in this chapter is that cycling will not achieve its potential for improving all ten policy areas until we have a new mobility strategy and the abandonment of the dominant ideology (Whitelegg, 2016) and its replacement by a kinder, evidence-based, sustainable, people-centred set of principles. These principles and policies will deliver a reduction in car use, a large increase in walking and cycling and transform streets from the current socially destructive 'traffic sewer' model into a socially restorative and community enhancing alternative (Appleyard, 1981; Hart and Parkhurst, 2011)

It is, therefore, appropriate, in pursuit of paradigm shift, to move the focus of discussion to public health, quality of life, costs of health care and to adopt a deeper, wider, system change perspective that will then create a more fertile environment and policy context that will encourage cycling policies and increases in cycling levels. In this shift, it is essential to deploy as much evidence as possible on public health and individual health and utilise the positive examples of Vision Zero and Energiewende to show that shift is not only desirable but also possible.

What is the current transport paradigm?

This can be summarised very succinctly in the national transport forecasting activity of three countries: Sweden, Germany and the UK. Forecasting is itself a deeply flawed process that has been described as 'predict and provide' (Kenworthy, 2012). Forecasts embed the concept of uninterrupted growth in vehicle numbers and vehicle-kms in transport policy and thinking and simultaneously exclude the option of a reduction based on a significant shift in travel choice from car to alternatives, including cycling, and this defines the paradigm. The foundation of the current transport paradigm is its use of traditional forecasting techniques and the absence of methodologies that would embrace the potential for a shift away from the car, for example, backcasting (Miola, 2008).

- In Sweden, official transport forecasts predict a 25 per cent increase in vehicle-kms by 2030 on a 2010 base, (Trafikverket, 2015).
- In the UK, the Department of Transport (2018) has predicted a growth in traffic of between 17 per cent and 51 per cent by 2050 on a 2015 base. This number is then used in all road-building projects to justify the need for the new roads. This produces a self-fulfilling prophecy: a very different forecast would result from a very different process (Miola, 2008). The self-fulling prophecy and the absolute rejection of any reduction in vehicle-kms is the defining characteristic of the current transport paradigm.
- In Germany the forecasts show an increase of 10 per cent in vehicle-kms (cars) by 2030 on a 2010 base and a 39 per cent increase in lorries (Bundesministerium fuer Verkehr und digitale Infrastruktur, 2018).

Paradigm shift and the importance of a wide-ranging public health and individual health perspective to produce a transformation of policies and attitudes

Paradigm shift is possible in transport and mobility, but will require a strong and sustained discussion around the benefits that flow from this shift. Health benefits are central to this transformation. There is a huge volume of evidence to show that cycling is beneficial to physical and mental well-being (British Medical Association, 1992; Andersen et al, 2000; Cavill and Davis, 2007; Pucher and Buehler, 2012b). This evidence has been summarised by Cycling England (2018):

- Cyclists can expect to live for at least two years longer on average than non–cyclists (Paffenbarger et al, 1986).
- Occasional and regular cyclists enjoy a level of fitness equivalent to being between five and ten years younger (Tuxworth et al, 1986).
- Cycling as part of normal daily activities can yield much the same improvements in physical performance as specific training programmes (Hendriksen, 1996).
- In 2003 there were around 40,000 deaths per year due to physical inactivity and 113 deaths due to cycling (Cavill and Davis, 2007).
- Studies between countries show that the higher the rate of cycling the lower the cyclists' death and injury rate (Jacobsen, 2003).
- The Health Select Committee said that meeting the Government's cycling target would do more to tackle childhood obesity than

any other measure (*Parliamentary Health Select Committee Report on Obesity*, House of Commons, 2004).

The 1992 report by the British Medical Association was researched and written by Mayer Hillman at the Policy Studies Institute in London and, more than 25 years later, is still relevant to the debate around cycling, safety, health and risk. In spite of the fact that it was commissioned and published by one of the world's leading professional medical bodies, it has not had the impact that might have been expected. The report gives a detailed explanation of the health benefits of cycling and adopts an evidence-based quantitative approach by comparing cycling rates in the Netherlands and the UK, and life expectancy at different ages in these two countries. The report is unusual in that it compares the life expectancy of UK cyclists killed in road accidents with the benefits associated with cycling itself, and epidemiological studies suggesting that the physical exercise associated with cycling can add an extra 2.5 years of life to those carrying out modest levels of cycling. The total of life-years lost (1989 data) as a result of cycling fatalities was 11,324 and Mayer Hillman comments:

> In this chapter a form of cost-benefit analysis of cycling has been attempted by comparing life-years lost through cycling accidents to life-years gained through regular exercise. Although a direct quantitative analysis is not possible due to lack of conclusive data, existing evidence would suggest that, even in the current hostile traffic environment, the benefits gained from regular cycling are likely to outweigh the loss of life through cycling accidents for the current population of regular cyclists. (British Medical Association, 1992: 121)

Is cycling dangerous and does this act as a deterrent to an increase in cycling?

Risk emerges as a central concern for considerations of change. 'In particular, it is argued that there needs to be a much more integrated approach to transport policy that combines interventions to make walking and (especially) cycling as risk-free as possible with restrictions on car use and attitudinal shifts in the ways in which motorists view other road users' (Pooley et al, 2013a). The national pro-cycling lobby group in England, Cycling England (see Box 5.1), provides one perspective on this issue.

Box 5.1: Cycling risk

Many people say that they do not cycle because they are worried about the risk. But consider the facts:

- The actual risk of cycling is small – one cyclist death per 33 million kilometres of cycling. This distance would take the average cyclist 21,000 years to cycle.
- Cycle casualties are declining: in 2004 deaths had declined to 134 from the 1994–98 average of 186, and all casualties among cyclists were down from 24,385 to 16,648 respectively.
- Off-road routes are safer, and use is growing rapidly. Cycling trips on the National Cycle Network have grown year on year since it began in 1995. In 2004 there were 100.2 million cycle trips, an 11.1 per cent increase since 2003, including increased usage due to new routes.
- A sedentary lifestyle poses clear risks to our health: in 2003 there were 57,000 cardiovascular disease deaths and over 10,000 cancer deaths that could be attributed to physical inactivity. In the same year 113 cyclists were killed on the road.

Source: www.cyclingengland.co.uk/health4.php

There is no doubt that road traffic danger and the perception of risk is a deterrent to cycling. Hillman et al (1990) identified this as the main reason for the profound decline in children's independent mobility between 1971 and 1990. Examining patterns of walking and cycling to school for children of different ages we concluded: 'In our English surveys in 1971, we found that 80 per cent of 7 and 8 year old children were allowed to go to school on their own. By 1990, this figure had dropped to 9 per cent' (Hillman et al, 1990: 106).

Another powerful source of empirical evidence identifying perception of risk and fear of traffic can be found in the work of Appleyard (1981) and a UK study that repeated the work of Appelyard in Bristol 2006 (Hart and Parkhurst, 2011). Other recent research has further confirmed the link between road traffic danger, perception of risk and deterrence. Aldred and Crosweller (2015) carried out an online diary survey of cycle trips and 'near misses'. One in four of the response recorded 'near misses' that were 'very scary'.

It is clear in the published literature that perception of risk is a significant barrier to an increase in cycling. Put very bluntly, many of those who are inclined to consider cycling as an option for their journeys will not make the switch from car to bike because they think 'it is too dangerous'. Perception matters (Hokstad and Vatn, 2008). Aldred and Goodman (2018) are clear on this point: 'Although multiple factors may act as barriers to cycling, the most common reason that people give for not cycling is perceived risk' (Horton, 2007; Thornton et al, 2010; Lawson et al, 2013). Hence, in the invaluable study by Pooley et al (2013b), provision of adequate segregated infrastructure was identified as crucial in changing patterns of walking and cycling.

Is statistical information on risk, death and injury to cyclists useful?

In one sense the answer to this question is 'no'. The 'safest' roads in the UK for cyclists and pedestrians are motorways because they are banned. The road identified by Appleyard with very little pedestrian activity because residents are fearful of traffic danger are very 'safe', because pedestrians do not use the street and opt for social isolation and immobility rather than run the risk of crossing the road. Data on death and injury tells us very little about danger and the impact of traffic levels and traffic speed on deterring walking and cycling and yet (in the UK) it is the most important consideration when discussing road safety (Davis, 2018). Vision Zero inverts that logic of road safety schemes based on death and injury levels. Instead, it imposes meaningful measures to reduce road traffic danger, including system-wide, default limits of 30 km/h on all roads carrying a mixture of pedestrian, cyclists and motorised vehicles and junction re-modelling to eliminate cycling deaths and serious injuries (Killed and Seriously Injured [KSIs]) at these locations.

Fortunately, we have a great deal of empirical evidence from the work of John Pucher at Rutgers University in the US, and these data reveal that the safety of cyclists varies enormously by country.

Also we know a great deal about Smeed's Law and the relationship between cycling rates and safety: the more cycling that takes pace, the safer it is (Jacobsen, 2003). A recent report from the Wuppertal Institute in Germany draws attention to the huge variations in bicycle safety in the 13 cities that are ranked on a variety of sustainable transport criteria (Kodukula et al, 2018), summarised in Table 5.2.

The importance of the work of Jacobsen (2003) and the city rankings published by the Wuppertal Institute (Kodukula et al, 2018) show that the safety of cyclists is dependent on the amount of cycling and on the thoroughness, consistency and funding of pro-cycling interventions. In the language of statistics taught to geographers in the late 1960s, the dependent variables are fatalities and/or crashes per kilometre travelled

Table 5.2: Road safety ranking for cycling in 13 cities

City	Share of cycling trips (%)	Annual cycling fatalities	Crashes for every 1 million cycle trips
Copenhagen	29	5	0.7
Amsterdam	32	5	1.2
Madrid	6	1	1.6
Oslo	7	1	2.3
Budapest	2	2	6.7
Vienna	7	2	7.6
Moscow	3	5	9.4
Paris	3	3	10.4
Zurich	8	2	11.3
Berlin	13	15	14.3
Rome	1	25	15.3
Brussels	3	2	21.4
London	2	8	22.3

Note: Data on road safety varies widely depending on the definitions of a crash and a fatality. In many cities fatality is considered relevant to the accident if the victim dies within 30 days of the crash. Similarly, actual crash numbers in cities are usually higher, as not all crashes are reported. Here we considered the numbers that are reported from official sources.

Source: Kodukula et al, 2018: 22

or thousands of residents, and the independent variables are measures of cycle infrastructure funding (especially segregated bike tracks) and fundamental road safety interventions including 30 km/h (20 mph) and car-free streets.

Pucher and Buehler (2012a) have listed 15 pro-cycling, evidence-based interventions that deliver increases in cycling rates and numbers. To put it very simply, we can have whatever level of cycle safety we want. It is illogical, flawed and unscientific to rely on KSI data for cyclists in any one location or in any one time period as if this is a meaningful statistic rather than the result of whatever mixture of pro-cycling policies have been adopted or not adopted.

The current paradigm accepts that cycling is risky and that the perception of road traffic danger and risk deters an increase in the quantity of cycling. Cycling cannot prosper within a paradigm that embraces year-on-year increases in vehicle numbers and vehicle-kms driven and a level of risk and danger that is known to deter the take-up of cycling. It is essential to challenge the current paradigm and substitute a new paradigm based on a total safe system concept and the explicit commitment to the eradication of death and serious injury in the road traffic environment (Elvik, 2003; 2008). This is already in place in the Swedish 'Vision Zero' road safety policy. It is also in place under different names in Norway and the Netherlands but it is not in place generally in the EU-28 (Elvebakk and Steiro, 2009).

Vision Zero and transformation: the urgent need for paradigm shift

The responsibility for road safety has traditionally been placed on the individual road user rather than on the designers of the system. Road safety has tended to focus on encouraging good behaviour by road users via licensing, testing, education, training and publicity. Sweden is among those countries with the lowest number of traffic fatalities in relation to its population. However, in spite of this excellent record, in 1997 the Swedish Parliament introduced a new approach to road safety called 'Vision Zero' (Whitelegg and Haq, 2006).

Vision Zero is based on a refusal to accept human deaths or lifelong suffering as a result of road traffic accidents (Elvik, 1999; Elvik and Amundsen, 2000). Swedish fatalities in 2015 were 26 per million inhabitants, 23 per 10 billion kilometres and 56 per million passenger cars, and on all three measures the lowest of any major nation state in the EU (European Commission, 2017). The EU-27 average in 2015 was 51 fatalities per million inhabitants, 54 per 10 billion kilometres and 104 per million passenger cars (European Commission, 2017). The decline in fatalities in Sweden, 55.6 per cent in the period 2001– 15, was higher than the two countries normally regarded as good performers in road safety (Netherlands and the UK).

Paradigm shift requires very practical and tangible changes in several policy areas that synergistically feed through to create the right conditions for paradigm shift. The position adopted in this chapter is that this can be achieved by the adoption of Vision Zero, the Swedish road safety policy. Vision Zero is an example of paradigm shift that has already taken place in transport, is beneficial for the achievement of high levels of cycling, and has been in place since October 1977. Vision Zero is based on the ethical imperative that: 'It can never be ethically acceptable that people are killed or seriously injured when moving within the road system' (Tingvall and Haworth, 1999; see also Fahlquist, 2006). To make this shift it is necessary to ensure that there is connection between policy areas. In other words it requires policy infrastructures that can cope with thinking about and implementing practical and tangible changes in several policy areas at once so that they can work synergistically. Oslo, which has adopted a Vision Zero policy, now ranks first in road safety (and in air quality) among

European cities through, as Elvebakk (2007) shows, extending the discussion beyond the technical aspects of road safety into the ethical.

The Energiewende

Vision Zero is a paradigm shift that has already taken place. It is a totally different way of formulating policies on traffic, transport, public health and alternatives to the car. Another example of paradigm shift is also in place and this is the 'Energiewende' or energy transformation in Germany (Lechtenboehmer and Samadi, 2013) and has more than a passing relevance to transport and cycling. The conceptual links between energy policy and transport policy are especially strong. Both have been dominated for decades by an unquestioned assumption that more is good and should be supported by heavy investment in new infrastructure. In the case of electricity generation this meant more power stations should be built and in the case of transport more roads, airports and high-speed rail must be built. In both cases, the subject of demand management (reduction in the consumption of electricity in the case of energy and the replacement of car trips by cycling, walking and public transport) was often discussed but not rigorously implemented. In both cases it was recognised that there are sound arguments for reducing the need to travel and reducing the amount of electricity used, but this did not alter the fundamental trajectory of more is better.

In energy, the paradigm has clearly shifted whereas in transport, it has not. It is now quite normal to talk about energy efficiency in the home, workplace and other buildings and thereby find ways to reduce consumption. This is also associated with a strong policy emphasis on renewable energy to shift the mode of production from fossil fuel–rich and dangerous technologies (nuclear, for example) to zero-carbon and benign technologies (for example, wind, wave and solar). In transport, none of this shift has occurred. Politicians and other decision-takers have learned the language of demand management and the many advantages that flow from increasing the use of walking, cycling and public transport, but the dominant paradigm is still about economic growth and the need for additional infrastructure that promotes the maximum consumption of time (speed) and space (distance).

Germany has now taken the energy debate to the stage of a fundamental paradigm shift (Lechtenboehmer and Samadi, 2013) based on the closure of nuclear power stations and the 100 per cent phasing out of fossil fuel electricity generation. The Energiewende maps perfectly onto transport and cycling. If we are to bring about a serious shift in pro-cycling policies there has to be deep-rooted cultural, attitudinal and political change in favour of sustainable mobility, walking and cycling. Here is where the hard work begins. Truly transformational policy will not be aimed at providing more for cycling and cyclists while leaving the hegemony of car dominance unchallenged. Cycling infrastructures presented as an add-on or a bonus to existing road regimes cannot perform that transformative role because they do not challenge the prevailing paradigm. In the worst case, they entrench the existing paradigm by making its continuation apparently more tolerable, providing marginal benefits for a small and marginal segment of the population.

Conclusion

Cycling has not yet achieved the priority status that is merited by its wide-ranging social, economic, health and environmental benefits. There are no financial, logistic or technical problems associated with the design and delivery of world-best, excellent cycling infrastructure and facilities, but cycling does not fit within the current paradigm that promotes motorised transport. Cycling requires a fundamental shift in transport and mobility policy with a strong emphasis on accessibility, reducing the need to travel and providing a high-quality street environment not dominated by motorised transport.

We have now had over three decades of high-quality academic, scientific and policy analysis on cycling and we know how to make it very safe indeed and how to achieve modal shares of more than 25 per cent in the vast majority of urban areas. In the UK, the modal share for cycling rarely exceeds 2 per cent, and the paradigm that maintains this poor level of performance is deeply entrenched. It is now necessary to change this paradigm and to create a fertile context for the adoption of a new paradigm. Paradigm shift has already taken place in road safety in the case of the Swedish Vision Zero policy and in Germany in the case of energy sources. Goepel (2016) has also identified ways of intervening to achieve paradigm shift, and more effort is needed to accelerate that process in the world of sustainable transport.

The transformational experiences of Vision Zero and the 'Energiewende' reveal the ways in which the totality of mobility and transport thinking can be transformed. Paradigm shift is more likely if we make wider connections and links with public health, fiscal consequences, the costs of providing health care, the incidence of serious diseases related to a lack of physical activity (WHO, 2018) and the quality of life of all of us in an ageing demography. This is the process identified by Goepel (2016) as 'Mindshift' and it requires a full-scale assault on four paradigmatic pillars:

- The current paradigm is far more expensive than one based on sustainable mobility. As the amount of walking and cycling go up, so the cost, public and private, of running a city goes down (Vivier, 2006).
- The current paradigm actually damages public health and increases the costs of providing health services (WHO, 2018).
- The current paradigm is unethical in that it accepts death and serious injury in road traffic in a way that would not be tolerated in aviation, rail services or lifts in high-rise office blocks.
- The current paradigm is socially regressive. It rewards the relatively rich and punishes the relatively poor and it deprives children of life chances (Wann et al, 2011).

At the moment, the connections are poorly developed but the opportunities are there for cooperation. Cooperation between health providers, hospitals, doctors, public health specialists, economists, political scientists, elected politicians and urban designers to scope an alternative vison for cities and regions based on smaller numbers of vehicles. The full weight of Vision Zero can produce safe streets for children and older people, and solve air quality and greenhouse gas problems within the same framework (Whitelegg et al, 2010; Whitelegg, 2016). A carefully integrated coordination of health policy, fiscal policy, urban design, public health and quality of life interventions will accelerate paradigm shift, and that requires a shift of emphasis from all those involved with any aspect of sustainable transport and mobility so more effort is devoted to the 'bigger picture' issues than is currently the case.

References

Aldred, R. and Crosweller, S. (2015) 'Investigating the rates and impacts of near misses and related incidents among UK cyclists', *Journal of Transport & Health*, 2(3): 379–93.

Aldred, R. and Goodman, A. (2018) 'Predictors of the frequency and subjective experience of cycling near misses: findings from the first two years of the UK Near Miss Project', *Accident Analysis and Prevention*, 110: 161–70.

Andersen, L.B., Schnohr, P., Schroll, M. and Hein, H. (2000) 'All-cause mortality associated with physical activity during leisure time, work, sports, and cycling to work', *Archive of Internal Medicine*, 160(11): 1621–8.

Appleyard, D. (1981) *Liveable Streets*, Berkeley: University of California Press.

Bailey, S. (1987) *Sex, Drink and Fast Cars*, Pantheon Books.

Banister, D. (2005) *Unsustainable Transport. City Transport in the New Century*, London: Routledge.

British Medical Association (1992) *Cycling: Towards Health and Safety*, BMA, Oxford University Press, British Medical Association.

Bundesministerium fuer Verkehr und digitale Infrastruktur (2018) *Verkehrsprognose 2030*, www.bmvi.de/SharedDocs/DE/Artikel/G/verkehrsprognose-2030.html?nn=12830

Cavill, N. and Davis, A. (2007) *Cycling and Health. What's the Evidence?*, London: Cycling England.

Cross, G. (2018) *Machines of Youth. America's Car Obsession*, Chicago: University of Chicago Press.

Cycling England (2018) 'Cycling and health: Did you know…?', www.cyclingengland.co.uk/health3.php

Davis, A. (2018) 'Essential evidence on a page No.136: Near misses and related incidents among UK cyclists', https://travelwest.info/project/ee-136-near-misses-related-incidents-among-uk-cyclists

Department of Transport (2018) *Road Traffic Forecasts 2018, Moving Britain Ahead* https://assets.publishing.service.gov.uk/government/uploads/system/uploads/attachment_data/file/740399/road-traffic-forecasts-2018.pdf

Elvebakk, B. (2007) 'Vision Zero: remaking road safety', *Mobilities*, 2(3): 425–41.

Elvebakk, B. and Steiro, T. (2009) 'First principles, second hand: perceptions and interpretations of vision zero in Norway', *Safety Science*, 47(7): 958–66.

Elvik, R. (1999) 'Can injury prevention efforts go too far? Reflections on some possible implications of Vision Zero for road accident fatalities', *Accident Analysis and Prevention* 31(3): 265–86.

Elvik, R. (2003) 'How would setting policy priorities according to cost-benefit analyses affect the provision of road safety?', *Accident Analysis and Prevention* 35(4): 557–70.

Elvik, R. (2008) 'Road safety management by objectives: a critical analysis of the Norwegian approach', *Accident Analysis and Prevention*, 40(3): 1115–22.

Elvik, R. and Amundsen, A.H. (2000) *Improving road safety in Sweden. Main report*. TOI Report 490, Oslo Institute of Transport Economics.

European Commission (2017) *EU Transport in Figures*, https://ec.europa.eu/transport/sites/transport/files/pocketbook2017.pdf

Fahlquist, J.N. (2006) 'Responsibility ascriptions and Vision Zero', *Accident Analysis and Prevention*, 38(6): 1113–18.

Goepel, M. (2016) *The Great Mindshift*, http://wupperinst.org/en/a/wi/a/s/ad/3597

Hart, J. and Parkhurst, G. (2011) 'Driven to excess: impacts of motor vehicles on the quality of life of residents of three streets in Bristol UK', *World Transport Policy & Practice*, 17(2): 12–30.

Hendriksen, I. (1996) *The Effect of Commuter Cycling on Physical Performance and on Coronary Heart Disease Risk Factors*, Amsterdam: Free University.

Hillman, M. Adams, J. and Whitelegg, J. (1990) *One false move. A study of children's independent mobility*. Policy Studies Institute, London.

Hokstad, P. and Vatn, J. (2008) 'Ethical dilemmas in traffic safety work', *Safety Science*, 46(10): 1435–49.

Horton, D. (2007) 'Fear of cycling', in D. Horton, P. Rosen and P. Cox (eds) *Cycling and Society*, Aldershot, UK: Ashgate.

House of Commons (2004) *Parliamentary Health Select Committee Report on Obesity*. The Stationery Office, HC23-1, May.

Jacobsen, P.L. (2003) 'Safety in numbers: more walkers and bicyclists, safer walking and bicycling', *Injury Prevention*, 9(3): 205–9.

Kenworthy, J. (2012) 'Don't shoot me I'm only the transport planner (apologies to Sir Elton John)', *World Transport Policy and Practice*, 18(4): 6–26.

Kodukula, S., Rudolph, F., Jansen, U. and Amon, E. (2018) *Living. Moving. Breathing*, Wuppertal: Wuppertal Institute, http://www.greenpeace.de/sites/www.greenpeace.de/files/publications/living.moving.breathing.20180604.pdf

Koglin, T. (2013) *Vélomobility – A critical analysis of planning and space*. Doctoral Dissertation, Lund University, Department of Technology and society, Transport and Roads, 2013, Bulletin 284.

Koglin, T. (2015a) 'Organisation does matter. Planning for cyclists in Stockholm and Copenhagen', *Transport Policy*, 39: 55–62.

Koglin, T. (2015b) 'Vélomobility and the politics of transport planning', *GeoJournal*, 80(4): 569–86.

Koglin, T. and Rye, T. (2014) 'The marginalisation of bicycling in modernist urban transport planning', *Journal of Transport and Health*, 1(4): 214–22.

Kuhn, T.S. (1962) *The Structure of Scientific Revolutions*, Chicago: University of Chicago Press.

Lawson, A.R., Pakrashi, V., Ghosh, B. and Szeto W.Y. (2013) 'Perception of safety of cyclists in Dublin City', *Accident Analysis and Prevention*, 50: 499–511.

Lechtenboehmer, S. and Samadi, S. (2013) 'Blown by the wind. Replacing nuclear power in German electricity generation', *Environmental Science and Policy*, 25: 234–41.

Miola, A. (2008) *Backcasting approach for sustainable mobility*, JRC Scientific and Technical Reports, Ispra, Italy.

Paffenbarger R., Hyde, R.T., Wing, A.L. and Hesieh, C.C. (1986) 'Physical activity, all-cause mortality and longevity of college alumni', *New England Journal of Medicine*, 314(10): 605–13.

Pooley, C.G., Jones, T., Tight, M., Horton, D., Scheldeman, G., Jopson, A. and Strano, E. (2013a) 'Policies for promoting walking and cycling in England: a view from the street', *Transport Policy*, 27: 66–72.

Pooley, C.G., Jones, T., Tight, M., Horton, D., Scheldeman, G., Jopson, A. and Strano, E. (2013b) *Promoting Walking and Cycling: New Perspectives on Sustainable Travel*, Bristol: Policy Press.

Pucher, J. and Buehler, R. (2012a) *Cycling Cities*, Cambridge, MA: The MIT Press.

Pucher, J. and Buehler, R. (2012b) 'International overview: cycling trends in Western Europe, North America and Australia', in J. Pucher and R. Buehler (eds) *City Cycling*, Cambridge, MA: The MIT Press, pp 9–29.

Sachs, W. (1992) *For Love of the Automobile. Looking Back into the History of our Desires*, Berkley: University of California Press.

Thornton, A., Bunt, K., Dalziel, D. and Simon, A. (2010) *Climate change and transport choices: Segmentation study*. Interim report by TNS-BMRB, London, Department for Transport.

Tingvall, C. and Haworth, N. (1999) 'Vision Zero: an ethical approach to safety and mobility', *6th International Conference on Road Safety and Traffic Enforcement Beyond 2000*, Melbourne, Australia, 6–7 September.

Trafikverket (2015) *RAPPORT Prognos för personresor 2030 Trafikverkets basprognos 2015*.

Tuxworth, W., Nevill, A.M., White, C. and Jenkins, C. (1986) 'Health, fitness, physical activity and morbidity of middle aged male factory workers', *British Journal of Industrial Medicine*, 43 (11): 733–53.

Vivier, J. (2006) *Mobility in cities database. Better mobility for people worldwide. Analysis and recommendations*, UITP (Union Internationale Transports Publique), Brussels.

Wann, J., Poulter, D. and Purcell, C. (2011) 'Reduced sensitivity to visual looming inflates the risk posed by speeding vehicles when children try to cross the road', *Psychological Science*, 22(4): 429–34.

Whitelegg, J. (2016) *Mobility: A New Urban Design and Transport Planning Philosophy for a Sustainable Future*, Shropshire: Straw Barnes Press.

Whitelegg, J. (2017) *The Economic case: jobs, inward investment and regeneration. Evidence presented to the public inquiry into the case for the M4 relief road in South Wales (UK)*, http://bailey.persona-pi.com/Public-Inquiries/M4-Newport/Third%20Parties/M4%20-%20Proofs/Gwent%20Wildlife%20Trust/Prof%20John%20Whitelegg%20-%20Proof%20of%20Evidence%20FINAL1.pdf

Whitelegg, J. and Haq, G. (2006) *Vision Zero: Adopting a target of zero for road traffic fatalities and serious injuries*, Stockholm Environment Institute, http://citeseerx.ist.psu.edu/viewdoc/download;jsessionid=76C61F21835BFC79315BA8D20727D536?doi=10.1.1.463.7565&rep=rep1&type=pdf

Whitelegg, J., Haq, G., Cambridge, H. and Vallack, H. (2010) *Towards a zero carbon vision for UK transport*, Stockholm Environment Institute, www.sei-international.org/mediamanager/documents/Publications/SEI-ProjectReport-Whitelegg-TowardsAZeroCarbonVisionForUK Transport-2010.pdf

World Health Organization (WHO) (2018) *Physical Activity for Health. More active people for a healthier world. Draft Global Action Plan on Physical Activity, 2018–2030*, www.who.int/ncds/prevention/physical-activity/gappa/

6

What constructs a cycle city?
A comparison of policy narratives
in Newcastle and Bremen

Katja Leyendecker

Contextual

Transport cycling in all its variant forms – from the personal to the political – challenges the socio-technical system of automobility (Urry, 2004). In a resistance to automobility, vélomobility studies, such as Koglin (2014) and Cox (2019), are slowly emerging under the new mobilities model (Sheller and Urry, 2006). At the heart of these studies is the careful investigation of current imbalances and impasses for sustainable transport and inclusive societies. The work presented in this chapter forms part of the author's PhD project: an ethnographic investigation into women activists campaigning for cycleways in Bremen and Newcastle (Leyendecker, forthcoming), funded by Northumbria University in Newcastle, UK. Through reflexive autoethnography, study of cycling infrastructures is revealed as not simply a concern for dissociated observation but of everyday personal experience. Thus this chapter is written in the first person to highlight that not only is the personal political, but when analysing everyday experiences conveyed by urban space, infrastructural interventions and the decision-making process that create them, the political is also personal. While this chapter focuses specifically on the policy documentation, its impacts are experienced as affect. This chapter seeks to advance assertions from previous chapters, namely that there is a moral political dimension to infrastructure as a socio-technical assemblage (Cox, Chapter 1, this volume), that a modernist approach to transport planning hinders its development (Koglin, Chapter 3, this volume) and that the interpretation of policies results in a value-action gap for cycling (Whitelegg, Chapter 5, this volume).

My experience of the UK in comparison to other European contexts confirms the findings that cycling as a personal and social practice in the UK remains too readily stigmatised (Horton, 2007; Aldred, 2010) as well as marginalised in transport spaces (Koglin and Rye, 2014). To allow transport governance to progress beyond its current focus on changing individual behaviour (Spotswood, 2016) would involve democratising the transport agenda: we must acknowledge the strong influence that urban design exerts on our transport choices. As both Pucher and Buehler (2012) and Pooley et al (2013) have expressly pointed out: cycleways protected from motor traffic, along main roads in particular, fulfil a basic material need for citizens who wish to cycle their everyday journeys. In sum, the demands made by transport cycling are inherently about re-designing our urban-built environments for societal inclusion, spatial and environmental justice. Urban space is a limited resource and hence contested, making the sustainable transport challenge undeniably political in its nature. Reinforcing Cox's argument (Chapter 1, this volume), I point out that spatial reallocation is vital for increasing the cycling constituent, as is the inclusion of social aspects in the politics and design processes of utility cycling.

What further problematises the utility-cycling endeavour is that the underlying strata of politics and justice are often hidden. In order to make transport politics visible (however fleeting and temporary these instances may be), this chapter examines the transport policies in two cities. Extending Whitelegg's discussions in Chapter 5 (this volume), I examine policy in more detail. More precisely, I apply the principles of phronesis as used by Flyvbjerg in his important and influential analysis of policy making (Flyvbjerg, 2001; Flyvbjerg et al, 2012) to critically investigate how these two policies narrate the use of space. Put simply, phronesis is the third Aristotelian category of knowledge. It stands alongside the universal truth claimed by epistemé and the technical know-how of techné. It is grounded in the practical knowledge of how to act on social problems in particular contexts, deriving from engagement with those particular contextual problems. I apply my very own critical expert view stemming from my experience as cycle activist and environmental engineer living, working and cycling in the UK and Germany. In particular, I examine the two cities' policy visions of space for cycling and for car parking (as a potential source of linear space for cycling to create a cycle network, rather than cycle parking). I then draw on the policy narratives and the cities' everyday realities to discuss implications for transport governance and local democracy addressing politicians, practitioners and activists.

A tale of two cities

The city of Bremen in Germany has a settled and deep connection to everyday cycling. This is demonstrated by Bremen's pervasive cycling infrastructure, resulting in 23.4 per cent cycle mode share (Ahrens, 2016). In comparison, the city of Newcastle in Northeast England, UK, has declared its ambitions to become a cycle city (NCC, 2013) but has as yet struggled to construct cycling into its urban fabric, showing a correspondingly low 0.9 per cent cycle mode share (Tyne & Wear, 2011). As the chapter progresses, I give a brief history of each city before generating their policy narratives and discussing the findings. As a final step, I exploit transition theories (Geels and Schot, 2007) to reflect on the prospects of change in both cities, also drawing on my ethnographic experience gained when living in the cities of Bremen and Newcastle. What narratives are constructed by the policies in the two cities? Is there a signposted pathway to a model cycle city?

To assure the reader, I am keen to acknowledge that any policy text should be read with great caution and reservation. The policy process takes ideas and ideologies, an often tacit and unconscious process, to fashion and formalise a policy (Stone, 1989; Stone, 2002). Any plan concerned with the future, such as a policy, can only ever express a hopeful prediction: without the complementation of political power, resolve and sufficient resources and public support, policies may struggle in their implementation phase, as Whitelegg notes in his chapter (this volume). However, while the policy text itself is only dry ink, it would have nonetheless been written with some considerable blood, sweat and tears in the policy process (Ingold and Monaghan, 2016; compare both Martin and Feddes et al in this volume). To recap my approach, I am applying Flyvbjerg's phronetic principles of social science to establish a narrative analysis of the policy text. The social must be inserted in the technical (Vreugdenhil and Williams, 2013; Koglin, Chapter 3 this volume; 2017) to stand a chance of system-wide paradigm shift of the cultural and political decision-making (Whitelegg, Chapter 5, this volume). While a narrative cannot give due depth to a policy's backstories it nonetheless offers the reader a looking glass. A policy reflects ideas of the future, the essence of which I seek to extract and then interpret. Resulting from that critical policy-assessment process are two condensed narratives about cycle space and car-parking space, presented in the following two sections.

Bremen

Bremen has 550,000 inhabitants and is situated in a flat North-German topography on the banks of the River Weser. The city has a colonial sea-faring history, and retains a commercial and industrial heritage to this day, also providing a culture and education hub for the surrounding region. Considering its everyday transport reality, Bremen is a cycling city: as its policy states, 'Cycling has a long tradition in Bremen. This is also evident in Bremen's comprehensive cycle infrastructure. Physically-separated cycle tracks exist on most major roads sections and in many side streets' (Bremen, 2014: 67). With nearly a quarter of all trips completed by bike (Ahrens, 2016), cycling makes for a prominent display in Bremen's cityscape. People of all ages and abilities cycle. The city's pertinent policy is the Transport Development Plan 2025 (*Verkehrsentwicklungsplan*) referred to hereafter as the VEP. Adopted in 2014, its planning horizon stretches to the year 2025 determining a long-term trajectory for the city, necessarily envisioning the future. In the foreword, the city's senior transport politician (*Senator für Umwelt, Bau und Verkehr*) takes pains to thank the citizens of Bremen for their dialogic involvement in the making of the policy (*Bürgerdialog*) reflecting Bremen's longer history of specific dialogic citizen-state processes dating back to the 1970s. The dialogic element of the policy production process won Bremen a European award (EC, 2015). An integral and central part of the dialogic element was the establishing of a steering group (*Projektbeirat*). I feel obliged to critically remark at this point that the group consisting of one chair and 25 representatives was overwhelmingly (85 per cent) presented by men (Bremen, 2014: 183) and that the double page introducing the *Projektbeirat* in the VEP only consisted of comments from male steering-group members (Bremen, 2014: 10–11). Thus inclusivity and engagement only goes so far.

Car parking

In relation to the spatial measure of car parking, the VEP opens by managing the reader's expectations: 'analysis of stationary motor vehicle traffic can only be treated on a general level in the city-wide plan' (Bremen, 2014: 54). It continues: 'There are enough parking spaces in Bremen city centre' (Bremen, 2014: 54), however, 'there is no adequate [Park and Ride] offer on all corridors' (Bremen, 2014: 55). The small-grain architecture of buildings and streets, typical for Bremen's urban fabric, 'results in high parking pressures in these areas, so that in some cases emergency routes, sidewalks and intersections are filled with parked cars' (Bremen, 2014: 55) and 'the already narrow roadside spaces in the affected areas for pedestrians and cyclists are further reduced, with significant restrictions on short-trip mobility and accessibility' (Bremen, 2014: 169). This provides justification for 'measures of car-parking management and space monitoring [being] provided in the action plan' (Bremen, 2014: 169). The VEP explains that the localities where space scarcity is most pressing will be prioritised and, in order to 'make the public space barrier-free and accessible, especially in residential areas, the parking space will gradually be reduced in favour of short-trip mobilities' (Bremen, 2014: 169). These actions are combined with a city-centre parking strategy, implementation and enforcement of parking and stopping bans and the promotion of sustainable modes. A parking-permit system is already in use in a number of neighbourhood areas and a car club is in operation (Bremen, 2014).

Cycleways

Despite the already high cycle mode share in Bremen, the VEP's vision remains ambitious and states that the 'potential for cycling has by far not been exhausted in Bremen yet' (Bremen, 2014: 66). Bremen's cycle network consists of '390 km of main routes, in line with quality requirements for everyday-cycling' (Bremen, 2014: 66) with the 'main-route classification in the cycling network [to] be taken into account in future planning to give high priority to the interests of cycling' (Bremen, 2014: 66). '[T]he network has optimisation potential' (Bremen, 2014: 67) with regard to 'travelling speed' (Bremen, 2014: 67, *Reisegeschwindigkeit*). When Bremen undertook an infrastructure inventory, it accounted for '674 kilometres of kerb-protected cycleways along roads' (Bremen, 2014: 68) making this cycle infrastructure the norm in Bremen. After the discussion of adequate widths for kerb-protected cycleways (*Bordsteinradwege*) the VEP concluded that the 'existing infrastructure is thus increasingly reaching its limits in many places and is not future-compatible' (Bremen, 2014: 68). The policy proceeds by lamenting Bremen's so-called 'culture of kerb-protected cycling' (Bremen, 2014: 68). Studies have shown that this specific cycling culture results in 96 per cent of people choosing *Bordsteinradwege* over on-road cycling options even without the mandatory use of the cycleway (Bremen, 2014: 68, footnote 9). The stated reasons for this collective behaviour are comfort and safety, according to feedback collected from 'the citizens' forums and regional committees' (Bremen,

2014: 68) held during the dialogic consultation process. The VEP then continues to describe on-road cycling solutions the city has implemented over recent years, and clearly links the 'attractiveness of the cycle network [with] the quality of the infrastructure' (Bremen, 2014: 69). As part of the VEP process, a gap analysis was carried out to identify deficiencies in the network. The policy further states that '[network] improvement remains a longer-term and on-going task requiring effective strategies' (Bremen, 2014: 69) and that 'Bremen has to turn ever more goal-oriented due to the obsolete, non-state-of-the-art and thus only partly future-compatible cycle infrastructure' (Bremen, 2014: 142). The chapter on cycling in the VEP culminates in a substantial list of measures, ranging from the improvement of individual locations (streets and junctions) to prime cycle routes (*Premiumrouten*) to be planned and built.

Discussion

In sum, Bremen's transport policy, VEP, promises to implement spatial reallocation: this will be accomplished both through car-parking elements (most notably by reducing car parking) and improvements to the cycle network. In contrast to the clearly stated vision for car-parking reduction, however, the policy's pitch for cycling measures is less clear. The VEP refrains from dissolving the conflict between the wants and needs of the 96 per cent of people who use *Bordsteinradwege* for their perceived comfort and safety and the interests of the council as the transport authority. Since 2016, Germany's national cycle campaign ADFC (*Allgemeiner Deutscher Fahrrad-Club*) officially supports protected cycleways. A motion was accepted with an overwhelming majority at the ADFC's annual general meeting (*Bundeshauptversammlung*) resolving the question of adequate cycle infrastructure. However, historical voices for on-road (vehicular) cycling remain at the local ADFC level, as I observed in Bremen. This disparity is also demonstrated between people's preference for cycle tracks (as acknowledged notably in the VEP) and the council's technical preference of on-road solution. Hence, the post-policy outlook for cycling is unresolved: will existing cycle tracks be improved and widened (to satisfy the people's expressed choice) or will the council execute their technical solution favouring on-road cycling (technocratic solution)?

From personal observations of Bremen, the cycle infrastructure is a noticeable and prominent feature in the city's urban design and much to be lauded. Rat-running in the remaining streets has been cut to a great extent (compared to Newcastle, for example) while permeability for walking and cycling has usually been retained. This creates an adequate secondary cycle network. Nearly all main roads have been fitted with a separate space for cycling, usually elevated from the road on a kerb and running alongside pedestrian pavements, creating a substantial primary network, although I do not hesitate to add that many cycle tracks leave much to be desired regarding widths and surface quality. The presence alone of infrastructure is no guarantee that it is easy or pleasant to use: infrastructure must also meet a threshold quality to be effective for the user. Over recent years Bremen council has removed some kerb-protected cycleways, and replaced these with painted cycle lanes on the road or Cycle Streets (*Fahrradstraßen*). Bremen's Cycle Streets, as I experienced them, do not cut motor-traffic levels and hence result in regular confrontation between cyclists and drivers. The impact of the recent changes on the city's transport system is not (yet) fully determinable. One such indicator useful to consult would be the cycle mode share. The latest representative statistics recorded a slight decline in cycling mode share between 2008 and 2013: from 24.8 per cent (Ahrens, 2010) to 23.4 per cent (Ahrens, 2016). Albeit small, this decline should be of keen interest to Bremen's polity considering the VEP goal 'not only to keep the high share of cycling in Bremen's modal split, but also to increase it by a targeted, effective and perceptible improvement of cycling' (Bremen, 2014: 142).

Newcastle

Newcastle in the northeast of England is home to 280,000 residents, who live in a moderately flat terrain overlooking the relatively steep north bank of the River Tyne (opposite Gateshead with 120,000 residents on the south side). In mobility terms, Newcastle and Gateshead form an urban agglomeration referred to here as NewcastleGateshead. Policy making is distinct between the two cities but they share a common core local plan as described further on. Like Bremen, the city has an industrial history, especially in the mining and shipbuilding trades; it also functions as a regional hub providing cultural and educational services to Northeast England. As for transport, I conclude that Newcastle is a car city in my analysis of the 2011 household survey (Tyne & Wear 2011). Unfortunately, data gathering methods in Newcastle are not entirely transparent, neither routinely carried out nor published widely. Hence data needs to be interrogated in order to identify modal shares (as the local cycle campaign group routinely has done). I calculated that 55 per cent of all trips are undertaken by car (Bremen 36 per cent), while under 1 per cent are made by bike (Bremen 23 per cent). Newcastle's key transport policy is incorporated in its Local Plan 'Planning for the Future 2010–2030' (NCC and GMBC, 2015), setting the spatial development path for Newcastle (and Gateshead)'s land-use planning. The plan was adopted in 2015 after a series of local protests seeking to highlight the plan's lack of environmental and social sustainability (for example, Moss, 2012) resulting in public inquiries and visitation by national inspectors. The policy's foreword signed by the council leader describes the city's struggle, between Newcastle's past history and future generations, growth and sustainability, community and business. As a 'spatial vision' (NCC and GMBC, 2015: 21) the policy sets out to '[i]mprove sustainable access to, within and around the Urban Core by promoting fast and direct public transport links to the heart of the Urban Core, increasing walking and cycling and minimising through traffic' (NCC and GMBC, 2015: 39). According to the policy, '[t]ransport and accessibility are fundamental to the delivery of the Plan's spatial strategy' (NCC and GMBC, 2015: 84). Newcastle has already provided a city-wide 20 mph (30 km/h) speed limit for residential areas, implemented in stages from 2010 to 2011 (Proctor, 2012).

Car parking

The policy recognises car-parking management as a feature of 'enhancement and delivery of an integrated transport network to support sustainable development and economic growth' (NCC and GMBC, 2015: 86). It also suggests that through the 'management of car parking locations, supply and pricing' (NCC and GMBC, 2015: 86) Newcastle, together with its policy partner Gateshead, will 'develop a joint car parking strategy to manage demand' (NCC and GMBC, 2015: 90), reduce commuter long-stay parking, promote short-stay parking for shoppers and introduce parking charges in shopping areas 'where this can be achieved without threatening the vitality and viability of the centre' (NCC and GMBC, 2015: 90). Gradually 'surface car parks and on street car parking will be more restricted' (NCC and GMBC, 2015: 146). The policy commends the 'great success in promoting use of car parks outside of peak times' (NCC and GMBC, 2015: 146) recognising the 'Alive after 5' (NCC and GMBC, 2015: 146) scheme that, since 2010, has permitted free car parking in Newcastle city centre after 17:00 in collaboration between the council and city-centre businesses. The policy announces that 'further opportunities [of this kind] will be explored' (NCC and GMBC, 2015: 146). Overall, the policy refers to car parking in the city centre in some detail, but leaves the approach to car parking more open in areas outside the city centre (existing neighbourhoods and the areas designated for new housing development).

Cycleways

With regard to spatial policy measures for sustainable transport, it is 'important that new development is located in the most sustainable locations and accessible by a choice of travel modes, including walking, cycling and public transport' (NCC and GMBC, 2015: 84). The policy goes on to list reasons: 'reduce the need for people to travel, minimise congestion, improve road safety and meet climate change reduction targets' (NCC and GMBC, 2015: 84) improving public health and quality of life 'while still acknowledging the need to cater for the private car' (NCC and GMBC, 2015: 85). The policy also outlines a transport hierarchy: 'Walking, Cycling, Public Transport (including taxis), Freight and Car Traffic' (NCC and GMBC, 2015: 88). The council 'will work with partners to create a strategic cycle network across the plan area that provides sustainable access to jobs and services […] formed from a mixture of on-road lanes (sometimes mixed with other modes), shared-use paths, off-road routes and recommended routes through traffic-free areas' (NCC and GMBC, 2015: 88). For the city centre, the policy states that 'there will be schemes which continue to enhance cycling infrastructure' (NCC and GMBC, 2015: 138). In addition, the council 'will improve conditions for cyclists' (NCC and GMBC, 2015: 138), through the removal of through traffic from the city centre, promising 'there will be greater priority and a more attractive environment for cyclists' (NCC and GMBC, 2015: 138). Several schematic maps are included in the policy, roughly outlining seven planned cycle routes originating from the city centre.

Discussion

In sum, the NewcastleGateshead policy sets out plans for car parking in Newcastle city centre, but does not clearly link car parking to spatial tensions in the urban design. The overall narrative in the policy is contradictory in respect of advancing sustainable travel, most obviously in the promotion of a free parking scheme, 'Alive after 5' (after successful lobbying of the council by city business groups). The importance, and the lobbying influence of the retail industry on the policy, can be inferred from policy statements as 'short-stay parking for shoppers [...] will be promoted' (NCC and GMBC, 2015: 90) and 'without threatening the vitality and viability of the centre' (NCC and GMBC, 2015: 90). As for the car-parking elements in the policy, the city centre attracts the bulk of policy measures – the surrounding neighbourhoods and new housing areas receive less attention with regard to car parking. For cycling, the lack of a strong narrative is evident in the policy. The more apparent notion to that effect – 'while still acknowledging the need to cater for the private car' (NCC and GMBC, 2015: 85) – appears entirely unprompted and relates only disjointedly to the policy text. The policy nonetheless predicts that 'there will be a considerable increase in cycling over the next few years' (NCC and GMBC, 2015: 138) without identifying mechanisms through which this might be achieved. Spatial catering for cycling (so vital for de-stigmatising, democratising and diversifying cycling) is only weakly outlined and it lacks overall prominence and clarity in the policy text. The need for action is clearly stated in the policy (climate change, public health, and so on), however, linking this firmly to spatial plans and actions has not been achieved. Beyond the engineering 'mixture of on-road lanes (sometimes mixed with other modes), shared-use paths, off-road routes and recommended routes through traffic-free areas' (NCC and GMBC, 2015: 88), the reader of the policy is left wondering what kind of cycle network the council envisages and what kind of cycle infrastructure it might propose for the routes. Compared to Bremen's policy process, no critical (gap) analysis has been carried out in Newcastle. Judging from the policy content, Newcastle council is hesitant to look back and learn from the past: a past which for decades into the present, has failed to increase from a 1 per cent cycling mode share.

Weaving blanket narratives

Here, I want to acknowledge a considerable difference in the respective purpose of the two cities' policies. Bremen's VEP is exclusively concerned with traffic and transport, while the primary purpose of Newcastle's Local Plan is land-use allocation and new housing developments. With that difference in clerical and political purpose in mind, Newcastle's policy does, however, state that '[t]ransport and accessibility are fundamental to the delivery of the Plan's spatial strategy' (NCC and GMBC, 2015: 84). It is hence fair, I propose, to deduce that transport has a reasonable focus in Newcastle's policy text. Further, Newcastle's policy was a joint undertaking with Gateshead, the municipality on the opposite bank of the River Tyne. This makes sense for land-use and transport planning as it combines a coherent conurbation, yet it would also be fair to presume that working jointly across two independent councils may complicate policy production (and implementation). This municipal cooperation, however, matters less for the public consultation process. Yet, Newcastle council did experience complications when consulting the public on the Local Plan; protests erupted in the city seeking to highlight the plan's lack of environmental and social sustainability (Moss, 2012). Resistance to the draft policy formed rapidly at the very start of the consultation process, indicating that it came as a shock to members of the public. The public protests and inquiries could indicate a disjuncture between the council and civic society. This procedural detail marks a stark contrast to Bremen's engagement process, winning awards (EC, 2015) and the transport senator's pride in an active citizenry partaking in the dialogue (*Bürgerdialog*). (Nevertheless, the apparent lack of diversity in Bremen's VEP steering group, a central instrument to citizen participation, leaves room for improvement in Bremen.)

The policies' forewords, both undersigned by politicians, warrant a cautious comparison. Bremen's 300-word introduction in the VEP is purely and plainly highlighting the aspect of cooperation in the production of the policy. The senator is obviously pleased with the end product: the policy document arises from community engagement and exchange. In Newcastle, the words of the council leader are much more tentative. Newcastle's foreword draws on the notion of an ongoing struggle: a struggle between the past and the future, encompassing tensions between growth and sustainability, community and business. The foreword acknowledges these opposing forces, but leaves the tensions unresolved; unsettling the reader who seeks resolution and resolve. This uncertainty continues in the policy. While Newcastle's policy itself is functional (that is, it allocates land for house building), it also leaves the contextual tensions of environmental and social changes, industrial past and high-tech future, unaddressed.

Car parking is a political issue. Local politicians have typically found it challenging to develop a rhetoric for car parking reduction (or motor traffic reduction for that matter). Yet the provision of car parking has long been known to attract motor traffic and hinder the transition to active modes. The fiscal and spatial management of car parking is a vital component in any sustainable transport policy. According to Shoup (2011) there is no such thing as free car parking, for the cost and damages are simply externalised. There are notable differences between the policy approaches of Bremen and Newcastle to car-parking space. Bremen's policy is relatively straightforward. To reduce car parking over time to create space for walking, cycling and make neighbourhoods accessible and liveable, in the policy's own phrase, 'in favour of short-trip mobilities' (Bremen, 2014: 169). Even so, it should be noted that there are no clear implementation plans how to achieve a car parking reduction in Bremen's city centre or neighbourhoods. In comparison, Newcastle's approach is to mandate the production of a car-parking strategy for the city centre, with the policy's stated aim to gradually restrict city-centre car parking (reducing on-street and parking lots while continuing to support off-peak parking provision through the 'Alive after 5' arrangement with the traders). To my knowledge, the car-parking strategy had not been progressed at the time of writing. Similar to Bremen, neither implementation steps nor details are outlined in the Newcastle policy. The major difference between Newcastle's and Bremen's approach is that Newcastle's policy further enlarges the ambiguity in its approach to car parking. The Local Plan lists a variety of measures contradicting a transport transition away from car use. Newcastle wants to shift from long-stay parking to short-stay arrangements (maximising turnover), and to increase free car-parking schemes. Both policy elements would attract more motor traffic into the city centre. This decidedly puts in question the meaning of the policy's planned 'management of car parking locations, supply and pricing' (NCC and GMBC, 2015: 86), for Newcastle's city centre.

Both cities are laudably aiming higher for the cycle mode share; cycling is to increase under the respective policies (although neither policy gives a specific target or rate of increase). Exploring cycling's spatial element in the policies, both cities plan to develop their cycle networks. Further details are sparse in Newcastle; and an anxiety about reducing car use remains present in the policy as it expresses 'the need to cater for the private car' (NCC and GMBC, 2015: 85).

The loss of cohesion in Bremen's policy is intriguing too: the VEP's narrative gets stuck between storylines: what the people expressedly prefer, referred to as the 'culture of kerb-protected cycling' (Bremen, 2014: 68) in the VEP supported by studies showing 96 per cent of people choosing *Bordsteinradwege* over on-road cycling options even without the mandatory use of the cycleway (Bremen, 2014: 68, footnote 9) and the council's preferred technocratic solution of on-road cycling. The narrative, as told in the Bremen policy, firmly sides with council technocrats. The favouring of the technical solution happens even without providing further explanation creating the 'circular logic' between interventionist and technocratic approaches that Cox highlights in Chapter 1 (this volume). Recent projects are named in the VEP; these are projects that have actually removed cycle tracks, not installed or improved them (Wachmannstraße and Hamburger Straße). Acting fundamentally against the expressions of the user majority who choose to use dedicated cycle tracks over on-road cycling (as the VEP laments), these recent schemes dismantling tracks could well be an imposition on its citizens, and would warrant further explanation and careful investigation by the council. We should note here, that the solution favoured in the policy is also the simpler solution in technical terms because only two traffic streams need to be catered for in the street design: walking as one, combined motor traffic and cycling as the other, supporting Koglin's description (Chapter 3, this volume) of technocratic modernist management of transport planning and Whitelegg's argument for the need of a paradigmatic shift in culture and politics (Chapter 5, this volume). Further, I have no knowledge that Bremen officially monitors these spatial innovations (mixing cycling with motor vehicles on Cycle Streets or on-road cycle lanes), thereby not entering a virtuous cycle of continuous technical learning and improvement.

Judging from the dry ink of policy narrative analysis, where are these two cities on the transport-transition trajectory? Both cities claim in their policies that an increase in cycling is sought per se. As I have referenced in the introductory paragraphs, dedicated space for cycling (cycle tracks, protected bike lanes, along main roads) is the minimum basic requirement for all-ability, everyday cycling (Pucher and Buehler, 2012). Bremen has this kind of infrastructure largely in place (especially when compared to Newcastle). Newcastle, too, seeks to develop a cycle network. The basic ideational building blocks are in place. Yet comparing the actual infrastructural initiatives linked to these strategies, both are ambiguous. Bremen has recently removed cycle tracks, and Newcastle leaves wholly unaddressed how space might be claimed for cycleways. Car parking on roads stakes a major claim on urban space and thus warrants close consideration. Both policies are critical about car parking, but only to a degree. Newcastle, especially, is lost in a tug of war: car-parking management and city-centre traders lobbying the council for more car parking (and furthermore, more free car parking at that), hence continuing to attract more motor traffic (for example, see Shoup, 2011).

Both policies retain contradictions, demonstrating that older and newer paradigms currently co-exist. Ideally, any policy would plot a smooth transition path. If, however, given the identified policy inconsistencies, progress was made in implementing the policies, how likely would a smooth transition pathway be in either Bremen or Newcastle? The multi-level perspective (MLP) outlined by Geels

Table 6.1: Comparative policy situation

Policy measure	Bremen, North Germany	Newcastle, Northeast England
Population	550,000	280,000
History	Sea-faring, colonial	Roman, ship-building, mining
Today	Regional centre, university city	Regional centre, university city
Transport policy	Verkehrsentwicklungsplan 2025 (adopted 2014)	Part of Local Plan 2010–2030 (adopted 2015)
Topography	Generally flat	Relatively flat with steep bank to River Tyne
Car parking	CITY CENTRE City centre has sufficient car parking, more P&R is needed on corridors	CITY CENTRE • City centre must be managed, • A car-parking strategy will be developed, • Gradually car parking space will be restricted in the city centre (but) free car parking scheme is successful and should be proliferated
	NEIGHBOURHOODS Parked cars blocking access (for sustainable modes and emergency routes), gradual reduction of parking space	NEIGHBOURHOODS No clear narrative emerges
Space for cycling, cycle tracks	• Aiming to increase cycle mode share, • Infrastructure: Bremen's cycling culture versus technocratic approach, • Substantial and detailed list of planned improvements	• Increase cycle share, • Create a strategic cycle network, • Schematic maps, • Design/type/quality of cycle infrastructure unaddressed

and Schot (2007) consists of three levels (landscape, socio-technical regime and niche levels) and four transition pathways (transformation, reconfiguration, technological substitution, and de-alignment and re-alignment). The policy originator is the council level (regime). The transformation pathway is the traditional path – it is slow and the council-regime level largely retains control. Let us then presume the absence of landscape pressures that are often unpredictable (market failures, environmental disasters, and so on), we can look more closely at the likely interaction between the council-regime and niche (civic society) in light of the policies' contradictions.

Bremen's major contradiction is the council's technocratic favouring of on-road cycle lanes as the solution (resulting in the removal of cycle tracks) while welcoming wide civic involvement in the policy-making process. Should Bremen further follow the on-road cycling strategy, a conflict could erupt between the council's projects and civic society groups flagging the contradiction. When living in Bremen and conducting my fieldwork, I observed the formation and mobilisation of local groups (niche level) to exactly that effect. This is a recent development, and it is too early in the policy implementation process to predict the council (regime level) reaction or adaptation to these pressures.

Newcastle's major policy contradiction is a much more fundamental one than Bremen's. The Newcastle policy has not yet articulated the spatial question: it wants cycling, but how will space for cycling be generated? Not having recognised space as a limited resource and its related contested and political nature, implementation has the potential to be on a rocky path. The conflict is again likely to play out in the public arena, especially since the policy-making process was much less dialogic, deliberative and participatory in Newcastle in the first place (when compared to Bremen). Indeed, recent council plans stemming from the Local Plan have, yet again, met protesters marching to bring attention to the plan's lack of environmental and social consideration (Hodgson, 2016). This time, Newcastle council agreed to meet the objectors, and a series of meetings was facilitated through the council. Nearly three years later, at the time of writing, while the objector group have released their recommendations, Newcastle officials have not yet managed to respond, most recently citing a consultation on air pollution for the reason of their delay (Holland, 2019).

Overall, the transport sector worldwide is in flux and disrupted by new technologies (for example, the use of mobile phones, free-floating bike share systems, to name only a couple), and the overall transport pathway is likely to follow a combination of reconfiguration, technological substitution and re/de-alignment, coupled with council-favoured and council-controlled transformation path. I suggest that one problem with the application of the MLP concept for transport transition is that it does not split out the political and technical aspects on the socio-technical regime level when in reality the technocratic management of transport planning (Koglin, this volume) and the de-socialisation of cycling politics (Cox, this volume) hinder system-wide paradigmatic change (Whitelegg, this volume).

Future headings and footnotes

Cities are spatial entities as well as social spaces standing in interaction, as explained in Chapter 1. Urban design enables and disables citizens' choices depending on spatial affordances. We know, in abundance, that cycling is good for people, the planet and various pockets and pecuniaries (Pucher et al, 1999; Sallis et al, 2006; Woodcock and Aldred, 2008; Garrard et al, 2012). We also know that dedicated space, especially along main roads, is the very basic requirement for cycling to become an everyday form of transport for the general public (Pucher and Buehler, 2012). However, an increasing move towards cycling means reconsidering space currently afforded to the car. Not surprisingly, the move away from the car is also contentious, requires considerable political and technical planning and resolve. To illuminate, however softly, the mode shift towards cycling, I have outlined in this chapter the transport policy narratives for two cities, Bremen and Newcastle. I looked at two types of spaces, cycling and car parking. The two cities under consideration have entirely different starting points for climbing the ladder of transport transition, with Bremen a cycle city and Newcastle a car city in comparison.

The chapter has critically assessed the transport planning policies for spatial reallocation measures (from car parking towards cycling) applying Flyvbjerg's phronetic principles. The analytical process identified some irregularities in the policy narratives. In Bremen, there is a contradiction between the council's policy engagement approach and its technical preference of on-road cycling (cycle lanes and Cycle Streets). Bremen's policy avows to have listened to the citizens, but stands in contrast to the council-favoured solution of on-road cycling. In Bremen's infrastructure proposal, a purely technocratic approach wins out over the choice expressed by cyclists in Bremen. Compared to Bremen, Newcastle's contradiction, however, is much more fundamental in nature. The Newcastle policy does not even acknowledge urban space as a limited resource that requires political steer and leadership. There is a glaring contradiction in the aim of Newcastle's policy: car parking is both to be reduced as well as increased in turnover and made available free of charge at times of low use. A clear link between car parking and environmental and social degradation is not made in the policy, where economic voices of city retailers win out.

Both policies contain irregularities in their processes and implementation, highlighting the current co-existence of old and new paradigms. This, to me, indicates that old paradigms are contested and shifting in Bremen and in Newcastle. MLP transition theory (Geels and Schot, 2007) tells us that a trajectory can be influenced by bottom-up resistances and forces (from below, in the niche level). The policy assessment, however, indicates that transport today is ruled by the socio-technical system of automobility (free car parking in Newcastle) and its technocratic practices (removing cycle tracks along main roads in Bremen) confirming Koglin's observations (Chapter 3, this volume). In opposition to a purely technocratic system, community groups, both professional and citizen-led, can construct alternative narratives that help envision new trajectories and futures. These grassroot organisations, however, have to be built and nurtured by local democratic processes. Both councils show on ongoing deep struggle with socio-technical automobility. The policies somewhat seek to curb car use, but the presence and dominance of the private car is palpable in the policy narratives. A system-wide paradigm shift indeed is needed, as demanded by Whitelegg (Chapter 5, this volume). The immediate outstanding transport questions for the two cities are these: Bremen requires answers to the quality of the cycling infrastructure it wants to build for the citizens. This should include the monitoring and evaluation of recent street changes and taking a critical view on the city's deteriorating cycle mode share. Newcastle officials (politicians and technocrats) must first accept urban space as a political asset and frontier, to then throw open their heavy council gates and let citizens assist in the policy process and implementation thereby jumpstarting local participatory democracy. Whether it may be Bremen or Newcastle, for a city to thrive and prosper it needs contented citizens.

Acknowledgements

I am grateful for the many discussions with Sally Watson in Newcastle and Beatrix Wupperman in Bremen about the transport policies in their respective cities. Their local insights and keen observations assisted my thought development and analysis of the policy texts.

References

Ahrens, G.-A. (2010) Sonderauswertung zur Verkehrserhebung 'Mobilität in Städten – SrV 2008' Städtevergleich. Dresden: Technische Universität Dresden, p. 67.

Ahrens, G.-A. (2016) Sonderauswertung zum Forschungsprojekt 'Mobilität in Städten – SrV 2013' Städtevergleich. Dresden: Technische Universität Dresden, p. 130.

Aldred, R. (2010) '"On the outside": constructing cycling citizenship', *Social & Cultural Geography*, 11(1): 35–52.

Bremen (2014) *Verkehrsentwicklungsplan Bremen 2025*. Bremen: Senator für Bau Umwelt und Verkehr, Freie Hansestadt Bremen.

Cox, P. (2019) *Cycling: A Sociology of Velomobility*, Abingdon: Routledge.

EC (2015) *Bremen and Östersund announced sustainable urban mobility winners in Europe*. Available at: /transport/themes/urban/news/2015-03-23-award-winners_en (Accessed: 19 May 2018).

Flyvbjerg, B. (2001) *Making Social Science Matter: Why Social Inquiry Fails and How It Can Succeed Again*, Cambridge: Cambridge University Press.

Flyvbjerg, B., Landman, T. and Schram, S. (2012) *Real Social Science: Applied Phronesis*, Cambridge: Cambridge University Press.

Garrard, J., Rissel, C. and Bauman, A. (2012) 'Health benefits of cycling', in J. Pucher and R. Buehler (eds) *City Cycling*, Cambridge, MA: The MIT Press, pp 31–56.

Geels, F.W. and Schot, J. (2007) 'Typology of sociotechnical transition pathways', *Research Policy*, 36(3): 399–417.

Hodgson, B. (2016) 'Residents to march in protest against controversial Blue House roundabout plan', *Chronicle*. Available at: www.chroniclelive.co.uk/news/north-east-news/residents-march-protest-against-controversial-11774629 (Accessed: 13 June 2018).

Holland, D. (2019) 'Blue House Roundabout plan on hold due to pollution crisis', *Chronicle*. Available at: www.chroniclelive.co.uk/news/north-east-news/blue-house-roundabout-plan-hold-16037706 (Accessed: 15 April 2019).

Horton, D. (2007) 'Fear of cycling', in D. Horton, P. Rosen and P. Cox (eds) *Cycling and Society*, Abingdon, UK: Routledge, pp 133–52.

Ingold, J. and Monaghan, M. (2016) 'Evidence translation: an exploration of policy makers' use of evidence', *Policy & Politics*, 44(2): 171–90.

Koglin, T. (2014) 'Vélomobility and the politics of transport planning', *GeoJournal*, 80(4): 569–86.

Koglin, T. (2017) 'Urban mobilities and materialities – a critical reflection of a "sustainable" development project', *Applied Mobilities*, 2(1): 32–49.

Koglin, T. and Rye, T. (2014) 'The marginalisation of bicycling in Modernist urban transport planning', *Journal of Transport & Health*, 1(4): 214–22.

Leyendecker, K. (forthcoming) *Women activists' experience of local cycle politics*. PhD. Northumbria University.

Moss, R. (2012) 'Green Belt protests on the march', *BBC News*, 10 February. Available at: www.bbc.com/news/uk-england-16987389 (Accessed: 10 June 2018).

NCC (2013) '*Newcastle fit for cycling – Cycle City Ambition bid*'. Available at: https://streetsforpeopleorguk.files.wordpress.com/2017/07/ncc_cca_extension_0_ccaf2_extension_bid_0.pdf

NCC and GMBC (2015) '*Planning for the Future – Core Strategy and Urban Core Plan for Gateshead and Newcastle upon Tyne 2010–2030* (adopted March 2015)'.

Pooley, C. G., Jone, T., Tight, M., Horton, D., Scheldeman, G., Dominelli, L. and Strano, E. (2013) *Promoting Walking and Cycling: New Perspectives on Sustainable Travel*, Bristol: Policy Press.

Proctor, K. (2012) 'Newcastle's 20mph speed limits reduce accidents', *Chronicle*. Available at: www.chroniclelive.co.uk/news/local-news/newcastles-20mph-speed-limits-reduce-1371127 (Accessed: 26 September 2018).

Pucher, J.R. and Buehler, R. (eds) (2012) *City Cycling*, Cambridge, MA: The MIT Press.

Pucher, J., Charles, K. and Schimek, P. (1999) 'Bicycling renaissance in North America? Recent trends and alternative policies to promote bicycling', *Transportation Research Part A: Policy and Practice*, 33(7/8): 625–54.

Sallis, J.F., Cervero, R.B., Ascher, W., Henderson, K.A., Kraft, M.K. and Kerr, J. (2006) 'An ecological approach to creating active living communities', *Annual Review of Public Health*, 27: 297–322.

Sheller, M. and Urry, J. (2006) 'The new mobilities paradigm', *Environment and Planning A: Economy and Space*, 38(2): 207–26.

Shoup, D. (2011) *The High Cost of Free Parking*, Updated edition, Chicago: APA Press.

Spotswood, F. (ed) (2016) *Beyond Behaviour Change*, Bristol: Policy Press.

Stone, D.A. (1989) 'Causal stories and the formation of policy agendas', *Political Science Quarterly*, 104(2): 281–300.

Stone, D.A. (2002) *Policy Paradox: The Art of Political Decision Making* (2nd revised edition), New York: W.W. Norton & Company.

Tyne & Wear (2011) *Housetravel survey data*, Tyne and Wear Joint Transport Working Group.

Urry, J. (2004) 'The "system" of automobility', *Theory, Culture & Society*, 21(4–5): 25–39.

Vreugdenhil, R. and Williams, S. (2013) 'White line fever: a sociotechnical perspective on the contested implementation of an urban bike lane network', *Area*, 45(3): 283–91.

Woodcock, J. and Aldred, R. (2008) 'Cars, corporations, and commodities: consequences for the social determinants of health', *Emerging Themes in Epidemiology*, 5(4).

7

Hard work in paradise.
The contested making of
Amsterdam as a cycling city

Fred Feddes, Marjolein de Lange
and Marco te Brömmelstroet

Introduction

In 1900, there were approximately 200 motorcars in the Netherlands; today it is close to 8.5 million, or one car for every two people. Amsterdam alone has over 250,000 cars. These numbers indicate that the Netherlands has followed the general mobilisation trend in the Western world, reaching an even higher car density than most countries in terms of vehicles per square kilometre (www.nationmaster. com). Yet in one significant aspect, it has taken an exceptional course in mobility patterns, only comparable to parts of Denmark and a handful of other urban areas across the globe (Pucher and Buehler, 2012). Despite being fully motorised, it has maintained and fostered a vital mainstream practice of cycling and bicycle infrastructure, especially in larger and midsized cities such as Utrecht, Zwolle and Groningen (Harms et al, 2016). Amsterdam is the most prominent and internationally best-known example of this phenomenon. Some say that in the Netherlands everybody cycles. It is indeed true that almost everybody cycles at least once a week, and the diversity of cyclists is a unique and often acknowledged feature. The fact that cycling levels are as high, if not higher, for women than for men is an especially radical difference from most other cycling contexts. The same goes for the remarkably high cycling levels among both teenagers and the elderly (Harms et al, 2014). There are, however, continuous concerns about especially non-Western migrant populations that, although they cycle more than similar populations in other countries, cycle less overall than the non-migrant population (although this varies according to gender and degree of urbanisation, see Van der Kloof, 2015). This correlation is further blurred by spatial variables that relate to the neighbourhoods in which migrant populations are represented. In addition, cycling and the bicycles used in Amsterdam are recently changing from a 'national habitus' of conspicuous non-consumption (Kuipers, 2013) to a symbol of cosmopolitan distinction, especially of the upper middle class (Boterman, 2018).

Outsiders often present Amsterdam as little less than a cycling paradise (for example, Pucher and Buehler, 2008). Indeed, although in other Dutch cities cyclists are more appreciative of cycling conditions, and those cities often boast higher cycling levels (Harms et al, 2014), Amsterdam is a more pleasant and safer place to ride than most cities around the globe. However, it is not a tranquil paradise and its conditions can never be taken for granted. Within a continuously contested (inter)national mobility landscape, the cycling city takes hard work to establish and maintain. This hard work comes in many shapes and forms, such as activism, policy making, alertness, endurance, expertise, diplomacy, playfulness. In addition, it takes cooperation and competition between many different actors. There is no stable end state. No matter how much has been achieved in the past, continued effort is needed to maintain and improve the cycling city, to avert current threats and to face new challenges in the following decades.

In this chapter, drawing on a broader body of research into the history of cycle activism and its role in shaping Amsterdam as a cycling city (Feddes and de Lange, 2019), we examine four important contributory elements. First, favourable qualities of the urban structure, some dating from long before the existence of the bicycle. Second, there is a wider social and political context of the 1960s and 1970s when cycling found new impetus despite severe external threat. Third is the subsequent construction of a systemic cycling city in which the relation between bicycle activism, (local) government, and the broader 'bicycle culture' is examined. Finally, we will discuss the roles played by cycling activists organised in Fietsersbond, and the city government of Amsterdam.

Favourable (pre-existing) conditions for the cycle city

Historic Amsterdam, like most cities in the Netherlands, has a compact urban form that unintentionally facilitates cycling. Its 17th-century extensions (Canal Ring, Jordaan, Plantage) are superb examples of land-efficient and rational planning. The fine-grained traffic system was designed primarily for pedestrians and freight barges. As early as the 16th century Amsterdam introduced control measures such as one-way traffic, limited access for carriages and designated parking areas (Didde, 1992: 17). The city maintained its compact form during successive expansions in the later 19th century and the early 20th century. These developments with relatively high density were organised in new rings surrounding the semi-circular historic city. New systems of public transport were introduced to provide for increased internal travel distances, but in the early 20th century, the bicycle was popularly adopted as a mass means of individual transport (Oldenziel and de la Bruhèze, 2011; Oosterhuis, 2015). It was discovered to be surprisingly well-suited to the size that Amsterdam had acquired by then. Amsterdam became a bike city almost by coincidence (Jordan, 2013).

Amsterdam missed out on the 19th-century international trend of carving out wide and monumental boulevards in the historic urban fabric, exemplified in Haussmann's Parisian boulevards (Sennett, 2018). Such boulevards unintentionally paved the way for mass motorisation: when motor cars arrived, these spacious layouts offered significant absorption capacity before the city became congested. Amsterdam lacked these 19th-century spaces; in other words, it lacked an important pre-existing condition favouring motorised traffic. Quite a number of (private initiative) boulevard plans were launched in Amsterdam during the second half of the 19th century, albeit on a relatively modest scale, but most failed to materialise due to lack of funding and a mostly passive city government.

Consequently, the introduction of motor cars almost immediately posed problems in the narrow streets of Amsterdam. Rising heritage awareness became influential in decision-making. From an early stage, major interventions in the famous, monumental Canal Ring were deemed unacceptable. In the late 19th century, social and political pressure increasingly turned against the filling-in of inner-city canals, as these were now defined as crucial spatial elements of the city's unique historic identity. A municipal plan from 1900 to infill in the Reguliersgracht sparked strong and well-organised protests, initiated among the city's cultural elite and spreading in ever-wider circles. The later Rokin infill was a pyrrhic victory, achieved only after strong controversy, and it turned out to be an incident rather than a meaningful link in a new traffic system. Whether and how the city should accommodate the demands of motorisation was always a matter of debate. As the city council stated in 1927, 'either the (existing) city should be adapted to the needs of modern traffic, by breaking down houses and filling in canals, or the new traffic should adapt to the possibilities of the old city' (Hessels et al, 1985).

Pre-war prognosis expected car density in Amsterdam to rise to a maximum of 40 cars per 1,000 inhabitants (Poelstra, 1985). However, this level had more than tripled to 128 cars by 1965, and by 1980 it had again doubled to 250 (Poelstra, 1985). This significant motorisation rendered all pre-war plans useless. For decades, until well into the 1970s, the city government struggled to grasp the enormity of the traffic problem, seemingly incapable of systemic, well-thought-out policies and practices. It is revealing that the best-known traffic plan from the 1950s was a back-of-an-envelope type of suggestion made by the Head of Police, Hendrik Kaasjager, in 1956 (Rooijendijk, 2005). Kaasjager suggested the infill of approximately 15 km of inner-city canals in order to create an inner and an outer automobile ring for smooth circulation and lots of parking space. The idea was instantly met with such massive outcry that within a week the city council had to distance itself from it (Rooijendijk, 2005). Amsterdam's spatial history offers a mixed picture for the following decades: a major traffic breakthrough was realised in later years on the Wibautstraat-Weesperstraat-IJtunnel route, but many other plans failed or shrank, including visionary 1960s suggestions (by Jokinen, an American traffic engineer) to transform Singelgracht, the ring canal surrounding the historic centre into an urban highway under the title 'Give the city a chance' (Jokinen, 1967). When these plans backfired, there was no ready alternative solution available. But in the Kaasjager debate, for the first time a clear limit was set to the car's power to dictate the city's development, thus opening a window to a shifting power balance in the future (compare Freudendal-Pedersen's description of Copenhagen, Chapter 9, this volume).

In its 1934 General Extension Plan (Algemeen Uitbreidingsplan (AUP)), Amsterdam pioneered urban planning explicitly based on systematic bicycle use. This long-term extension plan, with Cornelis van Eesteren as chief designer, was meant to guide the city's development until the year 2000. It broke with previous urban models by emphasising the principles of a 'functional city', spatially separating housing, work and recreation, and assigning generous spaces for mobility. Its housing quarters offered far more space, light, fresh air and greenery than the existing city. This could only be achieved by lowering housing and population densities; but then, inevitably, distances for regular movements within the city would increase. The AUP designers tried to balance spaciousness and accessibility, by establishing a 30-minute maximum one-way commute as a planning rule, and then pragmatically basing their calculations on 'the bicycle, which according to its numbers is by far the most important private means of transportation' (Gemeente Amsterdam, 1934). The AUP included two maps indicating that almost all the housing would be within 30 minutes cycle travel from the main work areas.

The economic crisis of the 1930s and the Second World War delayed execution of the AUP. During the post-war era (until 1965) it continued to serve as the general framework. Many aspects of the AUP were altered but the principles of a bicycle-scaled city and the separation of traffic modes in main roads remained. Consequently, the AUP-extension areas are bicycle-friendly, while simultaneously facilitating higher degrees of motorisation.

Culture clash (1960s, 1970s)

In the early post-war years, the city government chose not to prioritise inner-city issues. It faced two major urban tasks: to repair and renew the older parts of the city, and to build large stocks of new housing both to accommodate the post-war population boom and to allow working-class people to trade in their run-down inner-city quarters for a more pleasant and healthier environment. The second task was prioritised, and executed along AUP lines, as this was considered the quickest way to counter the acute housing shortage. As a consequence, the older parts of the city had to wait. 1950s inner-city Amsterdam offered a depressing sight that is almost unimaginable today. This is strikingly recorded by documentary photographers including Frits Weeda, Ed van der Elsken, Aart Klein and Boris Kowadlo.

In hindsight, the planning void proved to be a blessing in disguise. The long period of neglect and indecisiveness created the opportunity to make imaginative and creative plans without being limited by a focus on immediate implementation. These plans were then discussed, amended or rejected. Others could present counter-plans, do more research, forge coalitions, resist, rethink and redirect. The heated debate between 'modernists' and 'conservationists' sparked by the Kaasjager plan is just one example from this period. The lengthy period of stagnation and uncertainty about the future opened up new opportunities, new chances, new concepts and possible surprises for the old city (Rooijendijk, 2005).

During this long period, a major shift in orientation developed in the appreciation of cycles in the transport mix. Adjudged by its position in the city's policies, the official status of the bicyclebegan to evaporate. However, from the mid-1960s, its fortunes began to turn, as a cultural, social and political counter-force gradually gained momentum. A diverse range of influences contributed to this shift.

Figure 7.1: Children playing on Waterlooplein at the end of a market day, circa 1956–1958

Source: Chris de Ruig, Amsterdam City Archives

Mainstream traffic planning

Mainstream planning concepts in Amsterdam in the 1960s resembled those in other European cities. Run-down city quarters (for example, Jordaan, Nieuwmarktbuurt) were to be demolished, a central business district established and modern traffic would get more space. As in the influential British report, *Traffic in Towns* (Buchanan, 1963), and in the German report, *Stadtverkehr: Gestern, Heute, Morgen* (Sill, 1965), the traffic concept assumed that people would either travel in a motorised mode (private car or public transport) or on foot. Those examples are very similar to what happened in Sweden and led to a rationalisation in planning, as Koglin argues in Chapter 3 (this volume). Extensive studies and debate were undertaken on planning a network of partially underground urban railways ('stadsspoorwegnet') to cater for future mobility demands. Ultimately, a slimmed-down version of the initially designed metro network was executed (Davids, 2000).

Cycles, although still a major feature of Amsterdam's streets, were spectacularly absent in these visions of the future. This was partly the outcome of a strictly logical line of thought also used in *Traffic in Towns* (Buchanan, 1963). As cities expanded and densities decreased, people would live further away from their jobs; daily commuting distances would increase so much that it would no longer be attractive to cycle to work. All energies, therefore, should be focused on new transport modes better fitted to future travel demands. In other words, mass cycle use would soon be outdated by progress and prosperity, whether one liked it or not. This seemingly neutral reasoning was often charged with sentiments that suggested that bicycles were a symbol of backwardness. The mayor of Amsterdam, Van Hall, offered a revealing example in 1964, when he boasted that during a period of 17 years, he had had to succumb to cycling only once (Jordan 2013: 294–5).

While government officials ignored cycling as a realistic policy option, they did realise the advantages of the bike. It did so in its policy memorandum on the inner city from 1968, while arguing why public transport needed extra attention: 'Now that a mode of transport that is as economical in the use of space as the bicycle is diminishing, transport must be concentrated on public transport' (Gemeente Amsterdam, 1968: 11). The remark is as striking as it is fleeting: the scarcity of space was a major problem, the bicycle was acknowledged for its spatial economy and yet the bicycle was not considered as potentially part of the solution.

Demographic transformation

Official planning concepts were based on an assessment of major demographic trends; but planners did not seem to recognise an important upcoming phenomenon: the coming of age of the first post-war 'baby boom' generation. During the 1960s, this generation came to the city to study, to express themselves and to enjoy life in unprecedentedly large numbers. They introduced new social and cultural values that diverted from those of their parents, for example in family formation. They created a new and vital youth culture. And they used and valued the city in a distinctly different way, subsequently reshaping the city. Political scientist Herman de Liagre Böhl (2010) succinctly summed up this transformation of Amsterdam's identity in the 1960s and 1970s, 'from a worker's city to a youth city'.

Looking for affordable housing, the new urban dwellers discovered the vacated working-class quarters. For them, many of the negative qualifications of these quarters were irrelevant. Small apartments that had been bad housing for large families were fine if occupied by just one or two. High density was an advantage because it meant that all relevant services and locations were easily accessible: just hop on your bike and you are there. When faced with poor maintenance their attitude was not to wait for the authorities, but either to do it yourself, or start an action group and urge negligent authorities to act.

As perceptions of the city shifted, so too did perceptions of urban mobility. Cars were no longer the preferred mode of transport. Instead of being markers of progress or prosperity, they were seen as a nuisance and a threat, as well as impractical. Public transport was not an attractive alternative for a variety of reasons. Transport lines designed for the worker's city did not necessarily cater well for the youth city; trams and buses were trapped in congestion; and a youth culture that celebrated freedom preferred individual over collective mobility. Additionally, implementation of ambitious public transport schemes such as the metro proved to be complex, controversial and expensive.

Cycles were rediscovered as a great instrument for moving through the city swiftly and autonomously. They were an instrument of freedom; not just metaphorically, not just as an ideological or political *symbol* of freedom, but also, and perhaps foremost, as a highly flexible travel mode in day-to-day practice (see also Vivanco, 2013; Day, 2016). Arguably, the baby boom generation could disregard the car's symbolism of success and prosperity precisely because they were the first generation that had grown up familiar with car culture right from the start.

This emergent culture clashed with the conventional social code on many levels. It soon engaged itself in social activism and politics, thus organising the counter-culture into effective means of political influence. Generally, it aimed at pushing alternative ideological goals. It focused on a variety of issues, from university democracy to sexuality to law and order; in Amsterdam, it also had a strong focus on urban issues and city politics.

Provo and Kabouter

The 'Provo' movement that started in 1965 used irony and playful provocation as its main weapons (Duivenvoorden, 2009). Provo was in fact a very small movement without much direct impact, yet it introduced new ideas and values that would become highly influential. The authorities were confused by their actions and often overreacted. Through their power play, Provo managed to set the agenda for the next decade. Provo's playfulness was deceptive; no matter how unserious their style seemed, they were addressing urgent and grave issues, such as the steeply rising number of traffic fatalities and injuries.

In its *Annual Report* for 1965, the city government reported a total number of 31,868 traffic accidents, in which 93 people died and 5,655 were injured (Gemeente Amsterdam, 1966: 58). Traffic mortality continued to grow, reaching a high of 114 fatalities in Amsterdam in 1970 (Gemeente Amsterdam, 2016: 11–12).

One of Provo's great successes was the 'White Bicycle Plan' introduced by Luud Schimmelpennink in 1965: ban motorised traffic from the centre of the city and distribute a great number of unlocked bicycles, free for anyone to use. In practice, the plan was a total failure. There were never more than a handful of white bikes available and most were almost immediately stolen, but as a rhetorical device its effect was enormous. It generated much publicity, putting the bicycle back in the spotlight as a hip and highly fashionable means of transport, as a superior piece of technology (precisely because of its simplicity) and as an obvious instrument for a revamped society. In following years, the white bicycle would become an almost mythical worldwide symbol of a better world, even featuring on the bed that John Lennon and Yoko Ono famously shared at the Amsterdam Hilton in 1969.

Provo only existed for two years and was succeeded by the 'Kabouter (Gnome)' movement, which aimed to take a step further in the pursuit of change. Among their wide range of plans, urban liveability and banning cars were once again prominent (Tasman, 1996) as indicated by the slogan to 'reclaim the asphalt'. Reflecting an internationally emergent consciousness, environmental pollution was added to the range of arguments. They did not shy away from confrontational actions such as damaging cars or undertaking sit-down demonstrations to block car traffic. The sit-down demonstration campaign in the narrow Leidsestraat was highly effective. The first action took place in April 1970, and by July, car traffic was permanently banned from the street. In the same period, the Kabouter party entered the city council with a significant five seats. Kabouter and Provo were among a large number of related action groups, too numerous to cover individually here, but the presence of strongly anti-car movements such as Amsterdam Autovrij and De Lastige Amsterdammer also needs acknowledgement.

Urban warfare in the Nieuwmarkt neighbourhood

Confrontation between two sets of values and views on the city's development – the official planning doctrine and the emerging alternative view – escalated in the Nieuwmarkt area in the 1970s. The city wanted to build a metro line between Central Station and the new

Bijlmermeer suburb. The inner-city route would go underground, but because of the soft soil on which Amsterdam is constructed, the tunnel would have to be dug instead of drilled. A huge part of the old Nieuwmarkt neighbourhood was due to be demolished and replaced with an inner-city highway on top of the metro, and the route lined with large-scale office buildings. In resistance to these plans, the 1950s heritage movement and the 1960s counter-culture forged an unlikely, but powerful alliance.

The heritage movement, with Geurt Brinkgreve as a leading figure, took a strategic approach by buying the House De Pinto, an historic building from 1605, situated right in the middle of the projected four-lane road (see Figure 7.2). They asked the Dutch queen to open the building renovation project. Demolishing this monumental house would now be all but impossible for the city. An alternative routing was briefly considered that would turn the house into an island with two traffic lanes on each side. Meanwhile, squatters occupied many of the vacant housing and work spaces in the Nieuwmarkt area and started to renovate them. They strongly opposed the metro plan, both by 'direct action' and formal protest, such as speaking to city council and using the legal system to raise objections. One of the squatters

Figure 7.2: The demolition trail for the metro line construction through the Nieuwmarkt quarter

Source: Gerhard Jaeger

that engaged in this was Auke Bijlsma, who later even became city councillor for PvdA (Social Democrats).

The city government had backed itself into a corner. It could not possibly abandon the metro plan a mere kilometre from Central Station. Consequently, it pushed forward; even waging heavy fighting with squatters in 1975, but the price paid was high and other plans were given up. The urban highway to Central Station was abandoned in 1972 (with a minimal 22 to 21 vote in the city council) and the Sint Antoniesbreestraat kept its historic 12m width, respecting the situation of the House De Pinto. The Nieuwmarkt area was rebuilt as a fine-grained (social) housing and work area instead of a central business district.

Nieuwmarkt marked a turnaround in the city's policy. In 1972, social democratic Alderman Han Lammers (of the largest council party PvdA) reflected: 'Slowly, city governments have retraced their steps' (Hessels et al, 1985: 77). However, it took until 1978 before a new team of Aldermen substantially adopted a new, small-scale approach to housing and mobility into the city government policy.

Children's city

A further aspect of the shifting perspective was a changing view on the position of families and children in the city. A number of action groups focused on children's interests, such as sufficient playing space, safe routes to school, and safe streets where children could learn to ride their bicycles. One highly influential movement was 'Stop de Kindermoord' (Stop child murder). It protested against the horrendous dangers of traffic (with traffic as the highest cause of chidren's death in Europe), and against the authorities' apathy and fatalism on the issue. Founded in 1973 by a journalist in the province of Brabant who lost a young daughter in a traffic accident, and shortly afterwards almost lost a second daughter, Stop de Kindermoord resonated strongly across the country, especially in Amsterdam. The action group voiced a previously latent concern. It mobilised parents, teachers, journalists, other citizens and politicians. Even right-wing politicians who traditionally promoted automobile interests could not ignore the outcry.

Building the cycling city

While the promotion of cycling was an apparently natural ingredient of most of the citizens' movements mentioned earlier, specific cycling-oriented movements also emerged in the early 1970s. They recognised how the promotion of cycling could serve many interests simultaneously. Towards the end of the 1970s, the city government became more receptive to cycling interests and the concept of a bicycle-friendly city planning. The fundamental choice for these movements was between influencing policy making from the outside, or joining government in a collective effort.

Amsterdam Fietst was first staged in 1973 by diverse action groups including Stop de Kindermoord, Amsterdam Autovrij, the emergent ENWB (which later became Fietsersbond, the cyclists' union), Nieuwmarkt activists, neighbourhood groups and environmentalists. They organised large bicycle demonstrations demanding a more liveable city, greater (road) safety, fewer cars and a better position for cyclists (Amsterdam Fietst, 1977). The first edition of the festival attracted many participants, and it continued to grow as an annual event. It showed the power of the alternative movement through its preferred mode of mobility. It was fun but it came with a serious political agenda. In Amsterdam, the bicycle movement was large, well organised and eye-catching. Dramatic pictures of Museum Square full of demonstrating cyclists were published in many international newspapers (see, for example, *The Herald Tribune*, 5 June 1977).

The 1977 Amsterdam Fietst was particularly significant for its influence on the local elections of 1978. Participants urged politicians to change traffic policy and meet protestors' demands (*Report Amsterdam Fietst 1977*) to:

- stop building parking garages in built-up urban areas;
- locate car parks at the city edges, improve the tram network, stimulate city-friendly transport of people and goods;
- reduce the maximum speed for car drivers within the city to 20 km/h;
- improve and expand bicycle facilities;
- save energy and materials by rolling back car traffic.

To increase pressure, the 1978 Amsterdam Fietst demonstration was announced to take place one week before the local elections. To coincide, action group Amsterdam Fietst published their study detailing how political parties had previously voted on traffic. The new city council proclaimed the 'compact city' to be its priority. Cycling was to be a crucial part of it. Published in draft form in 1976, the Verkeerscirculatieplan (VCP, Traffic Circulation Plan) constituted the major policy document for traffic. It offered an extensive investigation into the state of traffic in Amsterdam, and detailed management measures. The draft was a hybrid of old and new concepts. It aimed to reduce 'non-essential car traffic' but wanted to do this mostly by promoting public transport, especially for commuting, and strategically building parking garages. The attitude towards cycling was hesitantly changing; the VCP introduced a first sketch of a main bicycle network, while also proposing to ban cyclists from some streets for the sake of trams and cars.

After the 1978 elections, the VCP was amended to offer substantially more attention to cycling (Gemeente Amsterdam, 1978). Its acceptance in 1979 marked the paradigm shift towards a cycling-positive policy that is still consequential today. A crucial aim was 'the creation of a network of direct routes on which the cyclist could safely and rapidly reach amenities and job locations from the housing neighbourhoods' (Gemeente Amsterdam, 1978). This change was partially fuelled by the '*Bottleneck Report*' that the cyclist's organisation ENWB had recently prepared (ENWB, 1977). At the heart of the report was an inventory of the 300 worst bottlenecks that cyclists experienced daily. The ENWB remained active on the streets, but also got involved in systematically analysing bottlenecks for cyclists and suggesting solutions to policy makers. A report of the social democratic faction in the city council sketched the outlines of cycling policy (Van der Vlis et al, 1978). After the elections, Van der Vlis became alderman for traffic.

In becoming a political actor, the ENWB faced a dilemma as well as a strategic choice. Should they (idealistically) stick uncompromisingly to their principles, or should they (pragmatically) seek solutions feasible within the existing framework and within a reasonable time period? Should they refrain from involvement in the city government, or should they cooperate? The dilemma became even more acute when alderman (or: Deputy Mayor for Transport) Van de Vlis in 1978 asked ENWB to participate in a Werkgroep Fiets (Bicycle Working Group) together with city officials.

One branch within the cyclist's movement ('Fundi's') opposed cooperating with the city government, the (former) enemy, out of fear of being compromised. The other branch ('Realo's') regarded government as the key instrument towards achieving collective goals, and applauded its policy shift towards bicycle-awareness. ENWB members discussed the issue intensely and then decided with a 75 per cent vote that ENWB should cooperate with the city while also keeping up activism. We see here close parallels with the dilemmas facing Danish cycle activists, described in Emanuel's chapter (this volume).

This approach was already visible in the 1977 *Bottleneck Report*. Here, ENWB had expressed its principles while offering practical solutions that were not too far from the existing reality. The report suggested solutions feasible with the existing number of cars; it stated that the number of cars should preferably be lowered, but accepted that this outcome was not yet attainable. It chose to make small and realistic steps rather than limit itself to utopian visions that would have little chance of materialising.

The Bicycle Working Group and network planning

In a formally constituted Bicycle Working Group, ENWB met with representatives of all city departments involved with cycling issues. Initially, city officials were just as ill at ease as the activists, but in due time they learned to collaborate on improving infrastructure for cyclists and solving bottlenecks. In the process, they developed standard solutions that could be widely applied. Both parties realised their positions were different; the ENWB representatives could never forget their activist consciences, while the city officials also had to always consider a wide range of other interests.

To implement a more bicycle-oriented policy, the Working Group advised starting simultaneously from two opposite ends: by (1) designing and refining an overall cycling network for the entire city and; (2) tackling the many day-to-day bottlenecks for cyclists that could be solved relatively easily. Gradually, these two approaches would meet on the streets of Amsterdam.

The practical approach of solving bottlenecks was based on the ENWB *Bottleneck Report*, as well as on complaints by cyclists, and traffic safety data. The body of knowledge that Amsterdam cyclists collectively possess (including every crack in the asphalt, every nasty ridge and cycling-unfriendly traffic light) has since been one of the great strengths of the Amsterdam cyclists movement as well the city's bicycle officials. Solving bottlenecks led to introducing new circulation models, such as allowing cyclists to use one-way streets in both directions. A seemingly minor measure, but one significant for cyclists, was to clear street corners of parked cars. Reducing speed, introducing speed bumps and reducing the number of parking spaces were other measures taken to make streets more cycling-friendly and safe. Meanwhile, a citywide bicycle main network (Hoofdnet Fiets) was elaborated. The network concept was a convincing way to integrate the cyclists' position in the total traffic policy framework. There were already networks for cars and public transport, and an acknowledged bicycle network would help to warrant the status of cyclingin political and financial debates. Its form was extensively discussed, both within the Bicycle Working Group and amongst ENWB members.

The 1976 draft VCP had identified three main bicycle routes. It was a start, but also subject to criticism, doubt and amendment. A three-route network might be realistic for car drivers, but it was far too wide-meshed to be meaningful for cycling. After 1978, the concept was amended. First, the main network had to be adapted to cycling-relevant mesh size. Second, the network should not stop at these main routes, but connect to a far more fine-grained layer of cycling-friendly environments; essentially including every street.

The Main Bicycle Network plan was agreed in 1982. It consisted of existing and yet-to-be-built routes that would together form a connected network for swift, safe and attractive cycling. It also included a quality standard that defined quality requirements for safety, speed and comfort. All routes of the main bicycle network should meet these standards. Obviously, the network would require long-term implementation. The first improvements in the early 1980s were carried out in 'easy streets', especially neighbourhood streets, rather than in main roads where the traffic situation was more complex. The measures resembled the list of demands of *Amsterdam Fietst* back in 1978, such as reducing car speed and the number of cars; introducing 'one way for cars, two way for cyclists'; taking out parking spaces, especially at street corners; and repairing missing links for cyclists, such as improvements at junctions. On main roads, improvements for cyclists often demanded an entirely new layout. In these cases, work on the bicycle network was synchronised with other road maintenance and improvement programmes to make it financially feasible.

Since 1982, the bicycle network has served as a long-term policy tool, with (slight) adaptations made over time. By consistently working on cycling quality in every project on the bicycle main network over nearly 40 years, Amsterdam now boasts a Main Bicycle Network of which approximately 95 per cent meets the layout and design standards. This has helped to improve road safety and comfort for cyclists and served as the backbone of the cycling city.

Systemising knowledge and standards

While the Main Bicycle Network was gradually secured in the streets of the city, activists and city officials also cooperated on creating a structure of knowledge, expertise and quality standards. In this way, bicycle interests were embedded into both the policy and operational routine of the city. The necessity of such systemised expertise intensified in the 1980s when the Municipality of Amsterdam was subdivided into 'stadsdelen', administrative districts with considerable autonomy in a number of policy fields. Between 1981 and 1990 a total of 16 districts were established. Some have merged since then, reducing the number to seven districts today. Cycling policy was decentralised. To ensure continuity and connectivity, and to avoid policy fragmentation and expertise drain, the Bicycle Working Group systemised its knowledge and experience in the '*Handboek Fiets Amsterdam*' (1st edition, 1991). The handbook was a co-production of the City of Amsterdam and Fietsersbond, following the example of Fietsersbond's earlier 'Neighbourhoods for cycling' study (Slebos et al, 1987). It subsequently served as the guiding handbook for all city districts and played a pioneering role in creating consensus on what constitutes good bicycle-friendly infrastructure and policy. It was also the basis for the (inter)nationally famous CROW Design Manual for bicycle traffic (CROW, 1993).

A further step in systemising safety standards was taken in 1997 when Amsterdam, like all other road authorities in the Netherlands, committed to the new 'Systematic Safety' (Schepers et al, 2017). This road safety programme aims to design roads in such a way that the design, use and function of streets are in balance and that streets are inherently safe, especially for road users rendered vulnerable by motor traffic. Cars and cyclists are separated when needed, and speed and volumes of cars are reduced when necessary. For cyclists, Systematic Safety basically had two types of roads:

- Residential areas with low speeds and few cars. When both speed and traffic levels are low (30 km/h and less than 6,000 vehicle movements per 24 hrs) cars and cyclists can share the street. Speed is controlled by speed bumps and a consistent layout. Forgiving, rounded speed bumps effectively reduce car speeds but are also comfortable for bicyclists. At junctions in residential areas, roads are equal in terms of priority. An exception is allowed for important bicycle routes which sometimes have priority. Thus, some of Amsterdam's 'best' bicycle routes are through residential areas with no particular special features other than priority. In Amsterdam entering a residential area goes via an elevated entrance construction (elevated kerb).
- Distributor roads (main roads), for through traffic (more than 6,000 vehicle movements per 24 hrs) with a maximum speed of either 50 or 70 km/h. Separated bicycle tracks are necessary to avoid collisions at high speeds and so that cyclists are not compelled

to ride between parked and fast-moving cars. The challenge of building bicycle tracks on main roads is especially acute in the older parts of Amsterdam where streets are narrow and demand for space is high (from pedestrians, cyclists, cars, shops, terraces, car and bike parking, trees, public transport, and so on). With the commitment to Systematic Safety and the quality standard of the main bicycle network, with the vision and courage of politicians and civil servants, and the energy and expertise of citizens and Fietsersbond, many unpleasant and unsafe main roads in Amsterdam have been transformed into streets where everyone can cycle comfortably. In newer parts of the city (built from the 1950s onwards), segregated bike tracks along main roads were often included at the time they were built, as planned in AUP and later development plans.

During the past 40 years of bicycle policy and about 20 years of Systematic Safety the Amsterdam street system has gradually been transformed. Today, about 95 per cent of all streets meet Systematic Safety standards. As in Whitelegg's discussion of Vision Zero (Chapter 5, this volume), the planning and management of traffic has been paradigmatically transformed over this period. This is not to say that everything is always good, but that the car-dominant paradigm still prevalent in most cities is no longer tenable in this situation.

Roles and partners

Building an effective and pleasant bicycle city was never easy, and results could never be taken for granted. It took activists' power, political will, technical skills, the 'wisdom of the crowd' of cyclists, and perseverance. It is therefore pertinent to look finally at specific roles played by some of the most relevant partners.

Since its foundation in 1976, the *Fietsersbond Amsterdam* (Amsterdam Cyclists' Union) has been influential in developing Amsterdam into a cycling city. Co-organising the Amsterdam Fietst demonstrations in the 1970s, it has cooperated with the city since 1979 in the Bicycle Working Group and through other projects. Fietsersbond is a member-based organisation, with circa 35,000 members nationwide, including 4,000 in Amsterdam, of whom about 70 people are actively involved as volunteer unpaid workers. From 1982 to 2015 Fietsersbond had (first one, later two) staff, paid for by the city government in order to secure the professional input of the Fietsersbond's expertise into the city's organisation. Although both posts were terminated in 2015, the work they had been doing continues.

Fietsersbond has a wide range of activities that have been a vital part in creating and maintaining the bicycle city as it is known today. They include consulting and co-creating for good cycling inclusive infrastructure and policy, lobbying and activism, signalling and raising awareness for new issues, collecting and preserving detailed knowledge, offering information, and educational activities. Given this range of activities, the Fietsersbond has a surprisingly lightweight organisation that has relied mostly on the input of its dedicated volunteers. Between 1982 and 2015, the paid workers at Fietsersbond sat in the centre of a meshwork of contacts and knowledge about the city and the projects that were important for cyclists. While the city itself had few staff explicitly dedicated to cycling, Fietsersbond arguably maintained the best overview of relevant cycling knowledge in town. Other participants in planning processes in the city include traffic groups of community centres, organisations for pedestrians and disability groups, shopkeepers, the Chamber of Commerce, and environmental groups such as Milieudefensie. The municipal public transport company, GVB, is also often involved in the planning.

The city government officially leads the process of building a bicycle network, establishing policy, designing and assessing traffic plans, funding and organising the process. Since the 1970s, plans are discussed with the relevant members of society. In most cases, this meant that the city makes and executes plans while creating space for citizens to react. In the field of cycling policy, external input was far greater; the city government asked Fietsersbond to be involved in cooperating and co-creating. Even then, just a handful of people were involved (on a paid basis) on both sides.

After the establishment of the city districts in 1981–90 the results differ from district to district, depending both on the district council's political leanings and on personal basis. The more right-wing Zuid district leans towards favouring cars; here, introducing cycling facilities can be difficult whenever it means less space for cars. Both the west and east districts just outside the centre have a more pro-bicycle profile. The outlying districts of Nieuw West, Zuidoost and North have more space and longer distances, which allows space both for cars and planned cycle infrastructure from the start.

Conclusion

Amsterdam has not become a cycling city by accident or by default, but by a consistent series of crucial choices combined with decades-long hard work by many involved stakeholders. Although historic characteristics provided good starting conditions, Amsterdam has transformed itself over time into the cycling city we know today through continuous policy and planning (Harms et al, 2016), moved forward by cooperation and action of active citizens and cyclists.

The historic morphology of Amsterdam made the spatial challenges that rising car levels created apparent in an early stage. As early as 1927 city councillor Wibaut stated: 'either the (existing) city should be adapted to the needs of modern traffic, by breaking down houses and filling in canals, or the new traffic should adapt to the possibilities of the old city' (Hessels et al, 1985).

For a long time, Amsterdam has been trying to adapt to the needs of modern traffic; changes have come slowly, on a relatively small scale and constantly contested over time. This contestation reached its peak when an emblematic traffic plan for enlarging a street in the historic city centre was voted down by the smallest majority possible. With the help of active citizens, the old traffic (and related land use) policy was conclusively stopped and replaced with a new, small-scale-oriented planning paradigm.

Cyclists pointed the way to alternative policies: the good old bicycle would become the key element of the 'new traffic' paradigm, in which traffic adapted to the possibilities of the old city instead of vice versa. This policy materialised through making cycling safe and convenient in every street, working kerb by kerb, street by street, junction by junction with the dedication, patience and persistence of many stakeholders in the city. However, it is important to note that this required the political infrastructures to allow such engagement. In addition, improvement of the national railway network further supported city cycling by offering a good substitute for longer-distance travelling (Kager et al, 2016). Contrary to some description, several new highways have also been constructed around the city. Although some were much debated, these also helped to allow the city centre to limit the number of cars.

Contested future

This challenge is by no means finished. Many of the developments that started in the 1970s have created conditions that now create self-reinforcing feedback loops that further support cycling and walking. However, this does not mean that the future of Amsterdam is by definition one in which it remains a cycling city. As the authors, we want to stress that cycling levels are not as high in all parts of the city as in the city centre. In some neighbourhoods, car traffic still dominates (Nello-Deakin, 2019). Further, ongoing efforts are required to re-adapt a street design culture in which cycling and walking have claimed space within a car-dominated logic. With current numbers, new patterns have to be developed in which cycling and walking takes centre stage in how we design our streets (te Brömmelstroet et al, 2018).

If Amsterdam is widely regarded as a cyclists' paradise, the city has obtained this honorary title on the cheap. Much of the indispensable observational, analytical and conceptual expertise on which the success of the bike city is built was delivered for free by devoted citizens working towards a more liveable city.

Cooperation between activists and city officials was successful because of mutual trust and openness. The dedication and expertise of activists met political support of Council members. When Fietsersbond started cooperating with the city, some members feared that they would be compromised into agreeing with unfavourable city policies. In hindsight, it was not the cycle advocates that were influenced or compromised by cooperating with the city, but rather the other way around: city officials were enabled to make use of the cyclists' expertise and could therefore make better plans. Nevertheless, compromises have been made. Amsterdam is not the car-free city idealists had in mind, and the city remains woven into a tightly-knit network of motorways.

More recently, the city itself has employed more staff specialised in cycling, but this is still a modest number, considering the total number of officials responsible for traffic policy and for neighbourhood liveability, urban planning and sustainability issues. It is also a modest number, considering the enduring dominance of car-oriented thinking in the traffic expertise realm, and in policies from the Dutch national government. Active cooperation and input of Fietsersbond and other citizens remains of crucial importance to improve cycling quality.

Lessons learned

To use a bicycling metaphor: the speed and ease with which a cyclist moves forward depends partly, but not only, on the cyclist's efforts, but also on the wind. Is there a tailwind pushing you in the preferred direction, or do you have to struggle against a headwind?

Discussions on bicycle activism and policies focus mainly on the deliberate efforts, assessing possible and preferable strategies, instruments, best practices, and so on. The Amsterdam case as we present it offers a variety of examples and also leaves some major questions unanswered. This chapter elaborated on the interplay between activists and policy makers, on systemising knowledge and on implementing the bicycle infrastructure as a long-term programme. We stressed the importance of working patiently, persistently and systematically, with a 'main bicycle network' plan as probably the most important policy tool. To realise this (local) knowledge, enthusiasm and collaboration with relevant parties are of the essence; the world-leading cycling city as it is today was not created overnight, but took many decades of constant, consistent and hard effort to materialise.

This chapter also acknowledged the tailwinds that have helped Amsterdam in ways that cannot easily be replicated elsewhere. These favourable, partly pre-existing conditions for the cycle city include a compact urban form that has not been subjected to large-scale 19th-century modernisation, thus offering relatively unfavourable conditions for the motorcar and favourable conditions for its competitors, including the bicycle. Demographic transformation and cultural shifts in the 1960s and 1970s also gave cycling advocacy a major boost, and they did so just in time to preserve continuity in the transition towards the mass presence of bicycles in the city.

All these tailwind factors in the Amsterdam case have a historical and local specificity that makes them hard to replicate in a different city in a different time. From this case, advice on making those transitions in other cities is restricted. Delve into your own history and your own specifics, and be on the alert to find your own favourable winds. They will most likely be different from Amsterdam's.

References

Amsterdam Fietst (1977) *Report Amsterdam Fietst 1977*, Amsterdam: Amsterdam Fietst.

Amsterdam Fietst (1978) *4 jaar stadspolitiek*, Amsterdam: Amsterdam Fietst.

Boterman, W.R. (2018) 'Carrying class and gender: cargo bikes as symbolic markers of egalitarian gender roles of urban middle classes in Dutch inner cities', *Social & Cultural Geography*: 1–20.

Buchanan, C. (1963) *Traffic in Towns*, London: Ministry of Transport.

CROW (1993) *Design Manual for Bicycle Traffic*, Utrecht: CROW.

Davids, K. (2000) 'Sporen in de stad. De metro en de strijd om de ruimtelijke ordening in Amsterdam', *Historisch Tijdschrift Holland. Werken Aan een Open Amsterdam*, 32(3/4): 157–82.

Day, J. (2016) *Cyclogeography: Journeys of a London bicycle courier*, New York: New York Review of Books.

de Liagre Böhl, H. (2010) *Amsterdam op de helling. De strijd om stadsvernieuwing*, Amsterdam: Boom uitgeverij.

Didde, R. (1992) *Blik op oneindig*, Amsterdam: Ravijn.

Duivenvoorden, E. (2009) Magiër van een nieuw tijd. Het leven van Robert Jasper Grootveld, Amsterdam/Antwerpen: De Arbeiderspers.

ENWB Amsterdam (1977) *Knelpuntennota Amsterdam*, Amsterdam: ENWB Amsterdam.

Feddes, F. and de Lange, M. (2019) *Bike City Amsterdam: How Amsterdam Became the Cycling Capital of the World*, Amsterdam: uitg. Bas Lubberhuizen.

Gemeente Amsterdam (1934) *Algemeen Uitbreidingsplan van Amsterdam*, Afdeling Stadsontwikkeling, Van Publieke Werken.

Gemeente Amsterdam (1966) *Amsterdam '65, Stedelijk Jaarverslag*, Amsterdam.

Gemeente Amsterdam (1968) *Voorontwerp van de tweede nota over de Amsterdamse binnenstad*, Gemeenteblad 1968, Bijlage C, Amsterdam.

Gemeente Amsterdam (1978) *Het Verkeerscirculatieplan*, Dienst Infrastructuur, Verkeer en Vervoer, Gemeente Amsterdam.

Gemeente Amsterdam (2016) Meerjarenplan Verkeersveiligheid, Amsterdam

Harms, L., Bertolini, L. and te Brömmelstroet, M. (2014) 'Spatial and social variations in cycling patterns in a mature cycling country exploring differences and trends, *Journal of Transport & Health*, 1(4): 232–42.

Harms, L., Bertolini, L. and te Brömmelstroet, M. (2016) 'Performance of municipal cycling policies in medium-sized cities in the Netherlands since 2000', *Transport Reviews*, 36(1): 134–62.

Hessels, M., Hoffschulte, C. and Nouwens, H. (1985) 'Het AUP in de Binnenstad', in H. Hellinga (ed) *Algemeen Uitbreidingsplan 50 jaar Amsterdam*, Amsterdam: Amsterdamse Raad voor de Stedebouw.

Jokinen, D.A. (1967) *Geef de stad een kans: Een studie uitgevoerd*, Amsterdam: Stichting Weg.

Jordan, P. (2013) *In the City of Bikes: The Story of the Amsterdam Cyclist*, Harper Perennial.

Kager, R., Bertolini, L. and te Brömmelstroet, M. (2016) 'Characterisation of and reflections on the synergy of bicycles and public transport', *Transportation Research Part A: Policy and Practice*, 85: 208–19.

Kuipers, G. (2013) 'The rise and decline of national habitus: Dutch cycling culture and the shaping of national similarity', *European Journal of Social Theory*, 16(1): 17–35.

Nello-Deakin, S. (2019) 'Is there such a thing as a "fair" distribution of road space?', *Journal of Urban Design*, 24(5): 698–714, DOI: 10.1080/13574809.2019.1592664

Oldenziel, R. and de la Bruhèze, A.A. (2011) 'Contested spaces: bicycle lanes in urban Europe, 1900–1995'. *Transfers*, 1(2): 29–49.

Oosterhuis, H. (2015) 'Ingebakken gewoonte of buitenissige liefhebberij?', *Sociologie*, 11(1): 3–30.

Poelstra, H. (1985) 'Verkeer en vervoer in Amsterdam', in H. Hellinga (ed) *Algemeen Uitbreidingsplan 50 jaar Amsterdam*, Amsterdam: Amsterdamse Raad voor de Stedebouw.

Pucher, J. and Buehler, R. (2008) 'Making cycling irresistible: lessons from the Netherlands, Denmark and Germany'. *Transport reviews*, 28(4): 495–528.

Pucher, J. and Buehler, R. (eds) (2012) *City Cycling*, Cambridge, MA: The MIT Press.

Rooijendijk, C. (2005) *That City is Mine! Urban Ideal Images in Public Debates and City Plans, Amsterdam & Rotterdam 1945–1995*, Amsterdam: Amsterdam University Press.

Schepers, P., Twisk, D., Fishman, E., Fyhri, A. and Jensen, A. (2017) 'The Dutch road to a high level of cycling safety', *Safety Science*, 92: 264–73.

Sennett, R. (2018) *Building and Dwelling: Ethics for the City*, New York: Farrar, Straus and Giroux.

Sill, O. (1965) *Stadtverkehr: Gestern, Heute, Morgen*, München: Hermann Kaiser.

Slebos, C., Muller, S., de Jongh, D. and Guit, A. (1987) *Wijken voor de fiets: handboek fietsvoorzieningen en fietsbeleid*, Amsterdam: ENFB Amsterdam, https://fietsstadamsterdam.nl/wp-content/uploads/2019/05/1987-Wijken-voor-de-Fiets-cpctv2.pdf

Tasman, C. (1996) *Louter Kabouter. Kroniek van een beweging 1969–1974*, Amsterdam: Babylon-DeGeus

te Brömmelstroet, M., Nello-Deakin, S., Quillien, J. and Bhattacharya, I. (2018) 'Towards a pattern language for cycling environments: merging variables and narratives', *Applied Mobilities*, 1(2): 1–19.

Van der Kloof, A. (2015) 'Lessons learned through training immigrant women in the Netherlands to cycle', in P. Cox (ed) *Cycling Cultures*, Chester: University of Chester Press, pp 78–105.

Van der Vlis, Stoffel, K.C. and Mug, P. (1978) *Fietsen in Amsterdam, nota van de raadsleden vd Vlis, Stoffel en Mug*, Gemeente Amsterdam.

Vivanco, L.A. (2013) *Reconsidering the Bicycle: An Anthropological Perspective on a New (Old) Thing*, London: Routledge.

8

Conflictual politics of sustainability: cycling organisations and the Øresund crossing

Martin Emanuel

Introduction

Mobility history scholarship makes the point emphatically: as streets were reinterpreted as mainly for cars, cyclists were marginalised by means of legislation, police-control, planning and infrastructure provision, a process that sped up in the post-war period. To the extent that cycling prevailed, cyclists were rendered invisible by dominant actors within city traffic regimes (for example, Emanuel, 2011; 2012; Oldenziel et al, 2016; Männistö-Funk and Myllyntaus, 2018). Notwithstanding new interpretations of cycles as tools of sustainability, and indeed increased policy attention and rising levels of cycling in many city centres in the last few decades, the marginalisation of cyclists remains a reality – as becomes evident in many chapters of this volume. Whereas cycling today often receives growing attention as an important mode of mobility in overall traffic policy documents and in comprehensive urban planning documents, allocation of funds, especially on the regional level, remain aligned with infrastructural plans that cater for automobility and public transit (Emanuel, 2018). Moreover, as Koglin (Chapter 3, this volume) shows, cycling is still marginalised in Sweden's transport planning, often through rationalisations. Cycling does still not sufficiently belong to the dominant mobility paradigm to warrant full inclusion. How do cycling organisations navigate this discrepancy between policy attention and *realpolitik*? This chapter provides an example from the recent past that reveals the tensions between different factions within cycling advocacy: on the one hand those who seek a true transition, and on the other advocates who are more pragmatic vis-à-vis the dominant paradigm.

Since the 1970s, the cycle has come to serve as a symbol of a more humane and environmentally friendly society, often in contrast to a car-centred one. Cycling organisations usually consider themselves as part of the environmental movement, and the belief in the cycle as an environmentally friendly means of transportation is often a reason for individuals to engage in cycle advocacy (Horton, 2006). An alternative motivation to engage may be a sense of frustration due to perceived imbalances in how our transport systems are shaped to take different road users into consideration (Furness, 2010). These contrasting motivations are not irreconcilable. For example, urban cycle tracks are often highlighted as a means to promote an environmentally friendly mode while also securing cyclists' rights of access. But at times the perspectives conflict. The cycling organisations' approach to a fixed connection across Øresund is a case in point. (Note that the Danish spelling Øresund is used here; Swedish documentation uses the Swedish spelling Öresund).

In summer 1991, both Swedish and Danish Parliaments approved a governmental deal for a fixed transport connection across Øresund: a combined road and rail bridge with a four-lane motorway and double-track railway would provide a link between Copenhagen and Malmö. Nine years later, in the summer of 2000, the Øresund Bridge was inaugurated. It consisted of a high bridge giving way for passing boats on the Swedish shipping lanes, coupled with a lower bridge and tunnel under the Danish waterway. There was a long prehistory before the deal was signed. There were stages when the Øresund Bridge was planned with cycle tracks, yet the final construction had no such lanes, and it was, and still is, forbidden to ride on it. This chapter draws on detailed examination of the Danish Cyclists' Federation's (DCF) internal discussion papers and personal correspondence drawn from the personal files of Ernst Poulsen, one of the leading figures in those negotiations, further supplemented by an interview with Poulsen by the author (Poulsen, 2013, interview with Emanuel, 19 October). The chapter draws on another previously published in Swedish (Emanuel, 2015). While the previous chapter examines the Swedish cycle organisations' as well their perspectives are largely left out of the present text. The interested reader can also consult the chapter in Swedish for a more thorough annotation of primary sources. These primary sources are used to trace the trade-offs between environmental sustainability and rights of access made by the DCF in their consideration of and campaigning for cycle tracks on the Øresund Bridge.

From a strictly environmental perspective, a railway tunnel was the preferred solution, prioritising public transport and minimising increase in car traffic. If, however, a combined car and railway bridge should be built, cyclists (and pedestrians) should be given access to the bridge on the same conditions as motorists and train passengers, to fulfil the requirements of transport justice and equal rights. Both perspectives were represented within DCF; there were in fact two different factions, one representing each perspective, which meant a constant tug of war over what ought to be the organisation's official policy. This struggle is at the heart of this chapter.

Cycling organisations are often treated as homogeneous: like other organisations, they seldom are in practice. A further consideration is that organisations do not exist in a vacuum, but need to be considered in context. Aims and activities need to be understood as shaped in interplay with the surrounding environment rather than as endogenous productions. Cycling organisations are not uniform, homogeneous actors with easily identifiable aims, but it is not the heterogeneous character per se (expressed, for example in internal hierarchies and power struggles) that is of interest for this chapter. Rather, the study is located closer to what the organisation researcher W. Richard Scott (2003: 25–30) identifies as a third overall perspective of organisational theory. This places greater emphasis on processes than structures, at the same time considering organisational dependence on both context and environment. According to this view, an organisation is reproduced by shifting coalitions of members, all embedded in a broader context. The discussion that follows examines the heterogeneity of DCF in relation to changes in (part of) the environment in which the organisation worked and tried to influence: specifically, transport policy on a fixed link across Øresund.

The Øresund Bridge: from idea to decision

A fixed connection across Øresund had been imagined since at least the late 19th century (Idvall, 1997: 128–32; Blomquist and Jacobsson, 2002: 37–38). Private initiatives drew inspiration from the rapid development of the railways in Europe desiring to connect the Nordic countries to the emerging international railway network. A railway tunnel would reduce Sweden's isolation from continental Europe. During the 1930s, a connection across Øresund re-emerged as part of a large-scale motorway plan for Denmark presented by a Danish-Swedish consortium. It proposed a combined road and rail bridge between Malmö and Copenhagen, whose road section was equipped with walking and cycling lanes (*Motorveje med Broer over Storebælt og Øresund*, 1936: 42–3 and 72–8). The consortium argued that the connection would be financed with a differentiated toll depending on traffic mode; cyclists would have to pay like any other traffic.

Figure 8.1: The 1936 proposal for an Øresund bridge with cycle path, as part of a wider motorway scheme

Source: *Motorveje with the Storebælt og Broer over Øresund*

The proposal was submitted to both countries' governments, but left unattended because of the outbreak of the Second World War. New initiatives were taken up after the war by this and other consortia, which presented different plans for road and rail links in both northern (Helsingborg–Helsingør) and southern (Malmö–Copenhagen) reaches of the Sound. Following initial discussions in 1954 between the Swedish and Danish Governments, a joint Øresund Delegation was formed. In 1962 it presented a proposal for a combined car and railway bridge between Helsingborg and Helsingør, acknowledging the possibility of a future additional link in southern Øresund (Blomquist and Jacobsson, 2002: 38–40). Cycle tracks were not initially excluded, but the delegation made their final assessment that the link should be built without them as they would be 'extremely costly' (SOU, 1962: 30); according to the cost estimates such lanes would be between

5.4 and 13.3 per cent of the total cost (SOU, 1962: 83–103). No subsequently submitted road bridge plan allowed for cycles or pedestrians: all were for motorised traffic only.

The fixed connection's design and location, however, were subject to further investigation and vigorous debate (Blomquist and Jacobsson, 2002: 40–2). A Helsingborg–Helsingør connection was cheaper and better suited the Swedish state's desire for improved transport between Sweden and the continent. Critics argued that a bridge between Malmö and Copenhagen would give greater socio-economic benefits. In 1964 a Swedish state investigation was assigned to follow up on the material that the previous delegation had left behind. In its 1967 report it stronger emphasised the regional impact of a fixed link and advocated a connection at Malmö–Copenhagen (SOU, 1967).

In the late 1960s, intergovernmental negotiations created a package deal to include a six-lane road bridge between Malmö and Copenhagen, a new airport on the Danish island of Saltholm and a railway tunnel between Helsingborg and Helsingør (Blomquist and Jacobsson, 2002: 40–4). An agreement was signed in 1973, followed by a favourable majority decision in the Swedish Parliament. In the end, however, the oil crisis, a growing environmental movement and declining optimism dashed the plans. When the Danish Parliament voted down the airport at Saltholmen in 1975, it prompted the Swedes to break the agreement.

Another 16 years would pass before a new agreement on the Øresund connection was ratified. The process was a complicated history of political scheming and of lobbying from powerful industry interests (Falkemark, 1999: 68–78; Blomquist and Jacobsson, 2002: 45–52). Negotiations on a fixed link were resumed in the mid-1980s after successful lobbying by 'The European Roundtable of Industrialists', formed in 1982 by prominent European industrial leaders and led by Volvo's CEO Pehr G. Gyllenhammar. A Nordic offshoot of the Roundtable, the ScanLink Consortium, persuaded both Swedish and the Danish states to explore a fixed Øresund connection. A new Øresund Delegation appointed in the summer of 1984 suggested a submersed Helsingborg–Helsingør rail tunnel and a four-lane Malmö–Copenhagen highway bridge. In July 1987, the delegation forwarded a revised proposal of a combined car and railway bridge between Malmö and Copenhagen, whose road toll fees would also finance the railways. By this time, regional motivation for a fixed Øresund link had strengthened and a combined Malmö–Copenhagen bridge was recommended on the basis of its expected regional effects.

The final (spring 1991) agreement between the Swedish and Danish Governments for the Øresund crossing made no mention of cycle tracks. Later, in letters to Poulsen and the DCF, politicians and officials who were involved in the negotiations claimed that cycle tracks had initially been on their agenda, but were soon dismissed (Odell, 1992, personal communication to DCF, 3 April; Holdt, 1996, personal communication to Ernst Poulsen, 6 March). Thus there had been no meaningful discussion of cycle tracks in the planning process (Hök, 1991).

The lack of cycle access caught the attention of cycling organisations at a late stage. In autumn 1990 the Swedish Cyclists' Federation (Cykelfrämjandet) wooed the Swedish Road Administration's General-Director Lennart Johansson to take cyclists' needs into account in the planning stage. If a railway tunnel was built it was important to assure cyclists' rights to bring their bikes on trains. Johansson assured the Federation that the cyclists' needs would be taken into account, but was uncertain that cycle tracks would be the best way to go about it. It could become overly expensive for cyclists (who, like all others, must pay in order to use the bridge) and, in any case, the high bridge as well as the 2km-long tunnel would be unpleasant for cycling (*Cykling*, 1990). With this, it seems, the Swedish organisation was content.

On the Danish side, it was only in the spring of 1991 that the Øresund connection received full attention. For a considerable time, the DCF's focus had been on the Great Belt Bridge (between the Danish islands of Zealand and Funen), where it had tried in vain to ensure a cycle track. No one expected the Øresund Bridge to emerge as quickly as it did. The organisation was, like the Danish environmental movement at large, taken by surprise by the influential Social Democratic Party leadership's sudden reversal regarding the Øresund connection (Poulsen, 1992a; 1992b; 2013, interview with Emanuel, 19 October). In relation to Øresund, the Danish Social Democrats had advocated a train tunnel rather than a combined bridge. Within only a few months the Danish Social Democratic Party, pressured by the leadership of their Swedish sister party that insisted on a combined connection, made a complete U-turn, announced support for a bridge, and called on the Danish Government to enter into agreements with Sweden (Hedegaard Sørensen, 1993: 10–11, 119–125; Anshelm, 1995). At the beginning of March 1991, the Danish Government, consisting of the Conservative and Liberal Parties (*Konservative* and *Venstre*), closed a deal with Danish Social Democrats and Centre Democrats. When Danish traffic minister, Kaj Ikast, a conservative, shortly thereafter sent out a voluminous report on the environmental impact of building a bridge, it became the starting point for a Danish public debate about a fixed Øresund connection. The agreement between the two governments was signed on 23 April, and on 2 May Ikast presented a legislative proposal for a fixed connection across the Sound. The draft law was followed in May and June by a large variety of alternative proposals from engineering firms and scientists, but they were rejected without further examination. The parties behind the agreement were at this point determined to realise the combined bridge connection.

'It is realistic to cycle across Øresund'

The intense debate about environmental effects and alternative solutions in the spring of 1991 focused on the marine environment, but DCF tried to use the opportunity to lobby for cycle tracks. The Federation's first initiative was a letter on 31 May 1991 from DCF board member Ernst Poulsen to traffic minister Ikast. Using the example of the Golden Gate Bridge in San Francisco, which had cycle tracks, Poulsen enquired why the same thing would not be possible on the Øresund Bridge. Arguing against a cycle track, Ikast mentioned how these would not be profitable given the expected amount of cycle traffic. Furthermore, limited ventilation in the 2km-long tunnel would make cycling 'unacceptable' (Ikast, 1991, personal communication to Ernst Poulsen, 3 July).

In response, Poulsen (1991, personal communication to Kaj Ikast, 31 May; 12 July; 17 July) produced examples of tunnels in Europe where cycling *was* permitted and thus obviously possible. According to one calculation, he argued that the bridge would cover its costs within 30 years. Ikast's answer did not arrive until September 1991, after the Danish Parliament had ratified the intergovernmental agreement on the Øresund connection. A cycle track had been considered but, according to Ikast, rejected during the Danish-Swedish negotiations. The coalition agreement now 'precluded' it from being built; the case was 'closed'. At the same time, he stressed that the parties behind the agreement had made sure, through an amendment in the construction law, that rail transport of cycles on the bridge would be given special care (Ikast, 1991, personal communication to Ernst Poulsen, 11 September).

Ernst Poulsen continued his assiduous efforts to refute the arguments against a cycle track on the bridge put forward by the transport minister and others (Poulsen, 1991, personal communication to the traffic policy spokespersons of the Danish Socialist People's Party,

Social Democratic Party, Christian Democratic Party, and Social-Liberal Party, 13 August). He managed to get the Ministry to retract their claim that it would be impossible to cycle on the bridge. Also, his telephone survey with shipping companies operating the sound revealed that the number of cyclists ferrying their cycles across the strait was three times the number declared by the Ministry. With these details as a basis, Poulsen urged the traffic policy spokespersons of four political parties to demand a traffic forecast and cost calculation for widening the roadside to incorporate a lane for cycling and walking. In fact, a minority in Parliament proposed, in vain, a more thorough review of the environmental impacts and options, including cycling conditions (Blomquist and Jacobsson, 2002: 69–70).

The DCF, with Poulsen at the fore, had to work hard before reaching a breakthrough on the cycle track costing. The Danish Road Administration's (Vejdirektoratet) calculations showed the costs as more than double those claimed by the Federation. As the correspondence between the Transport Ministry and DCF and internal notes of DCF show, it was discovered too late that the Directorate had made its calculations on the basis of one-way cycle tracks on both sides of the connection, while the Federation had proposed a two-way cycle track on one side only (Krag, 1992; Brok et al, 1992: 112–16).

In February 1992, Poulsen's findings against the traffic ministry's arguments were released in a DCF report (Poulsen, 1992a), which was spread through a press release with the title '*It is realistic to cycle across Øresund*' (DCF, 1992a). The report called for a more realistic cost estimate of a cycle track (this was before they learned of the Directorate's assumption) and for cycling's positive environmental effects to be incorporated. It attracted little attention, but Poulsen kept trying. When the DCF released a slightly revised, carefully designed and illustrated version in the autumn (Poulsen, 1992b), the response was different (Figure 8.2). Poulsen now claimed that it was not only possible to construct cycle tracks at almost no extra cost (less than 1 per cent of the entire construction cost), they could also be utilised during maintenance work or for other necessities.

There were new arguments on attractiveness. Poulsen stressed that the bridge would not primarily be used for commuting, but for cycle tourism and excursions, and for this sort of cycling 17 km was not at all a particularly long distance. 'The physical hardships are … part of the experience,' wrote Poulsen, 'and thus the Øresund Bridge will be a magnet for cycle tourists.' In the early 1990s, 30–35,000 cyclists took the ferry across the channel. With cycle tracks on the bridge, he argued, 100,000 cyclists a year was a conservative estimate.

Figure 8.2: 'In Sådan cykler man over Øresund' ['This is how to cycle across Øresund'], Danish Cyclists' Federation's board member Ernst Poulsen collected his rebuttal to allegations that it was impossible to provide the bridge with a bicycle lane. Architect Peter Munch was hired to illustrate the Øresund connection, including a bicycle lane

Source: Peter Munch

In Poulsen's summary, one *could* cycle across Øresund. The real question was whether politicians *wanted* it to be possible. Rhetoric and practice went separate ways here, Poulsen argued. While talking about the environment, politicians spent the majority of resources on roads, bridges and tunnels that could not be used by either pedestrians or cyclists. A ban on walking and cycling on the connection would be detrimental to Denmark's image as a cycle-friendly country.

The report was circulated widely, including copies to all members of the Danish Parliament. Articles in several newspapers stressed the possibility of an Øresund Bridge cycle track. To the minister of transport, Kaj Ikast, however, the case was already closed (Ikast, 1992, personal communication to DCF/Poulsen, 19 November). In the Danish daily paper *Politiken*, he argued that it would be too dangerous to allow cyclists on the bridge, and to have cycles in the tunnel would be simply 'irresponsible' (Skaarup, 1992).

A moratorium on advocacy

Although the discussion thus far suggests that DCF favoured a bridge crossing with cycle tracks, this was not the whole story. The official position of the Federation was for a long time that no bridge should be built, full stop. Opposition to a bridge had grown since the formation of ScanLink in 1984, and culminated with the Swedish environmental examination later in the 1990s (Idvall, 2000: 75–90). In common with much of the Danish environmental movement, DCF was opposed in principle to a combined car and railway bridge and preferred a bored rail tunnel.

In particular the Federation's Brundtland Committee, which focused on environmental sustainability, worked diligently against the bridge. The Committee took its name from the 1987 Brundtland report, the result of a UN Commission (WCED) to examine the relationship between economic growth and environmental degradation. Faced with the Parliament decision on 14 August 1991, the Committee arranged a campaign against the 'motorway bridge' (DCF, 1991a). On 6 October, a smaller group of members occupied the site where the connection would connect to the road network on Amager with a 'tent camp', albeit only for a short while before eviction by the police (Sign. 'LI-Z', 1991, 'Kort Cyklist-Protest', 1991). Two days later, a three-day cycle demonstration began (Figure 8.3). Starting in Rødby Havn with Amager as its endpoint, the demonstration covered the stretch that the Federation feared would turn into a motorway if the Parliament voted in favour of the Øresund Bridge (DCF, 1991b; 1991c).

Figure 8.3: Drawing by 'RAK' (Rane Knudsen), from the press release on the Danish Cyclists' Federation's three-day demonstration by bicycle against the Øresund Bridge

Source: Rane Knudsen

From 1991 the official stance of DCF was to prefer a rail tunnel, but if a bridge was unavoidable, it should have a cycle track (DCF, 1991d). Bridge resistance was, over time, replaced by a new 'realist' standpoint: since the Øresund Bridge had been adopted in both Sweden and Denmark, then the Federation should exclusively lobby to give cyclists access to it (DCF, 1993a: 18).

The Brundtland Committee reacted strongly when DCF representatives proposed a pedestrian and cycle track as a means to give the bridge a 'softer profile' and to counter its 'motorway image' (Brundtland Committee, 1992). The Committee argued that Ernst Poulsen's approach was likely to give the impression that the organisation *wanted* a bridge, and repeatedly tried to defuse the lobby work for a cycle track on the bridge. At the Federation's national assemblies in 1991 and 1992 the Brundtland Committee (in 1992 joined by the organisation's Copenhagen Division) tried to change the statutory purpose of the organisation to stress sustainable transport rather than 'the special interests of cyclists'. If this stance was taken, then the Federation would have had to limit its advocacy to thwart the environmentally devastating combined link, not to lobby for cycle tracks (DCF, 1992b: 32).

Statute changes were outvoted and the Committee declared the matter dead in November 1992 (Brundtland Committee, 1992). Only a few months later, however, at the beginning of 1993, the Øresund connection was subject to renewed criticism from other quarters. Both the Swedish Licensing Board and the two governments' appointed international panel of experts independently rejected the existing plans for the Øresund Bridge. Extra costs incurred to ensure proper water flow gave further argument for bridge opponents (Falkemark, 1999: 106–8; Blomquist and Jacobsson, 2002: 70–3). Because of these further criticisms, the DCF's Brundtland Committee considered the topic 'reopened', with consequences for Federation's policy. Lars Georg Jensen (Brundtland Committee member and consultant at the Danish Society for Nature Conservation) criticised the DCF executive committee for its exclusive focus on cycle tracks on the bridge, arguing that it could only be seen as a support for a 'car bridge' now declared environmentally unsustainable. This would be very unfortunate for the public perception of the Federation. The organisation ought therefore to return to lobbying for a rail tunnel '*and only that*'; ensuring on-board cycle carriage (DCF's Brundtland Committee, 1993, personal communication from Jensen to DCF's Executive Committee, 1 March). DCF chair, Walther Knudsen, defended Ernst Poulsen's voluntary efforts in support of a cycle track, but agreed it was now time to keep a low profile on the issue, considering politicians' less solid support for the Øresund Bridge (Knudsen, 1993, personal communication to Jensen, 5 March). In March the same year the board of DCF took a decision in a similar spirit (DCF, 1993b).

At the DCF national assembly in Odense in May 1993, the Øresund connection became the subject of lively debate and multiple ballots. The board was criticised for prioritising cycle track advocacy over a rail tunnel, but proposals to completely stop the work with the cycle track was voted down. By a narrow margin, the assembly agreed on a wording that gave the demands of a railway tunnel higher priority than a cycle track on the bridge (DCF, 1993c; Poulsen, no year). The arrangement left open for both factions to push their own agenda, typical for a grassroots organisation where a large part of the resources is the work invested by the active members. At the same time the arrangement revealed a reversal of official priorities within the Federation, visible in the internal correspondence, and a stance reinforced by the Federation's objection to the Danish traffic ministry against the Øresund connection in early July 1993 (DCF, 1993, personal communication, Kjerulf Jensen to Trafikministeriet, 6 July).

This was not, however, an end to the disagreement. In the midst of all, it came to the bridge opponents' attention that Poulsen and Knudsen had invited the newly appointed social democratic traffic minister, Helge Mortensen, for a cycle test-ride on the Great Belt Bridge. This was explicitly intended to allow comparison with (potential) cycling on the Øresund Bridge (DCF, 1993, personal communication, Knudsen/ Poulsen to Mortensen, 16 June). Mortensen's public opposition to a cycle track was based on economics. He argued that the DCF had underestimated the costs of an adequate width cycle track and that the 800 riders per day required to make it profitable was unrealistic (Steen Nielsen, 1993). In a meeting with the Federation at the end of May 1993, however, Mortensen had asserted that it was still an open question, technical challenges notwithstanding (Krag, 1993). So in mid-June, as the decision-making process for the Øresund connection went into its final phase, the Federation invited Mortensen to the aforementioned ride. Although the tour apparently never happened, it still opened old wounds within the organisation. Poulsen had interpreted the national assembly's decision as carte blanche for continued advocacy for cycle tracks on the bridge, something Lars Georg Jensen and several other significant representatives within DCF sharply opposed (Østergård et al, 1993, personal communication, to DCF's Executive Committee and Knudsen, 2 July).

This time the opponents of the bridge were successful. Knudsen would later argue that the Copenhagen and Tårnby sections of the Federation obtained a moratorium on work in favour of cycle tracks on the bridge (Knudsen, 1995, personal communication to DCF's National Board, 6 November). In September 1993 he signed, as chairman of DCF and together with Charlotte Østergård, representative of the 'tunnel group' within the Federation, a joint press release stressing that the Øresund connection should be realised in the shape of a railway tunnel. A bridge with a motorway would encourage car traffic in a region with already high levels, they argued. A tunnel would instead attract motorists to public transport, which in turn would also improve the traffic environment for cyclists (Knudsen and Østergård, 1993). At this point in time, within DCF, the environmental concerns of stopping the bridge outweighed principles of cyclists' right of access.

A cycle track back on the agenda

The Swedish environmental trial of the Øresund connection continued (Falkemark, 1999: 109; Blomquist and Jacobsson, 2002: 72–78). In November 1993, the Swedish Water Court endorsed the Øresund Consortium's application, provided that a so-called 'zero solution' (that the salt and oxygen levels in the Baltic Sea was not affected) could be achieved. Disagreements within the Swedish Government (the Centre Party were dedicated bridge opponents) delayed the process.

But as the Øresund Consortium had undertaken several changes that would ensure a zero solution, the government gave its consent on 16 June 1994. The event did not lack drama: Centre Party leader and Minister of Environment, Olof Johansson, resigned in protest. Shortly thereafter, the Øresund Consortium received permits from the Licensing Board and the Water Court, again provided that a zero solution could be obtained. Construction began in autumn 1995.

With bridge construction appearing inevitable, lobbying for cycle access re-emerged as a legitimate activity for DCF, so, in summer 1995, Poulsen led new initiatives. A couple of things made the Federation hopeful. First, a group of students from Denmark Technical University (DTU) had been commissioned to investigate cycle track construction on the bridge. Their report (Hansen et al, 1994) rejected the counter arguments and included an elaborate design of a cycle track on the high bridge and in the tunnel (see Figure 8.4) that in its cheapest version would cost 210 million Danish kronor, matching the Road Administration's estimate. The second factor was unexpected support for DCF from former Volvo President, Pehr G. Gyllenhammar, arguably the chief proponent of the bridge during the 1980s. In a letter to Poulsen, he wrote that, 'there should be room for everyone

Figure 8.4: Postcard sent to traffic minister Jan Trøjborg to ask for reconsideration of the cycle facility. Drawing by Peter Munch shows the cycle track beneath the road and above the railway as proposed in DTU students' design

Source: Peter Munch

on the roads, and since the bridge will be the only fixed connection between the Scandinavian Peninsula and the Continent, cyclists should be able to travel on the bridge' (Gyllenhammar, 1995, personal communication to Poulsen, 6 June).

Emboldened, the DCF began a new media campaign. Several Danish politicians endorsed the call for cycle tracks on the bridge if technically feasible and affordable. Malmö's strongman Ilmar Reepalu also said that he was prepared to consider the idea (Perschard, 1995; DCF, 1995a; DCF, n.d.). But on the Swedish side it was difficult to reinvigorate the debate: the Swedish Cyclists' Federation lacked resources to push the issue (Swedish Cyclists' Federation, 1995, personal communication, Wathén to Poulsen, 7 August), and articles Poulsen sent to major Swedish newspapers were rejected.

Opposition from representatives of the Ministry of Traffic, the bridge consortium, and heavyweight traffic politicians at the national level in Denmark, however, was strong. Christian Democrat Arne Melchior, chairman of the Transport Committee of the Danish Parliament, argued that the DTU report was 'complete nonsense!' According to him, it was economically unjustifiable to construct cycle tracks given how little they would be used, according to 'all expertise' (Fris Jensen, 1995a). Representatives from the Øresund Consortium argued that it was too dangerous to have a cycle track on a motorway bridge and that there would be problems with ventilation in the tunnel and high wind speeds on the high bridge. The Consortium's administrative manager, Sven Landelius, stressed that they were determined to carry out their assignment: to build the bridge according to the signed agreements, that is, one without a cycle track (Fris Jensen, 1995b). The Swedish National Road Administration also suggested problems from exhaust and noise in the tunnel section, but most of all the Administration found DCF's estimate of 100,000 cyclists per year unrealistic. According to their estimates, the actual number would not justify the additional costs (Swedish National Road Administration, 1995, personal communication, Leif Adolfsson to the Swedish Cyclists' Federation, 10 August). Neither did the issue receive any public support from the most decisive Danish politicians, the Danish ministers of traffic and of the environment, Jan Trøjborg and Svend Auken ('Ingen støtte til cykelsti på bro', 1995; 'På frihjul om cykelsti', 1995).

The sceptics did thus not attach any particular importance to DCF's or the DTU students' claims that there was no obstacle to a cycle track on the Øresund connection. All the more surprising, therefore, was that the planning chief of the Ministry of Traffic's bridge division, Kurt Lykstoft Larsen, claimed that the DTU report did not contain anything new. Of course it was technically possible to create a cycle track, 'You can send people to the moon' he argued, but due to priorities of resource allocation a clear majority of the politicians had discarded the idea. To introduce a lane at this point would require new negotiations between Sweden and Denmark and with contractors. The latter would, according to Lykstoft Larsen, 'lick their lips' (Fris Jensen, 1995c).

Within the DCF, the new initiative for a cycle track offended those who opposed the bridge. Lars Georg Jensen urged the Copenhagen chapter to take action against the executive committee of the Federation, knowing that other environmental organisations were puzzled by DCF's agitation (Jensen, 1995, personal communication to the Board of DCF's Copenhagen Chapter, 24 August). This time, however, the bridge was so close to realisation that the critics within the organisation accepted Poulsen's advocacy. The chairman of the Copenhagen chapter, although stressing that his branch remained opposed to the bridge in principle, declared it a lost cause (DCF's Copenhagen Chapter, 1995, personal communication from Hjulmand to DCF's national board, 11 October; Hjulmand and Rasmussen, 1995, personal communication to Jensen, 20 September). Walther Knudsen (1995, personal communication to DCF's national board, 11 June), chairman of the national DCF board, also defended lobbying for a cycle track: despite potential criticism from the broader environmental movement, at this point, when the realisation of the Øresund Bridge seemed impossible to stop, the efforts to secure cyclists' right of access was legitimate enough.

Finale: no cycle track on the Bridge

DCF's next move was to demonstrate popular support for a cycle track on the Øresund Bridge (DCF, 1995b). Having produced a public poll showing about two thirds for and less than a quarter opposed, political response was mixed. In letters to DCF, several politicians believed that it was more important, or perhaps more reasonable, to secure space for cycles on public transport. In autumn 1995, however, social democratic MPs from the Environment Committee lent their support to cycle tracks, and called upon traffic minister Jan Trøjborg to reconsider the issue. They wrote to Poulsen that a cycle track would lend the bridge a greener profile and thus stronger public support. Martin Gleerup, environmental spokesperson, was quoted in the daily press: 'We have to show that Denmark is an environmentally pioneering country. Hence we should get to the bottom with this matter [the issue of a cycle track on the bridge].' (Boelskifte, 1995; 'Cykelsti på Øresund', 1995; Mose, 1995) Internal correspondence shows that DCF now focused on convincing the social democrats and traffic minister Jan Trøjborg, but he was dismissive (Trøjborg, 1995, personal communication to DCF, 6 October). Unexpectedly, it was Arne Melchior, previously critical, who convinced Trøjborg to have the Øresund Consortium look into the subject (Melchior, 1995, personal communication to Trøjborg, 20 October).

The Consortium's report contained a thorough review of why cycle tracks on the connection, in particular in the tunnel, were not appropriate (Øresund Consortium, 1995). High fixed costs made a separate cycle track unrealistic. Furthermore, noise, exhaust fumes, the claustrophobic feeling of cycling in the tunnel, as well as the discomfort of riding near high-speed trains and in the strong wind on the bridge were used to question the DCF's usage estimate. The full report was an argumentation *against* cycle tracks on the bridge, wrote Thomas Krag to Melchior (DCF, 1996, personal communication, Krag to Melchior, 24 January), hardly an unbiased investigation of the matter. Krag especially questioned the consortium's cost estimation of the tunnel, which was two to three times higher than both the assessments made by the students at DTU and the National Road Administration. For politicians, on the other hand, the report was a welcome confirmation that the project did not need to be revised. Trøjborg stressed that the contracts for tunnel construction were already signed and to change them would be 'colossally expensive … hundreds of millions.' (Fris Jensen, 1996) Three parties, the Liberal Party (Venstre), the conservatives and the Centre Democrats stood rock solid by the decision that cycling would not be possible on the bridge. To the Øresund Consortium, finally, the case was closed: 'We do not even have that proposal in our drawers. It is nothing we even speculate about any longer' (Nielsen, 1996).

The issue was dead. Further proposals from DCF in spring 1996 were cold-shouldered by the Øresund Consortium, and by Trøjborg and other politicians who advised them instead to constructively contribute to detailing the requirements of alternative transportation arrangements for cyclists on the Øresund connection (Brøndum, 1996, personal communication to Krag and Poulsen, 29 January; Christensen, 1996, personal communication to Krag, 13 March; Trøjborg, 1996, personal communication to DCF/Johannes Lund, 31 July). The Øresund Bridge opened to traffic in the summer of 2000. The inauguration was preceded by an event, Open Bridge, during which people could cycle across. A Swedish reporter argued that it showed that, in fact, it was not only possible but 'excellent to ride on the bridge and that few cyclists were uncomfortable in the tunnel' (Orrenius, 2000). But cyclists' access to the bridge was an exception. As one speaker reminded the participants: 'You are 42,000. It doesn't get any more than this. Never again will anyone be able to ride on the bridge' (O'Dell, 2002).

Conclusion

The microscale study of a five-year period and the discussions around a single infrastructure proposal presented in this chapter allows us to understand cycling organisations' perspectives on the resulting failure to construct any cycle-specific infrastructure. Today, as a cyclist you instead need to take your cycle on the train. In fact, cycle tracks were never really given serious consideration in the negotiations preceding the 1991 agreement. As the DCF, and in particular Ernst Poulsen, had to invest all their efforts to puncture the arguments against a cycle track that were being forwarded by reluctant civil servants, it meant that the Federation was unable to get the issue on the agenda in time to influence the Danish Parliament ahead of its decision to approve the intergovernmental agreement. That small cycle organisations would then be able to prompt the authorities and state-led consortia to modify their plans was almost hopeless. Yet they came surprisingly close to a breakthrough.

At the same time, we have seen how a significant group within DCF (the Brundtland Committee and the local chapters in the capital area) were critical of Ernst Poulsen's and the rest of the national board's lobby work for a cycle track. Aligned with the broader environmental movement, they did not want to see any bridge at all, and in their view, work to promote a cycle track could easily be mistaken as a support of the bridge. This position attained extra fuel when politicians and cycle track proponents within DCF spoke of a cycle track as a way to give the bridge a greener image.

Key people within DCF's Brundtland Committee were allied with the Danish environmental movement and concerned about the Federation's (and presumably their own) reputation among environmentalists. From their perspective, it mattered little how close to realisation the bridge was; it was in principle wrong for an organisation with environmental ambitions to give their indirect support to the bridge by advocating cycle tracks on it. Supporters of a cycle track on the bridge were idealistic about cyclists' rights of access to public infrastructures but pragmatic in relation to the environment. If the bridge was being built anyway, they argued, it should at least accommodate cycling. A third group, which I here have just mentioned in passing, was made up of the major local chapters in the capital area. Their loyalty was with the city: they took interest in both the (urban) environment and the rights of cyclists in (urban) traffic situations. But as they deemed a cycle track on the Øresund Bridge to be more relevant to recreational cycling (while the bridge would supposedly bring more traffic into an already congested Copenhagen), they reluctantly abandoned their resistance to the bridge only at a late stage. Bridge opponents/environmentalists/urban cyclists in DCF were up against its cycle track proponents/rights of access activists/recreational cyclists, and who had the upper hand, that is, who controlled the Federation's position to the outside world, depended on how inescapable the realisation of the bridge appeared to be.

In a case of complex and contentious politics over infrastructural provision, cyclists' voices raised questions about the way that the various crossing options provided for some forms of mobility and excluded others. Environmental objections and questions introduced a further dimension to the issues of justice, not just the politics of some social groups but the wider environment needed to be considered in seeking a just and inclusive solution. The arguments over what form the infrastructure should take and for whom it should provide had no easy answers and, as the case study shows, were deeply political and politicised. Further, the details of these arguments show that the discussions cannot be reduced to simple binaries. The arguments are both multiple and changing, according to both ideology and pragmatism.

References

Anshelm, J. (1995) *Socialdemokraterna och miljöfrågan: En studie av framstegstankens paradoxer*, Stockholm: Symposion.

Blomquist, C. and Jacobsson B. (2002) *Drömmar om framtiden – beslut om infrastruktur*, Lund: Studentlitteratur.

Boelskifte, E. (1995) 'Flertal ønster cykelsti over Øresund', *Jyllands-Posten*, 20 September.

Brok, M., Joenssen, R., Knudsen, K., Lodal, T. and Menné, M. (1992) 'Cykler Over Øresund, et case studium om magtrelationer', student report, Roskilde University.

Brundtland Committee (1992) 'Referat af møde i Brundtland-udvalget', 21 November.

'Cykelsti på Øresund' (1995) *Dagbladet Information*, 20 September.

Cykling (1990) [untitled] 1990(4): 24.

DCF (1991a) (Holm), DCF Press release, 6 August.

DCF (1991b) 'Tre-dages cykeldemonstration mod motorvejsbroerne', Press release (Krag), 8 August.

DCF (1991c) (Aggernæs) 'Velkommen til denne cyklistdemostration', DCF Press release, August.

DCF (1991d) 'Dansk Cyklist Forbunds holdning til en fast Øresunds-forbindelse', Dansk Cyklist Forbund, 1 August.

DCF (1992a) 'Det er realistiskt at cykle over Øresund', DCF Press release, 5 February.

DCF (1992b) 'Landsmøde Viborg 1992', Dansk Cyklist Forbund.

DCF (1993a) 'Landsmøde Odense 1993', Dansk Cyklist Forbund.

DCF (1993b) 'Referat af HB-møde 19 marts 1993 i Rømersgade'.

DCF (1993c) 'Referat fra Dansk Cyklist Forbunds Landsmøde i Odense 22–23 maj 1993'.

DCF (1995a) 'Politikere støtter cykelsti over Øresund', DCF press release, 18 July.

DCF (1995b) 'Gallupundersøgelse: Københavnerne vil have cykelsti på Øresundsforbindelsen', DCF press release, 18 September.

DCF (n.d.) 'Borgmestre i København og Malmö- vil undersøge Øresunds-cykelsti', DCF press release.

Emanuel, M. (2011) 'Constructing the cyclist: ideology and representations in urban traffic planning in Stockholm, 1930–70', *The Journal of Transport History*, 33(1): 67–91.

Emanuel, M. (2012) *Trafikslag på undantag: Cykeltrafiken i Stockholm 1930–1980*, Stockholm: Stockholmia.

Emanuel, M. (2015) 'Principer i klinch: Öresundsbron och cykelorganisationerna' (Clinching principles: the Öresund bridge and the cycling organizations), in N. Wormbs and T. Kaiserfeld (eds) *Med varm hand: Texter tillägnade Arne Kaijser*, Stockholm: KTH.

Emanuel, M. (2018) 'Waves of cycling policy: cycling, mobility, and urban planning in Stockholm since 1970', in T. Männistö-Funk and T. Myllyntaus (eds) *Invisible Bicycle: Parallel Histories and Different Timelines*, Leiden: Brill, pp 101–25.

Falkemark, G. (1999) *Politik, lobbyism och manipulation: Svensk trafikpolitik i verkligheten*, Nora: Nya Doxa.

Fris Jensen, P. (1995a) 'Uventet støtte til cyklestier over Øresund', *Dagbladet Information*, 13 July.

Fris Jensen, P. (1995b) 'Socialdemokrater vil cykle over Øresund', *Dagbladet Information*, 14 July.

Fris Jensen, P. (1995c) 'Modstridende svar om cykelsti på Øresundsbro', *Dagbladet Information*, 27 July.

Fris Jensen, P. (1996) 'Broen breder sig', *Information*, 9 January.

Furness, Z. (2010) *One Less Car: Cycling and the Politics of Automobility*, Philadelphia, PA: Temple University Press.

Hansen, P., Bentzen, M. and Dorte Koch, A. (1994) 'Cykel- och gangsti på Øresundsforbindelsen', student report, Denmark's Technical University (DTU), autumn 1994.

Hedegaard Sørensen, C. (1993) *Slår bro fra kyst til kyst? En analyse af Socialdemokratiet og Øresundsforbindelsen*, Højbjerg: Hovedland.

Hök, M. (1991) 'Bron stängs för cyklister?', *Sydsvenska Dagbladet*, 17 October.

Horton, D. (2006) 'Environmentalism and the Cycle', *Environmental Politics*, 15(1): 41–58.

Idvall, M. (1997) 'Nationen, regionen och den fasta förbindelsen: Ett hundraårigt statligt projekts betydelser i ett territoriellt perspektiv', in S. Tägil, F. Lindström and S. Ståhl (eds) *Öresundsregionen – visioner och verklighet*, Lund: Lund Univ. Press, pp 126–51.

Idvall, M. (2000) *Kartors kraft: Regionen som samhällsvision i Öresundsbrons tid*, Lund: Nordic Academic Press.

'Ingen støtte til cykelsti på bro' (1995) *Kristeligt Dagblad*, 27 July.

'Kort Cyklist-Protest' (1991) *Information*, 7 August.

Knudsen, W. and Østergård, C. (1993) DCF press release: 'Dansk Cyklist Forbund ønsker rene linier', 15 September.

Krag, T. (1992) 'Notat fra møde i Vejdirektoratets bro-afdeling den 7.4.1992', Dansk Cyklist Forbund, 9 April 1992.

Krag, T. (1993) 'Notat om møde med trafikminister Helge Mortensen den 24.5.1993'.

Männistö-Funk, T. and Myllyntaus, T. (eds) (2018) *Invisible Bicycle: Parallel Histories and Different Timelines,* Leiden: Brill.

Mose, P. (1995) 'Fornyet krav om cykelsti', *Politiken*, 21 September.

Motorveje med Broer over Storebælt og Øresund (1936), København: Christiani & Nielsen, Højgaard & Schultz A/S, Kampmann, Kierulff & Saxild A/S.

Nielsen, J. (1996) 'Flertal mod cykelsti til Sverige', *Politiken*, 9 January.

O'Dell, T. (2002) 'Regionauterna', in P.O. Berg, A. Linde-Laursen and O. Löfgren (eds) *Öresundsbron på uppmärksamhetens marknad: Regionbyggare i evenemangsbranschen*, Lund: Studentlitteratur, pp 97–113.

Oldenziel, R., Emanuel, M., Albert de la Bruhèze, A.A. and Veraart, F. (eds) (2016) *Cycling Cities: The European Experience: Hundred Years of Policy and Practice*, Eindhoven, Foundation of the History of Technology.

Øresund Consortium (1995) 'Cykelstier og alternative transportordninger på Øresundsforbindelsen', 20 December.

Orrenius, N. (2000) 'Varför kan man inte cykla på bron?', *Sydsvenskan*, 10 July.

'På frihjul om cykelsti' (1995) *Berlingske Tidende*, 27 July.

Perschard, V. (1995) 'Cykelstiprojekt kræver velvilje', *Berlingske Tidende*, 16 July.

Poulsen, E. (1992a) 'Cykler over Øresund. En rapport om cykel- och gangsti over Øresund', Dansk Cyklist Forbund, Februar.

Poulsen, E. (1992b) *Sådan cykler man over Øresund*, København: Dansk Cyklist Forbund.

Poulsen, E. (no year) 'Øresund: Hvem må – og hvem skal arbejde med hvad?'.

Scott, W.R. (2003) *Organizations: Rational, Natural, and Open Systems* (5th edn) Upper Saddle River, N.J.: Prentice Hall.

Sign. 'LI-Z' (1991) 'Protestlejr ryddet efter en halv time', *Berlingske Tidende*, 7 August.

Skaarup, J.P. (1992) 'På cykel over Øresund', *Politiken*, 19 October.

SOU (1962) 53. *Öresundsförbindelsen: Betänkande. D. 1, Utredningar och förslag.*

SOU (1967) 54. *Fasta förbindelser över Öresund: Översyn av Öresundsdelegationernas betänkande SOU 1962:53 och 54, Redogörelse, avgiven år 1967 av svenska och danska öresundsgrupperna.*

Steen Nielsen, J. (1993) 'Cykelforbud på Øresund', *Information*, 12 March.

9

Vélomobility in Copenhagen – a perfect world?

Malene Freudendal-Pedersen

'One feels very Danish and social democratic when one is cycling.'

'I guess I'm thinking that I have to bike because it is good for me with the 8–9 kilometres, actually really good. I can feel the difference, in my mood and in my body generally, so I feel guilty when I use the metro.'

'The bike gives the most freedom, the metro also has this thing that one doesn't need to think, but the bike means that you can just jump on and drive wherever you want. That's also why I couldn't imagine living in the countryside where you have to drive the same stretch every day by car. I was also brought up with cycling because I was raised in the city and my parents never transported us around the city. Some of the other parents were outraged about that …'

These quotations, taken from extended fieldwork interviews in Copenhagen, give a great sense of the emotional, embodied identity and cultural aspect of cycling that Copenhageners express when asked why they cycle. Whereas in many other places, cycling in a city is seen as a hazardous activity (Spinney, 2010a; Aldred, 2012) Copenhagen offers a different perspective. 'Copenhageners' use of bikes is not defined in terms of risk, but rather in terms of urban everyday life on the move, with the sensuous, kinetic, and emotional power of biking emerging as a key to urban spatiality and vitalism' (Jensen, 2013: 278). Copenhagen is often described as a model cycling city, whose approach should be duplicated throughout the world, and Copenhagen is without a doubt a city that prioritises vélomobility (City of Copenhagen, 2017). However, the downside is a somewhat self-satisfied cycling narrative in Copenhagen, which, I will argue, could also be a barrier to further development of Copenhagen as a cycling city.

This chapter discusses these dilemmas in light of qualitative research conducted with cyclists in Copenhagen. It takes a theoretical position rooted in mobility research, questioning dominant planning paradigms that conceptualise the future of cities and mobilities as a matter of more efficient technologies rather than of social cohesion, integration and connectivity (Urry, 2007; Freudendal-Pedersen et al, 2016). The story of Copenhagen as a cycling city is also a story of 'collaborative storytelling' understood through communicative planning theory and the 'argumentative turn' (Healey, 1997; Fischer and Gottweis, 2012). The chapter discusses opportunities to create stories in which space is made for cyclists by questioning the dominance of the car. Thirty qualitative interviews and five focus groups of five to seven people form the empirical ground on which the discussion is based. Participants were an equal number of men and women between the ages of 22 and 73, as well as a group of 14-year-olds. As is very common in Copenhagen, my interviewees use a variety of transport modes and cannot be labelled solely as car drivers, public transport users, cyclists, or through any other unitary mobility identity. The interviewees are all middle class. In Denmark, due to the welfare society, the middle class is both extensive and possesses a lot of power when it comes to validating and recreating stories (Freudendal-Pedersen, 2014b). Specifically, I will discuss the storytelling produced about, and reproduced by, Copenhagen cyclists. This builds on a larger body of analysis of the ways in which people legitimise their actions and decisions by the stories that they tell themselves and each other about those actions. Shared in communities, individual stories act as unexamined truths, justifying actions and absolving those who share those stories from further examination of their actions (Freudendal-Pedersen, 2005; 2009).

First, through discussing the politics of cycling in Copenhagen, I will show how cycling is used strategically as part of urban development. I will then turn to the role of storytelling in creating Copenhagen as a city of cyclists, where the infrastructure and the role it plays for the success of cycling in Copenhagen is based on an understanding of how materialities and meanings are interconnected. After this, I will show how infrastructures both provide opportunities and create inequalities, especially for kids and untrained cyclists. In concluding, I will outline the possibilities for creating different stories that can challenge the car-dominated culture also present in Copenhagen.

The politics of cycling in Copenhagen

In Copenhagen, cycling is used strategically as part of urban development (Jensen, 2013; Koglin, 2013; 2015), and, even if cycling is less dominant in most other Danish cities (with the exception of Odense, Aarhus and Aalborg), the health and safety of the cyclist are ingrained in Danish traffic laws. The government takes responsibility for providing resources for cycling. This creates a different situation from, for example the UK, where cycling is viewed as an individual choice that comes with individual responsibilities (Aldred, 2013). On top of the extended infrastructure provision in Copenhagen, the municipality also takes responsibility for promoting a 'cycling community' through government-funded campaigns, as well as by installing bike counters along the road. Tallying the number of cyclists communicates to the public that cyclists matter (Freudendal-Pedersen, 2015a; 2015b). This creation of a cycling community is not to be understood as a separate, closed community. Copenhagen municipality uses the strong cycling community as part of its strategy to create a liveable city with top ranking in the international city competition.

It is important to note, especially when discussing cycling, that Copenhagen does not equal Denmark. On the national scale, car traffic increased by 2.9 per cent, and cycle traffic declined by 3.1 per cent in the last quarter of 2015, compared to the last quarter of 2014 (Road Directory, 2016). Clearly, this increase in car traffic is incompatible with the aim of increasing cycling as an everyday form of transport in Denmark, and the politics behind this development also influence Copenhagen. It seems that no matter how much Copenhagen and Denmark wish to be low-carbon communities, putting restrictions on car traffic is still politically unfeasible. In this sense, the story of Copenhagen has many similarities to what Feddes, de Lange and Brömmelstroet narrate in their story of Amsterdam and the strong role the car plays there, even in a 'cycling city' (Chapter 7, this volume). In many European and North American cities, cycling is practised as a form of resistance to the car's dominance of urban space, a claim on the part of cyclists for the right to the city (Furness, 2007; 2010; Spinney, 2010b). Despite the dominant role the car still plays, cyclists in Copenhagen seldom adopt the attitude or politics of resistance that characterises cycling cultures in many other cities around the world. The few associations working on behalf of cyclists' rights use a polite, collaborative approach in keeping with the Danish equality mentality, which does not 'allow' for any outspoken inequalities (Freudendal-Pedersen, 2014b; 2015b). The empirical research with cyclists in

Copenhagen reveals that they feel that they do have the right to city space: in practice, in law, and as materialised in the built landscape. They would like this right to be expanded and more deeply embedded in practice, but, in many ways, they have also adopted the discourse that Copenhagen is the best cycling city in the world. How can we then ask for more?

At the same time, there is an underlying sense that there are asymmetrically structured antagonisms arising between cyclists and motor traffic on a daily basis in Copenhagen's overly congested transportation environment (Freudendal-Pedersen, 2014a: 2015a; 2015b;). Cresswell (2010: 22) argues that we need to also look at the represented meanings and experienced practices attached to movement to 'delineate the politics of mobility'. He asks: 'How are mobilities discursively constituted? What narratives have been constructed about mobility?' and observes that '[e]veryday language reveals some of the meanings that accompany the idea of movement' (Cresswell 2010: 21). Koglin and Rye (2014) have developed Cresswell's idea into the concept of vélomobility to develop a theoretical framework for including cycling in transport planning. What they describe in their article is also reflected in the way Copenhagen cyclists narrate their everyday cycling experiences; the fight between cars and bikes for city space exposes the underlying conflict between cars and cyclist that is always present:

> 'The aggression and the conflicts occur because there is so little space. Sometimes I drive too close to the car and sometimes I touch the hood and they think I'm aggressive and will destroy something or assert myself. There is not enough space and it means that we ride too close.'

> 'Before I started cycling, cyclists did not really exist for me, if I may put it that way. They were just there, they have always been there, and they take care of themselves. I do not think car drivers, for example, think one bit about how much more uncomfortable a pothole is for a two-wheeler. I really don't think so. Why should they? They don't experience it. I also think it's a little as if the car is the proper adult mode of transport people have because it is needed to solve real problems.'

In Copenhagen, cycling has moved from what Castells (1997) would call a 'resistance identity' – communities looking for free spaces for critical positions and breaking with institutions – into a 'project identity', trying to build up new institutions based on its own practice. Copenhagen municipality has played a major role in narrating this project identity, partly through their way of emphasising that: 'Copenhagen doesn't have cyclists, but merely people transporting themselves by bike' (Copenhagen Municipality, 2009). This is a normalisation of activity that in other countries is seen as something special and often dangerous (Horton, 2007; Spinney, 2009; Nixon, 2012; Aldred, 2013).

As the earlier quotations show, though, there is still status embedded in driving (or at least owning) a car. Car ownership in Copenhagen is constantly increasing, and the car remains a symbol of power and wealth (Freudendal-Pedersen, 2014b). Yet the project identity enforced by the 'we' created in opposition to the 'other' road-user is strong. These narratives reveal how the everyday language about cars and cycles is aligned with specific structural stories (see further on for details) produced and reproduced about societies' need for specific mobilities (Freudendal-Pedersen, 2009; 2015a).

Storytelling and structural stories about cycling infrastructures

The story of Copenhagen as a cycling city is a good example of what Fischer and Forester (1993) describe as the 'argumentative turn in policy analysis and planning'. It understands planning as storytelling and stands in the tradition of 'communicative action planning' (Sandercock, 1998), influenced by Habermas' work on communication and action planning. This recognises the power of stories to keep specific 'systems' in place but also as a main social activity that can initiate social change (Healey, 2007; Sandercock, 2011; Hajer, 2016). To transform, for example, the car-dependent city and the 'system of automobility' (Urry, 2004) including its predominant planning paradigm, requires new strong stories, for instance of the cycle as something that creates freedom. The cyclists of Copenhagen express both stories: not only that of the dominant car, but also that of cycling as freedom (Freudendal-Pedersen, 2018). These structural stories (Freudendal-Pedersen, 2009; 2015a) conceptualise a way of understanding what Cresswell is asking for when he puts forward the question of how mobilities are discursively constituted (Cresswell, 2010: 21). The structural stories are the everyday 'micro discourses' we use to guide practice. In this way, they influence mobility choices and, at the same time, they give reasons for those choices. Structural stories guide future choices while simultaneously functioning as an apparent rationality in giving the chosen reasons. Thus, the structural stories are spun into a net of cultural notions about mobile and flexible late modern life. They are spun into a 'sociality', where the centre of rotation, for example, is made up of mobility, individualisation and reflexivity (Giddens, 1991; Beck, 1992; Kesselring, 2008).

Different discourses can lead to the same structural story. A structural story that was very dominant in my work with cyclists in Copenhagen was that 'it is too dangerous for kids to bike'. This structural story may originate from various discourses such as 'the good parent' or 'real men have their own car'. Mobilities are a fundamental process in society, and structural stories surrounding mobility, across discourses, attempt to capture 'something' that, not alone, belongs to a specific discourse, a specific organisation or a specific place. As structural stories are formed in everyday practice, we need to recognise that politicians and planners also have everyday lives and the structural stories supporting this everyday life do not vanish when they step through the door at work. In line with this, Nixon (2012) describes how neotechnological automobilisation is the dominant response to many discussions regarding the future mobility of cities. He suggests that the fact that '... many transport decision-makers predominantly drive' is important here (Nixon, 2012: 1673). He also suggests that the discourse that frames this is that '...the neotechnological approach allows capture of the consumers' surplus and is less likely to disrupt capital accumulation' (Nixon, 2012: 1664).

Despite the focus on cycling, the neotechnological viewpoint is also very dominant in Copenhagen. The lock-in of the myth of 'prosperity through mobility' (Essebo, 2013) can always be used to argue for more car-oriented planning, where the story becomes that 'if we limit car-driving the welfare state is at risk'. This makes it even more antagonistic when Copenhagen municipality sets major goals for future cycling, while at the same time expanding the number of parking places in the inner city. This antagonism is clearly evident in the interviews when cyclists reflect upon cycling conditions in Copenhagen:

'It is sort of as if the car is the grown up transport mode. Investment in roads and expansions in roads for cars, I guess is crazily more expensive than anything made for cyclists. And it is also much more a subject discussed, much more than what we should do for cyclists. It is interesting with Bryggebroen (Copenhagen's first cycling bridge over the harbour). The first time I crossed it, it was dark and I couldn't find my way. In the beginning something was missing that took you to Dybbelsbro. And making that lane thing (Cykelslangen). I think it cost the same as the bridge. And then people discuss if it is ok to spend that much money on this. But before, when you crossed the bridge, you ended up at a staircase and needed to get off the bike and carry it up the stairs. One wouldn't do this with cars – then there would be chaos.'

Bryggebroen, which opened in 2006, is the first bridge built as part of a large system of inner-harbour pedestrian and cycle bridges in Copenhagen. The bridges provide significant shortcuts for cyclists as well as the opportunity to experience beautiful routes away from heavy traffic. Around 12,000 people cross the bridge (Bryggebroen) on an average weekday. Cykelslangen ('The Cycle Snake'), which opened in 2014, connects Bryggebroen with a train station (Dybbelsbro), a big road and the neighbourhood on the other side of the road. Between 2006 and 2014, cyclists needed either to go on an 800-metre detour or to get off the bike and push the cycle up the stairs on a slide. There is no doubt that the harbour bridges in Copenhagen are a major improvement for cyclists in the way they create a separate network of connections and relations that are independent of the roads. Still, it is quite interesting that cyclists had to wait eight years before there was a direct connection to the road and neighbourhood to which the bridge was intended to connect. This was due to fights over which specific project to choose and, in the first place, securing the funding for the connecting bridge. It is hard to imagine a situation like this happening if new connections were being built for cars. The earlier quotation expresses how there is an inequality in modes of mobilities when money spent on infrastructure is up for debate. In the introduction to this volume, Cox and Koglin (this volume) discuss how infrastructure is never neutral. Koglin (Chapter 3, this volume), who adds that transport planning is newer neutral, supplements this. Bryggebroen is a very good example of how creating infrastructure for cyclists is woven into political fights about urban spaces and infrastructures. This is also the focus for Leyendecker (Chapter 6, this volume) who shows how this can be seen in the two cities of Bremen and Newcastle, where transport is ruled from a socio-technical system with a lack of acknowledgement that urban space is a limited resource.

The consequences of the cycle success in Copenhagen

Copenhagen's everyday cyclists are neither visually identifiable (except by their bikes) nor associated with stereotyped images or visual signifiers, such as the Lycra and helmets of the UK (Aldred, 2013). Aldred and Jungnickel (2014) point out that cycling is associated with social identities such as those of class and gender, and discourses guiding practice and subcultures. They suggest that in order for cycling practices to be sustained they needs to be related with other practices, such as shopping, commuting to work or taking children to school. This is a major reason why cycling plays the role it does in Copenhagen, when cycling in the same way as other modes of transport in the city is linked to everyday practices. In my interviews I asked about everyday life organisation including mobility routines, activities people usually do, who does what in the household, and so on. One of the unintended consequences of the success of Copenhagen as a cycling city seemed to be the success itself.

'In many places the city is designed well for cyclists. It is annoying when there are holes in the bike paths, or if there aren't any bike paths. It is really nice when there are bike paths. The system we have with traffic lights for cyclists, where one gets a head start, that's really good. But I also think in many cases it would be really good if we could regulate the behaviour of the cyclists. There are many dangerous situations, also for other cyclists. When I have to choose a route for my kids I always choose bike paths or small residential streets.'

'When I pick up kids and buy groceries and transport kids to play dates it is always on a bike, most of the time in a cargo bike because it is too dangerous for the kids to bike.'

'My kids didn't bike without being accompanied by an adult until they were around ten. They haven't been biking that much in traffic because it is so hectic, and because school is within walking distance they haven't had the natural training. So I think they started late with biking independently. My son was 15 before he started cycling independently. You need to be alert to look out for yourself in bike traffic. My youngest, who is 12, is not allowed to bike to the city across Langebro (the bridge across the inner harbour with bike paths). Copenhagen is not working for kid cyclists because the grown-up cyclists are so tough. The cycle traffic is so intense and people just need to get going because they need to pick up kids or buy groceries, so they don't take care of kids on bikes in traffic. It is a little grotesque that this is how it is. I feel it is unsafe if my child has to drive in rush hour traffic, where people cycle in multiple layers and wind in and out between each other.'

'The worst thing is the fight with cars over space, or cycling behind somebody who is not used to cycling.'

Copenhagen municipality is aware of this problem and sets goals to establish a safer, more accessible cycle city. However, in many ways this is complicated by the wish for more cyclists. Safety is an important issue for cyclists in Copenhagen, and infrastructure is of great importance, not least for those teaching their kids how to cycle in the city. This constitutes a dilemma, because the fast cyclists, most often long-distance commuters, put a large emphasis on the flow on cycle paths. The mixture between fast, slow, experienced and inexperienced cyclists creates frustration and risky situations. Inexperienced cyclists often get hemmed in by the Copenhagen rush hour traffic and this is very often due to the fact that the inexperienced cyclist often does not know the unwritten rules of the cycle paths. The theme of the focus group, which I organised with 14-year-olds who were brought up in Copenhagen, was about their understanding of the unwritten rules. They were asked to list them, starting with the most important one. It only took them a few minutes to agree that the most important thing was: "Always look back before you overtake." Then came rules such as: "Don't place yourself in front at a crossing if you cycle slowly; don't overtake on the inside; always get back on the kerbside after an overpass; don't drive next to someone on a narrow cycle path", and so forth.

These young people who are experienced cyclists also prioritise the flow, and when the 'new' cyclist is unaware of these rules it can be unpleasant to cycle in Copenhagen. The biggest problem for the flow is the increased number of cyclists on the cycle paths. This puts Copenhagen in a situation where the only opportunity left is to start reclaiming space from car traffic, and this is difficult to imagine without conflicts. Currently it is also politically challenging.

Nevertheless, even if it is politically challenging, planners in Copenhagen are finding ways to make more space for cyclists in

Copenhagen. The municipality has made many 'simple' improvements to the infrastructure that can be viewed as small-scale reclaiming of street space. These projects, which are important for cyclists, include two-way cycle lanes on one-way streets (now only one-way for cars) and allowing cycling against one-way traffic (without cycle lanes). These streets without cycle lanes have a 30 km/h speed limit, which creates possibilities for visual contact between cars and bikes. Another big improvement is the redesign of two main arterial roads (Nørrebrogade and Amagerbrogade), where cars have had to cede road space to cyclists, pedestrians and buses. Even if these measures only constitute smaller parts of the Copenhagen infrastructure, they send very positive signals to cyclists.

> 'One of the really cool things is Nørrebrogade – it's really, really cool that you feel you are a priority and privileged and that people have considered you, that there is room for you. There are many places where the bike path is as wide as the road. It is a real priority.'

These planning projects play an important role in understanding why (and how) Copenhageners themselves contribute to maintaining the story about Copenhagen as the best cycling city in the world. Indeed, compared to many other cities, there is a significant difference in the prioritisation of cycling as everyday mobility. This positive story about being prioritised is interesting when compared to the increase in car ownership in Copenhagen, especially because we know that even if people own a car their daily commute is most often done by bicycle.

Storytelling about the bicycle as the only rational thing

In modernity, the car has become the symbol of something that provided the opportunity to escape locally embedded lives, thus becoming the primary symbol of freedom and independence (Freudendal-Pedersen, 2009; Sheller and Urry, 2000; Freudendal-Pedersen, 2009; Doughty and Murray, 2016). This is also a big part of why Copenhageners buy cars: because of the potential opportunity to go wherever one wants, whenever one wants. It might be the weekend trip to the holiday home or going on holiday, or just jumping in the car and driving. This idea of freedom is very strong, even if it has nothing to do with actual everyday practice (Freudendal-Pedersen, 2009). It seems there is a general understanding and acceptance 'that everybody has the right to have a car', almost as a fundamental human right. A very large amount of trips made by car are short enough to be substituted by the bike (Vivanco, 2013; Road Directory, 2016), and the fact that 62 per cent of Copenhageners (Miljøforvaltningen, 2017) cycle to work or school/college/university on a daily basis shows that it is possible to replace many everyday car trips with the cycle. In many cases, one could argue, the car is not a basic necessity but a tool for providing the individual with a feeling of freedom and flexibility in a stressful and fast-paced modern life.

Alongside this constitution of the car as a basic right, which is continuously powerful, cyclists are developing new storylines to counter this perception. Green et al (2012) identified a normative discourse supporting cycling in the city of London where few people actually do cycle and explain how interviewees: '… constituted car travel as a morally dubious choice which had to be defended, and cycling (in principle) as encapsulating "moral mobility". Cycling enabled the ultimate "citizen traveller" to traverse London, demonstrating knowledge of and belonging to the city, and (crucially) ecological commitment to the planet' (Green et al, 2012: 285). This normative discourse can also be found in Copenhagen:

> 'My normal mode of transport is cycling, and I will always do this as long as there is cycling distance to work, and I will always apply for jobs where I can bike to work. It is not only that both have to do with me and my own exercise, but also because I think it is totally crazy to drive around in here by car. It is totally crazy. There are way too many people driving in the city. I don't know how many Copenhageners that do it but from my perspective there is way too much commuting. And if I don't take the bike then I take a train. I have done that in periods when my bike was broken and when the weather was really bad.'

> 'I totally love it when I am cycling along the highway and then all the cars are standing still and I totally overtake the car queue.'

One of the powerful stories that both the municipality and the Copenhagen cyclist use is the flexibility and the speed of cycling compared to car driving. The work with cycling in Copenhagen shows that the freedom of mobility still associated with the car is also very much related to cycling in Copenhagen. However, it offers a different view from the one from 'inside the car' and, as such, provides us with an urban utopia where the significance of freedom through cycling is aligned with the attempt to create both liveable and greener cities. It also provides the opportunity to confront the fact that the growing car ownership in Copenhagen is working against the attempt to create this kind of city. And this is one of these situations where we can't have it all. Horton (2007) talks about the affective state in the dangers of cycling in car-dominated societies. With very little space available, cyclists rub shoulders with other cyclists and fight for space with cars, aware that any collision between the two different modes is likely to injure or even kill the cyclist. In this sense, the cyclist is always constructed as the soft and vulnerable part. According to Horton (2007), the fear entangled in this constitutes a major emotional barrier to cycling. In Copenhagen this barrier is less dominant, but very present in relation to kids. This constitutes a serious problem for Copenhagen in the wish to get more people on bikes. This fear can be a big barrier when the aim is to change the practice of more Copenhageners.

Concluding remarks

Using storytelling and highlighting the less dominant stories also present about everyday vélomobilities can be part of highlighting what Hajer (2015) calls the ontological expansion in planners. Brezina, Leth and Lemmerer (Chapter 4, this volume) discuss how it is easier for planners to make cycle-centred measures when strategic documents exist. And strategic documents are storytelling about the dreams and hopes for the future. The everyday narratives from cyclists in Copenhagen provide an important tool to understand how these embodied and semiotic infrastructures both impede and facilitate cycling in Copenhagen. These can be important tools for planners and politicians when making strategic documents, it provides the opportunity to question or re-conceptualise the 'normality' or 'taken-for-granted naturalness' of specific practices, such as driving kids to school by car. Communicative planning and storytelling offer tools to understand the significance of creating new 'utopias' involving everyday life rhythms, hopes, dreams and expectations (Sandercock, 2003; Fischer and Gottweis, 2012; Freudendal-Pedersen and Kesselring, 2016). At the same it also creates the possibility for coordination between different politics like health, fiscal and urban design that Whitelegg (Chapter 5, this volume) argues will accelerate the paradigm shift. These everyday stories also provide important storylines in the international city competition (guided by fiscal politics) where the liveable city is of high importance in attracting new companies to relocate and tourists to visit. When looking at what defines the liveable city in the international city competition the car is not to the fore and this might help politics and planning to give cycling a stronger stake in the fight for space (Harvey, 2005; Spinney, 2016). What is needed are new strong storylines that decouple freedom and flexibility from car use and as things principally provided by the car, and this could potentially break cycling's marginality in the urban future.

References

Aldred, R. (2012) 'Governing transport from welfare state to hollow state: the case of cycling in the UK', *Transport Policy*, 23: 95–102.

Aldred, R. (2013) 'Who are Londoners on bikes and what do they want? Negotiating identity and issue definition in a 'pop-up' cycle campaign', *Journal of Transport Geography*, 30: 194–201.

Aldred, R. and Jungnickel, K. (2014) 'Why culture matters for transport policy: the case of cycling in the UK', *Journal of Transport Geography*, 34: 78–87.

Beck, U. (1992) *Risk Society: Towards a New Modernity* (Published in Association with Theory, Culture & Society), London: SAGE Publications Ltd.

Castells, M. (1997) *The Power of Identity: The Information Age: Economy, Society, and Culture, Volume II*, New York: Wiley-Blackwell.

City of Copenhagen (2017) *Copenhagen City of Cyclists. Facts and Figures 2017*, City of Copenhagen: Technical and Environmental administration.

Copenhagen Municipality (2009) *City of Cyclists*, Copenhagen.

Cresswell, T. (2010) 'Towards a politics of mobility', *Environment and Planning D: Society and Space*, 28(1): 17–31.

Doughty, K. and Murray, L. (2016) 'Discourses of mobility: institutions, everyday lives and embodiment,' *Mobilities*, 11(2): 303–22.

Essebo, M. (2013) *Lock-in as Make-Believe*, School of Business, Economics and Law, University of Gothenburg.

Fischer, F. and Forester, J. (eds) (1993) *The Argumentative Turn in Policy Analysis and Planning*, Durham: Duke University Press.

Fischer, F. and Gottweis, H. (2012) 'The argumentative turn revisited', in F. Fischer and H. Gottweis (eds) *The Argumentative Turn Revisited*, Durham: Duke University Press, pp 1–27.

Freudendal-Pedersen, M. (2005) 'Structural stories, mobility and (un)freedom', in T.U. Thomsen, L. Drewes Nielsen and H. Gudmundsson (eds) *Social Perspectives on Mobility*, Farnham, UK: Ashgate, pp 29–45.

Freudendal-Pedersen, M. (2009) *Mobility in Daily Life: Between Freedom and Unfreedom*, Farnham: Ashgate Publishing, Ltd.

Freudendal-Pedersen, M. (2014a) 'Searching for ethics and responsibilities of everyday life mobilities', *Sociologica*, 1/2014: 1–23.

Freudendal-Pedersen, M. (2014b) 'Tracing the super rich and their mobilities in a Scandinavian welfare state', in T. Birtchnell and J. Caletío (eds) *Elite Mobilities*, Abingdon: Routledge, pp 209–25.

Freudendal-Pedersen, M. (2015a) 'Cyclists as part of the city's organism – structural stories on cycling in Copenhagen', *City & Society*, 27(1): 30–50.

Freudendal-Pedersen, M. (2015b) 'Whose commons are mobilities spaces? – The case of Copenhagen's cyclists', *ACME*, 14 (2): 598–621.

Freudendal-Pedersen, M. (2018) 'Engaging with sustainable urban mobilities in Western Europe: urban utopias seen through cycling in Copenhagen', in S. Low (ed) *The Routledge Handbook of Anthropology and the City*, New York and London: Routledge, pp 216–29.

Freudendal-Pedersen, M., and Kesselring, S. (2016) 'Mobilities, futures and the city. repositioning discourses – changing perspectives – rethinking policies', *Mobilities*, 11(4): 573–84.

Freudendal-Pedersen, M., Hannam, K. and Kesselring, S. (2016) 'Applied mobilities, transitions and opportunities', *Applied Mobilities*, 1(1): 1–9.

Furness, Z. (2007) 'Critical mass, urban space and vélomobility', *Mobilities*, 2(2): 299–319.

Furness, Z. (2010) *One Less Car: Bicycling and the Politics of Automobility (Sporting)*. Philadelphia: Temple University Press.

Giddens, A. (1991) *Modernity and Self-Identity: Self and Society in the Late Modern Age*. Stanford: Stanford University Press.

Green, J., Steinbach, R. and Datta, J. (2012) 'The travelling citizen: emergent discourses of moral mobility in a study of cycling in London', *Sociology*, 46(2): 272–89.

Hajer, M. (2015) 'On being smart about cities: seven considerations for a new urban planning and design', in A. Allen, A. Lampis and M. Swilling (eds) *Untamed Urbanism*, Oxon, New York: Routledge, pp 50–63.

Harvey, D. (2005) *A Brief History of Neoliberalism*, Oxford, UK: Oxford University Press.

Healey, P. (1997) *Collaborative Planning*, Vancouver: UBC Press.

Healey, P. (2007) *Urban Complexity and Spatial Strategies: Towards a Relational Planning for Our Times*, London and New York: Routledge.

Horton, D. (2007) 'Fear of cycling', in D. Horton, P. Rosen and P. Cox (eds) *Cycling and Society*, Hampshire: Ashgate, pp 133–52.

Jensen, A. (2013) 'The power of urban mobility: shaping experiences, emotions, and selves on a bike', in S. Witzgall, G. Vogl and S. Kesselring (eds) *New Mobilities Regimes in Art and Social Sciences*, Farnham: Ashgate, pp 273–86.

Kesselring, S. (2008) 'The mobile risk society', in S. Kesselring, V. Kaufmann and W. Canzler (eds) *Tracing Mobilities*, Aldershot: Ashgate, pp 77–104.

Koglin, T. (2013) *Vélomobility – A Critical Analysis of Planning and Space*, PhD: Faculty of Engineering, Lund University.

Koglin, T. (2015) 'Vélomobility and the politics of transport planning', *GeoJournal*, 80(4): 569–86.

Koglin, T. and Rye, T. (2014) 'The marginalisation of bicycling in Modernist urban transport planning', *Journal of Transport and Health*, 1(4): 214–22.

Miljøforvaltningen, Teknik (2017) *"Cykelregnskabet 2016"*, Copenhagen.

Nixon, D.V. (2012) 'A sense of momentum: mobility practices and dis/embodied landscapes of energy use', *Environment and Planning A: Economy and Space*, 44(7): 1661–78.

Road Directory (2016) *Key Numbers for Traffic in Denmark*. www.vejdirektoratet.dk/DA/viden_og_data/statistik/trafikken i tal/hvordan_udvikler_trafikken_sig/Sider/default.aspx

Sandercock, L. (1998) *Towards Cosmopolis. Planning for Multicultural Cities*, Chichester: Wiley.

Sandercock, L. (2003) 'Out of the closet: the importance of stories and storytelling in planning practice', *Planning Theory & Practice*, 4(1): 11–28.

Sandercock, L. (2011) 'Transformative planning practices – how and why cities change', in G. Baumann and S. Vertovec (eds) *Multiculturalism, Political Concepts in Sociology*, Abingdon: Routledge, pp 157–79.

Sheller, M.B. and Urry, J. (2000) 'The city and the car', *International Journal of Urban and Regional Research*, 24: 737–57.

Spinney, J. (2009) Cycling the city: movement, meaning and method', *Geography Compass*, 3(2): 817–35.

Spinney, J. (2010a) 'Improvising rhythms: re-reading urban time and space through everyday practices of cycling', in T. Edensor (ed) *Geographies of Rhythm: Nature, Place, Mobility and Bodies*, Farnham: Ashgate.

Spinney, J. (2010b) 'Performing resistance? Re-reading practices of urban cycling on London's South Bank', *Environment and Planning A*, 42(12): 2914–37.

Spinney, J. (2016) 'Fixing mobility in the neoliberal city: cycling policy and practice in London as a mode of political–economic and biopolitical governance', *Annals of the American Association of Geographers*, 106(2): 450–8.

Urry, J. (2004) 'The "system" of automobility', *Theory, Culture & Society*, 21: 25–39.

Urry, J. (2007) *Mobilities*, Cambridge: Polity Press.

Vivanco, L.A. (2013) *Reconsidering the Bicycle – An Anthropological Perspective on a New (Old) Thing*, New York and London: Routledge.

10

Navigating cycling infrastructure in Sofia, Bulgaria

Anna Plyushteva and Andrew Barnfield

Introduction

While cycling is a global and familiar practice, it includes human and non-human elements which are also highly contingent and locally specific. The focus of this chapter is cycling infrastructure in Sofia, the capital of Bulgaria. In recent years, the city has witnessed changes in every aspect of cycling, including the number of cyclists on the city's streets, the development of cycling infrastructure and the social and cultural significance of the bicycle as a mode of urban transport, among others. This chapter builds on our previous research on cycling in Sofia which examined the practices and affordances of travelling by bicycle in a post-socialist south-east European city (Barnfield and Plyushteva, 2016). By drawing attention to the situated, embodied, mundane and ambiguous elements of cycling, we sought to show how the bicycle acts as a small but important force shaping mobility in contemporary Sofia. We argued that the growth of cycling, rather than being symptomatic of increasing individualism, offered a counter-narrative to the perceived decline in public-oriented acts and affordances. Cycling in Sofia thus came to complicate what has been theorised as the cultural and spatial condition of privatism (Hirt, 2012). We also pointed to the shortcomings of infrastructural provision that erodes the capacity of cycling to contribute to convivial urban public life, while at the same time complicating the idea that Sofia can be located along a linear line of progress from less to more cycle-friendly cities.

The analysis presented in this chapter revisits and develops our discussion of cycling infrastructure in Sofia, by drawing together ethnographic observation, interviews with urban mobility activists, and document and media analysis from several research visits between 2013 and 2018. Continuing our approach of zooming in on a specific urban location and the situated interactions of people and infrastructures within it, in this chapter we focus on a cycle lane added to a central Sofia boulevard in 2017. In this process we echo the specific longitudinal frame used by Morgan (Chapter 2, this volume) although over a much shorter time period. Expanding our previous focus on the embodied practices of cycling, we discuss the decision-making processes which brought together politicians, municipal employees, mobility and cycling activists, local residents and various other actors. We then explore how these processes resulted in a particular set of hard and soft infrastructures for cycling. The chapter offers a longitudinal view of cycling infrastructure in an urban context and draws attention to the ongoing material and discursive transformations of Sofia's cycling culture. In doing so, the chapter also contributes new understandings of the barriers and frictions inherent in the prospect for an increasingly more prominent place for cycling in the city's everyday life.

Infrastructure and everyday politics

'The built environment, the material, physical and spatial forms of the city, is itself a representation of specific ideologies, of social, political, economic, and cultural relations and practices, of hierarchies and structures, which not only represent but also, inherently constitute the same relations and structures' (King, 1996: 4).

   In this chapter, we understand infrastructure to be more than a passive backdrop, 'a silent stage on which others perform' (Amin and Thrift, 2017: 3; see also Cox, Chapter 1, this volume). Infrastructures are not the hard, inert objects that they are often taken to be. They are part of dynamic assemblages in which users, objects, energy, law makers and laws acquire particular significances as a result of the relations which bind them. Infrastructure itself is a lively performer, and infrastructural relations shape everyday activities and the life of cities. To urban scholars and to city dwellers, infrastructure is crucial to the continuous reorganisation of urban spaces (Gandy, 2005; Graham, 2010; Harris, 2013). This perspective on infrastructure means that it cannot be viewed in exclusively technical terms. The socio-technical capacities of infrastructure, 'the technological materialities of the urban, the various flows this sustains, and the exercising of social and political power' means that infrastructure is intimately bound up with everyday politics in cities and the ongoing social inequalities they produce (Graham, 2002: 175). At the same time, while we agree with King and Graham that infrastructures embody power relations, they are mundane everyday objects as much as they are the physical manifestations of power and politics (Latour, 1991; Furlong, 2011). In this chapter, we work with this productive tension, approaching the politics of infrastructure through the timing and spacing of political life (Barry, 2010). The political importance of infrastructure arises in the particular circumstances and sites of its planning and use, and in the situatedness of its provision, maintenance and adoption (Nolte and Yacobi, 2015). Infrastructure then, is the very stuff of everyday politics in urban spaces.

Cycling in cities

While cycling may be seen as one identifiable practice involving a relatively stable set of movements and technologies, it can in fact take a number of distinct forms each requiring different skills, materials and spaces (Heinen et al, 2010; Horton and Parkin, 2012; Zhao, 2014). Cyclists have particular experiences of the urban environment, inhabiting rich and diverse sensory landscapes, navigating distinctive relations with drivers and pedestrians and negotiating the materialities of road surfaces, traffic signals and weather, among others (Gatersleben and Uzzell, 2007; Spinney, 2009; Aldred and Jungnickel, 2014; Latham and Wood, 2015; Barnfield and Plyushteva, 2016). The bicycles used in cities vary considerably in price, design and functionalities. There is an array of clothing, locks or securing devices and accessories. This makes cycling a relatively affordable, inclusive and democratic mode of transport, albeit within multiple socio-material and bodily constraints. Thus, cycling as an everyday practice is defined by a particular set of interactions with the urban environment. At the same time, these interactions can be experienced as both mundane and significant. While urban bicyclists may spend extensive periods of time on their bike, they may not see this as an expression of a particular identity or set of beliefs (Aldred, 2013: 197).

Urban mobility and cycling in Sofia

As the capital of Bulgaria, Sofia is the centre of the country's economic, political and cultural life, as well as its biggest city, with 1.2 million inhabitants in 2014 (Eurostat, 2018c). Since the collapse of state Socialism in 1989, the city has experienced notable changes in its urban form, including extensive peri-urban development, which have resulted in increased commuting distances and greater socio-economic segregation (Hirt, 2012). As a result, densities have remained low compared to other European capital cities – 157 people per sq km –

even as population has increased (Eurostat, 2018c). Public transport, already in steady decline since the 1960s, saw drastic cuts in funding after 1989. Nevertheless, the network of bus, trolleybus, tram, minibus, and since 1998 metro, is relatively comprehensive.

Post-socialist urbanism does not merely consist of physical changes in the urban fabric. Thus, Hirt, 2012: 3) argues that in its function as a medium of culture, urban space is itself the story of a post-socialist cultural condition. The rapid rise of the private in Sofia illustrates the way the cultural and material dimensions of post-socialist urbanism are interwoven (Barnfield, 2017; Tuvikene, 2018). Dramatic increases in private car ownership have characterised post-socialist urbanism across the Eastern European region. In Sofia, there were over 700,000 private cars in 2010, their numbers having doubled since 1995 (Grozdanov, 2011: 266). Car dependence has become a major challenge for the city, with 655 cars per 1,000 inhabitants in 2011, compared to 451 in Brussels, 290 in Berlin, 328 in Budapest and 541 in Prague (Eurostat, 2018b). The heavy traffic and poorly managed car parking has proved detrimental in terms of environmental degradation, public health and equality of access to urban spaces and resources. Air pollution in Sofia exceeds European Union limits (particulate matter PM10 concentrations exceed 50 $\mu g/m^3$) on approximately 82 days of the year (Eurostat, 2018a). Reliance on car transport is also often seen as a key factor in low physical activity rates (Williams, 2016).

Although no published studies on the topic are available, anecdotal evidence suggests that cycling rates in socialist Sofia were low, mainly as a combined result of the limited availability of cycling infrastructure, the extensive public transport network and the low status of cycling compared to both public transport and the private car. It was only after 2000 that the position of cycling began to change from marginality to relative visibility. This was felt in the city streets, but also in the rhetoric of local politicians, in media coverage and in everyday conversations. However, the share of cycling in 2012 remained low, at 2 per cent of all journeys (Tzvetkova, 2018). This coincided with the first attempts of local political actors to voice opposition to the unhindered dominance of the private car. However, being seen to restrict automobility remains a risky political move, as car ownership and heavy traffic are increasingly perceived as definitive of Sofia public life (see Leyendecker, Chapter 6, this volume, for an exploration of the difficulties of political buy-in for reducing cars and car parking in cities).

The challenges presented by everyday cycling in cities have often been discussed in terms of the insufficient or inadequate provision of cycling lanes (Sofia Municipality, 2012). This point certainly resonates with Sofia's residents, as the city provided only 49.5km of cycling lanes in 2015 (Sofia Urban Mobility Centre, 2016). Where cycle lanes have been constructed, their quality, safety and accessibility have attracted much criticism (Barnfield and Plyushteva, 2016). Increasingly heavy motorised traffic, competition between pedestrians and parked vehicles for the footpaths, and the poor condition of street surfaces mean that Sofia's few cycle lanes are separated by areas which can be very difficult to traverse on bicycle, making a route across the city challenging even for experienced cyclists.

Plans to renovate Dondukov Boulevard

Dondukov Boulevard is one of the historic arteries of central Sofia, stretching eastward from the cluster of Government buildings at Nezavisimost Square. Prior to the renovation, the streetscape of Dondukov Boulevard made no provision for cycling. Through the centre of the boulevard ran two tram tracks with one car lane and one parking lane on either side. Although driving on the tram tracks is forbidden, this rule was not (and is not) adequately enforced, and the practice remains widespread. As a result, the car dominated the road space in Dondukov. The sidewalks of the boulevard were fairly wide, but not smooth, with many sections of broken or damaged paving slabs (see Figure 10.1). These uneven surfaces presented a bigger obstacle to cycling on the sidewalk than the national traffic regulations which forbid it; as these rules are rarely enforced, cycling on the pavement takes place in many parts of Sofia where the physical environment permits it.

The Sofia Municipality plan for bicycle transport, published in 2012, envisaged the construction of a cycle path along the central Dondukov Boulevard to begin that same year, a plan quickly recognised as too ambitious given competing municipal priorities (Sofia Urban Mobility Centre, 2012). In 2016, Sofia Mayor Yordanka Fandakova, finally announced impending plans to renovate the boulevard. The road surface and water, heating and electric infrastructures required repair, but the renovation of the boulevard was to represent much more than this. The works were intended as a major step towards substantiating the Municipality's sustainable mobility rhetoric, of which local activists had often commented that it rings hollow (VeloEvolution, 2017).

Local transport infrastructure is part not only of networks and flows at the neighbourhood level, but is also embedded in circulations of policies, expertise and image-making with national and international

Figure 10.1: Visualisation and photo of Dondukov Boulevard in 2017 before renovation works

Source: Sofia Municipality and authors

reach (Wood, 2014). In an effort to demonstrate the strength of her commitment to promoting cycling and walking, in 2016 the Sofia Mayor commissioned a report from internationally acclaimed Danish urbanist Jan Gehl (Bulgarian News Agency, 2017). His recommendations were unequivocally endorsed by the Municipality, but local cycling activists were quick to voice concerns that they would remain on paper only (see Feddes, de Lange and te Brömmelstroet, this volume, on the political complexities behind cycling provision in Amsterdam).

The initial plans for Dondukov proposed different possible approaches to the introduction of cycle paths. This included segregated cycle lanes travelling both ways with the traffic flow; non-segregated cycle lanes; and a single two-way cycle lane situated on one side of the boulevard. The Municipality emphasised that the most suitable approach would be selected democratically through a public consultation.

The many publics of a boulevard and a cycle lane

The renovation of Dondukov was highly contentious. The public consultation process proved complex and frustrating for all actors, due to the extensive range of interconnected issues which had to be addressed.

A key matter was the type of surface to be used on the renovated boulevard. Historically, most of Dondukov Boulevard was paved with cobblestones, dating back to the early 20th century. Originally, the Municipality plans involved replacing cobblestones with asphalt – purportedly to reduce noise and dust, but according to local activists, because resurfacing with asphalt was financially beneficial, and because workers skilled at laying cobblestones were in increasingly short supply. However, the Ministry of Culture intervened in the debate, to declare that Dondukov must remain cobbled, in keeping with central Sofia's historic appearance. The cobbles were hastily given protected heritage status, blocking the Municipality's plans. Local residents' groups were divided on the matter – many were concerned with noise and pollution, while others prioritised heritage. Cyclists' organisations in turn voiced reservations about the combination of a cycle lane and cobblestones. The final decision announced by the Mayor, was to divide the boulevard into three sections: the westernmost section, closest to the historical centre, entirely paved with cobblestones; a second section using a combination of cobbles and asphalt and a third section of asphalt only. Local urbanism activists Spasi Sofia argued that this was an infrastructural vision which prioritised political compromise over tangible objectives for either mobility or public space, as it mainly aimed at avoiding confrontation with any group despite the many incompatible perspectives (Chaushev, 2017). The map critiquing the compromise and showing the three sections, published by Spasi Sofia under the headline 'The Dondukov Boulevard renovation – a little something for everyone' can be seen in Figure 10.2.

Immediately prior to the start of the works, the Municipality published a street visualisation that indicated that a new cycling pathway would be inserted on one side of the street, fully segregated from tram and vehicle traffic (Figure 10.3). On the one hand, this approach was deemed sufficient for the purpose of demonstrating that cycling was being taken seriously by the local authorities, with tangible infrastructure which would lend credibility to the act of cycling. Through the specific segregation of space, cycling would be demarcated as a legitimate means of transportation in the city. On the other hand, a single two-way cycle lane was the type of infrastructure which minimised the amount of space to be taken away from drivers and which compromised the level of safety and convenience afforded to cyclists.

The justification of the Municipality was based on the way the boulevard itself was to be reconfigured. The tram tracks which had to be renovated would have been re-positioned and run next to the segregated cycling lane with vehicle traffic on the opposite side of the boulevard. This was intended to make cycling more appealing to new cyclists by providing a felt level of safety and protection from the segregated lane: the tram lines acting as an additional buffer to motor traffic. The temptation for car drivers to stop on the cycling lane would have been removed.

The inclusion of a cycle lane and the exact form that cycling infrastructure should take, proved as contentious as the matter of

Figure 10.2: Compromise solution for the resurfacing of Dondukov Boulevard. Section 1 (left) corresponds to cobblestones, section 3 (right) to asphalt and section 2 (centre) to a combination of the two

Source: Spasi Sofia via Facebook, posted on 20 September 2017

Figure 10.3: Sofia Municipality visualisation of the intermediate plan for Dondukov Boulevard renovation

Source: Sofia Municipality

replacing cobbles with asphalt. Local organisations as well as cycling groups were vociferous in their condemnation of the plans with several protests held. However, there were many different reasons and opinions behind the protests. This included car drivers who did not want to concede any driving or parking space to cyclists. Another perspective was that of stakeholders concerned with heritage, who focused on the visual disruption a segregated cycle lane would introduce. Finally, sustainable transport campaigners demanded cycle lanes as part of a more radical re-think of mobility in Dondukov, including segregated tram tracks and protected tram stops (Spasi Sofia, 2017).

Those opposed to segregated cycle lanes repeatedly voiced concerns about being unable to park within close proximity of one of the boulevard's many shops, banks and institutions. Further objections to the most ambitious redesign – that of segregated tram tracks and cycle lanes on either side of single-file traffic – included concerns that emergency vehicles would not be able to pass in times of heavy traffic. Despite proponents' efforts to cite examples of tried and tested infrastructural solutions from other cities, public fears around the more radical approaches grew, and the Municipality lacked resolve to dispel the less substantiated objections. On the contrary – the Mayor's office adopted a strategy of appeasing critiques and repeatedly affirmed its commitment to finding a compromise solution that worked for everyone.

Realisation of the project

Construction work began on 5 June 2017. On 8 June, yet another protest was held against the way the Municipality was handling the project. The protest was organised by an alliance of local pressure groups and civil society organisations concerned with cycling and mobility more broadly. The protest attracted approximately 250 people and took the form of a march along Dondukov to the central municipal offices, which happen to be located nearby. The march briefly stopped traffic in Dondukov Boulevard, a strategy which added visibility to their five demands: quality public works; a cycle lane; separate tramway; pedestrian islands; authenticity (Spasi Sofia, 5 June 2017 via Facebook).

The construction works moved ahead at pace, even though the political debate and the resulting repeated redesign of the plans for the boulevard, were ongoing. Notably, the organisations that protested the Municipality's decisions were not in full agreement among themselves: some of them favoured cobblestones, others favoured asphalt. However, these actors had twofold reasons for working together. First, all demanded that whatever approach were to be chosen, a cycle path should be included in the design. Second, all voiced a concern that the renovation of Dondukov was being executed to the lowest possible standard in terms of materials and techniques, as had been the case with other high-profile public works in Sofia. However, the media portrayed the protest differently: the (extensive) media coverage reported that the protesters had gathered to demand Dondukov be resurfaced with cobblestones. The attempt to present the actual demands, which were more nuanced, while at the same time being more specific on the technical details of the infrastructure under construction, was not captured in the media discourse.

Renovation works were completed before the end of 2017. In its final form, the project did not involve moving the tramway from its central position to running alongside the space for cycling. The latter, however, retained its controversial place as a single two-way cycle lane along the southern side of Dondukov (Figure 10.4). Only the western section of the boulevard was paved with cobblestones, while the remainder of the boulevard was reconstructed with an asphalt surface. The Municipality claimed that the costs of the project spiralled as a result of the cobbles/asphalt uncertainties, which meant funding had to be cut from infrastructures for segregating cycling, trams and tram stops. For local activists, however, the Mayor and her administration had failed to take a stand against the dominance of the car once again.

Cycling on the renovated Dondukov Boulevard

The more ambitious visions for the boulevard as a space where different motorised and non-motorised mobilities could be given equal weight did not come to pass. Although the cycling lane was eventually partially segregated (the photo in Figure 10.4 was taken before this additional measure was implemented), this was done using small plastic barriers which neither prevented cars from entering, nor were sturdy enough to withstand this practice for long. By mid-2018, they had nearly disintegrated. Vehicle traffic flowed very close to cyclists as the total width of the two-way cycle lane was a mere 2.5 metres. A frequent sight on the renovated boulevard was cars stopping or parking on the cycling lane, forcing cyclists to swerve around them to avoid the obstruction. For cyclists who have to cycle towards oncoming traffic this additional hazard means that this part of the route is off-putting even to experienced cyclists. In addition, the single two-way cycle path on one side of the road makes turning into and out of the boulevard complex and risky. Through the new

Figure 10.4: Completed cycling infrastructure on Dondukov Boulevard

Source: Authors

infrastructure, the Municipality mostly re-enforced – subtly and not so subtly – that the boulevard is a place for fast-moving cars, which can also stop at will directly outside their destination. By contrast, bicycle parking in Dondukov remains scarce and of poor quality (Aldred and Jungnickel, 2013). In another reminder of the international reach of local cycling infrastructure politics, the sturdiest and most prominent bicycle stand can be found outside the building at Dondukov 54, occupied by the Embassy of Denmark.

In terms of its contribution to cycling infrastructure in Sofia, the Dondukov Boulevard renovation can at best be considered a partial success. Cyclists would have benefited from more radical traffic calming measures, such as a segregated tram track and full segregation between bicycle and car traffic. Instead, new infrastructural additions were arguably designed to 'compensate' drivers for the space that had been taken away from them. Thus, the busiest intersection along Dondukov Boulevard – with Vasil Levski Boulevard – was equipped with new, request-only pedestrian traffic lights. While this theoretically improved chances for cyclists to pass the intersection uninterrupted along with motorised traffic, in practice this was not the case, due to the high number of cars making left and right turns in all directions of the intersection. With no measures favouring pedestrian traffic over cars, cyclists were also inconvenienced, and endangered.

A further limitation on the impact of the new Dondukov cycle lane for bicycle mobility in the city more broadly, is the fact that at its western end, the boulevard joins Nezavisimost Square, one of the busiest and most car-dominated intersections in central Sofia. Navigating this intersection by bicycle is extremely difficult, as there is no provision for bicycle traffic, and car traffic is fast (even pedestrians have been forced underground, with a series of underpasses replacing ground-level crossings in the 1960s). Until this intersection is reorganised to slow down and limit traffic and welcome the full range of urban mobilities, the cycle lane in Dondukov Boulevard can only have limited utility.

Discussion and conclusion

The case study discussed in this chapter highlights two important dimensions of conceptualising cycling infrastructure. First, the process of planning and constructing a cycling lane for Dondukov points to the way diverse publics, processes, budgets and concerns are woven together in the politics of urban infrastructure. As the case study demonstrates, the 'technical' questions of surfaces and materials, widths and lengths, are indivisible from the socio-cultural processes through which heritage, noise and hazard are continuously re-negotiated. Second, the politics of a cycle lane are never confined to an individual street or square. As infrastructures can only be grasped in terms of their place and functions as part of heterogenous socio-technical networks (Graham and Marvin, 2001), so the questions raised by the Dondukov cycle lane are questions about Sofia-wide traffic flows and political priorities regarding urban space and mobility.

While the implementation of physical infrastructures for cycling in Dondukov Boulevard proved disappointing for many, the intensity of the debate demonstrated that significant changes in the infrastructural discourses in Sofia were taking place nonetheless. To insert cycling infrastructure into cities that have been dominated by the motor vehicle – this domination enabled and supported by a highly politicised set of laws, norms and infrastructures – is highly problematic. The case study of the Dondukov Boulevard renovation highlights dynamics recognisable in many cities across Europe. The boulevard may have a local character, feel and history, but increasingly its main job has become to maintain the smooth flow of vehicle traffic as part of a network of major arteries. Achieving this aim has been reliant on a highly regimented and hierarchical spatial division between vehicles and trams on the one hand, and pedestrians on the other. The boulevard's infrastructures of rails, cables, lights, road markings and paving slabs reflect this division. The resurgence of bicycle transport requires a fundamental rethinking of the hierarchy and its rules, which proved complex for reasons of space, politics, culture and finance. In the case of Dondukov, Sofia Municipality attempted the impossible task of providing infrastructure and space for cycling, without eroding provisions for motorised traffic. The process made visible the level of political commitment required in creating spaces for urban cycling, and the extent to which finding and shaping such spaces is a process of friction and tension, rather than compromise.

Nevertheless, the demands placed by cycling activists and other publics as part of the Dondukov renovation acquired unprecedented visibility, as these actors have gradually established themselves as an important part of Sofia's urban development debates. In the 2017–18 renovation of a key artery in central Sofia, Rakovski Street, many of the same problems were reproduced, but a cycle lane was constructed on either side of the two-way traffic. The contestation around Dondukov's resurfacing and cycle lane represented a turning point in the city's cycling infrastructure debate, which has increasingly become part of a broader debate on public procurement processes, nepotism and the ability of urban dwellers to have a say in the way infrastructure is planned, implemented and changed. This debate is still ongoing.

References

Aldred, R. (2013) 'Who are Londoners on bikes and what do they want? Negotiating identity and issue definition in a 'pop-up' cycle campaign', *Journal of Transport Geography*, 30: 194–201.

Aldred, R. and Jungnickel, K. (2013) 'Matter in or out of place? Bicycle parking strategies and their effects on people, practices and places', *Social & Cultural Geography*, 14(6): 604–24.

Aldred, R. and Jungnickel, K. (2014) 'Why culture matters for transport policy: the case of cycling in the UK', *Journal of Transport Geography*, 34: 78–87.

Amin, A. and Thrift, N. (2017) *Seeing like a City*, Cambridge: Malden, MA: Polity.

Barnfield, A (2017) 'Experiencing post-socialism: running and urban space in Sofia, Bulgaria', *European Urban and Regional Studies*, 24(4): 368–80.

Barnfield, A. and Plyushteva, A. (2016) 'Cycling in the post-socialist city: on travelling by bicycle in Sofia, Bulgaria', *Urban Studies*, 53(9): 1822–35.

Barry, A. (2010) 'Materialist politics: metallurgy', in B. Braun, S.J. Whatmore and I. Stengers (eds) *Political matter: Technoscience, democracy, and public life*, Minnesota: University of Minnesota Press, pp 89–118.

Bulgarian News Agency (2017) 'Danish Urban Designer Jan Gehl's Urban Planning Report on Sofia Provides for More Pedestrian Space, Bicycle Lanes', *Bulgarian News Agency*, Sofia. Available at: www.bta.bg/en/c/NW/id/1664537 (Accessed: 2 October 2018).

Chaushev, V (2017) The truth about Dondukov [Истината за Дондуков]. In: *Spasi Sofia*. Available at: http://spasisofia.org/ (Accessed: 31 July 2018).

Eurostat (2018a) *Environment – and Greater Cities*. Brussels: European Commission. Available at: https://ec.europa.eu/eurostat/data/database (Accessed: 1 November 2018).

Eurostat (2018b) *Perception survey results*, European Commission. Available at: https://ec.europa.eu/eurostat/data/database (Accessed: 4 October 2018).

Eurostat (2018c) *Population on 1 January by age groups and sex – cities and greater cities*, European Commission. Available at: https://ec.europa.eu/eurostat/data/database (Accessed: 4 October 2018).

Furlong, K. (2011) 'Small technologies, big change: rethinking infrastructure through STS and Geography', *Progress in Human Geography*, 35(4): 460–82.

Gandy, M. (2005) 'Cyborg urbanization: complexity and monstrosity in the contemporary city', *International Journal of Urban and Regional Research*, 29(1): 26–49.

Gatersleben, B. and Uzzell, D. (2007) 'Affective appraisals of the daily commute: comparing perceptions of drivers, cyclists, walkers, and users of public transport', *Environment and Behavior*, 39(3): 416–31.

Graham, S. (2002) 'On technology, infrastructure and the contemporary urban condition: a response to Coutard', *International Journal of Urban and Regional Research*, 26(1): 175–82.

Graham, S. (2010) *Cities Under Siege: The New Military Urbanism*, London: Verso.

Graham, S. and Marvin, S. (2001) *Splintering Urbanism: Networked Infrastructures, Technological Mobilities and the Urban Condition*, London: Routledge.

Grozdanov, V. (2011) 'Urban Mobility Problems in Sofia', *20th International Transport Conference 2011*, Sofia, Bulgaria, 4–5 November.

Harris, A. (2013) 'Concrete geographies: assembling global Mumbai through transport infrastructure', *City*, 17: 343–60.

Heinen, E., van Wee, B. and Maat, K. (2010) 'Commuting by bicycle: an overview of the literature', *Transport Reviews*, 30(1): 59–96.

Hirt, S. (2012) *Iron Curtains: Gates, Suburbs, and Privatization of Space in the Post-Socialist City*, Hoboken, N.J: Wiley & Sons.

Horton, D. and Parkin, J. (2012) 'Conclusion: towards a revolution in cycling', in J. Parkin (ed) *Cycling and Sustainability*, Bingley: Emerald, pp 303–25.

King, A.D. (1996) *Re-presenting the City. Ethnicity, Capital, and Culture in the 21st Century Metropolis*, New York: New York University Press.

Latham, A. and Wood, P. (2015) 'Inhabiting infrastructure: exploring the interactional spaces of urban cycling', *Environment and Planning A: Economy and Space*, 47(2): 300–19.

Latour, B. (1991) 'Technology is society made durable', in J. Law (ed) *A Sociology of Monsters: Essays on Power, Technology, and Domination*, London: Routledge, pp 103–30.

Nolte, A. and Yacobi, H. (2015) 'Politics, infrastructure and representation: the case of Jerusalem's Light Rail', *Cities*, 43: 28–36.

Sofia Municipality (2012) *Program for the development of bicycle transport in Sofia, 2012–2015*, Sofia: Sofia Municipality.

Sofia Urban Mobility Centre (2012) *Plan for the development of bicycle transport in the territory of the capital region municipality, 2012–2017*, Sofia: Sofia Urban Mobility Centre. Available at: www.sofiatraffic.bg/bg/cycling_not_working/340/plan-za-razvitie-na-velosipedniia (Accessed: 1 October 2018).

Sofia Urban Mobility Centre (2016) *Plan for the development of bicycle transport in the territory of the capital region municipality, 2016–2019*, Sofia: Sofia Urban Mobility Centre. Available at: www.sofproect.com/Veloalei.aspx?AspxAutoDetectCookieSupport=1 (Accessed: 3 October 2018).

Spasi Sofia (2017) 'Open Letter to Yordanka Fandakova regarding Dondukov Boulevard [Отворено писмо до Йорданка Фандъкова за бул. Дондуков]'. Available at: http://spasisofia.org (Accessed: 6 June 2018).

Spinney, J. (2009) 'Cycling the city: movement, meaning and method', *Geography Compass*, 3(2): 817–35.

Tuvikene, T. (2018) 'Post-socialist (auto)mobilities: modernity, freedom and citizenship', *Geography Compass*, 12(3): 1–12.

Tzvetkova, S. (2018) 'Development of bicycle transport in the city of Sofia as part of the concept for stable urban mobility', *Earth and Environmental Science*, 182(1): 1–7.

VeloEvolution (2017) 'Who approves rubbish cycle lanes for Sofia? [Кой одобрява калпавите велоалеи в София?]', *Cycling News*. Available at: http://velobg.org (Accessed: 10 July 2018).

Williams, K. (2016) *Spatial Planning, Urban Form and Sustainable Transport*, London: Routledge.

Wood, A. (2014) 'Learning through policy tourism: circulating bus rapid transit from South America to South Africa', *Environment and Planning A*: Economy and Space, 46(11): 2654–69.

Zhao, P. (2014) 'The impact of the built environment on bicycle commuting: evidence from Beijing', *Urban Studies*, 51(5): 1019–37.

11

Cycling advocacy in São Paulo: influence and effects in politics

Letícia Lindenberg Lemos

Introduction

Cycling has become an increasingly prevalent topic of research not only in the Global North but also in the South. In the North, it has been analysed as a strategy for improving both public and individual health (Dill, 2009; Fernández-Heredia et al, 2014; Taino et al, 2016), and through the lens of economic development (Flusche, 2012), social inclusion and gentrification (Stein, 2011; Daly, 2014; Hoffmann, 2016). In Brazil, studies have been conducted in the field of behaviour science and 'traffic psychology' (Pezzuto, 2002; Araújo et al, 2009), as well as social and economic analyses (Sá et al, 2016), and research on factors that might influence the use of bicycle that might serve to provide input on the planning of new infrastructure for cycling (Sousa, 2012).

This chapter seeks to contribute to the debate about cycling policies by examining the struggles that help bring cycling to the political agenda. In this sense, this chapter is tightly related to the study of Amsterdam in Chapter 7 (this volume), but from the perspective of a completely different urban context: São Paulo. Not only do the two cities differ dramatically in size and their respective share of bicycle users, but they also diverge in that advocacy for cycling infrastructure in São Paulo started in a context in which the urban form was already dominated by automotive-oriented transportation infrastructure. The initial political mobilisation for bicycling also occurred at a moment of political instability in the 1980s during the re-democratisation of the country, with the cycling agenda reaching the higher level of institutionalisation after one of the most massive protest movements in the history of Brazil.

In mid-2013, prompted by an increase in bus fares, a series of mass protests took place in São Paulo against the poor condition of the public transit system and urban circulation in general. Other issues were incorporated along the way, and these demonstrations became known as 'Jornadas de Junho' (Protests of June). Led by the Movement for Free Fares (in Portuguese, *Movimento Passe Livre*), this was 'one of those moments in which society's capacity to intervene on politics widens, sweeping away the fragile certainties that mark the routine game of institutional politics' (Tatagiba, 2014: 35). The 2013 demonstrations were held in several Brazilian cities and invoked the Right to the City (Lefebvre, 1968), a concept that was translated in this moment to mean free access, without turnstiles, to quality public services. The concept of the Right to the City had been proposed by Lefebvre in 1968 in his homonymous book (Lefebvre, 1968) and was adopted in Brazil by the housing movements during the re-democratisation process. Its meaning was adapted and redefined over the years in Brazil and was used to support calls for the right to housing and to justify demands for infrastructure and urban amenities on the outskirts of the cities (Tavolari, 2016).

In addition to having the fare reduced to its pre-protest levels, the 2013 protests marked the beginning of the installation of 400km of cycling infrastructure, as has been previously specified in the mayor's office's plan for the 2013–16 period (São Paulo, 2013). The infrastructure built between 2013 and 2016 marked, for the first time in the history of the city's mobility policies, a reduction in the space for automobiles in order to create space for bicycles: on some streets, lanes previously marked as parking spaces were turned into bike lanes.

The mayor's plan included several hundred kilometres of bike tracks and lanes, and there was a political decision to build infrastructure for commuter-oriented cycling – also one of the critical responses of the Executive to the Protests of June 2013. However, the strengthening of cycling issues in mobility policies cannot be explained merely as due to the understanding of the mayor about the importance of cycling as a means of promoting sustainable mobility. In order to analyse this change of the distribution of space on the streets of São Paulo, however small it may have been, one must examine the issue with a broader perspective, and more specifically one must consider how the State and Civil Society are mutually constituted (Skocpol 1992; Amenta et al, 2002; 2010; Houtzager, 2003; Gurza Lavalle and Szwako, 2015).

Prior to 2013, cycling infrastructure was limited and disconnected. It was composed of unconnected segments, in almost half of the total of these segments it was hard for cyclists to access and it provided insufficient protection for cyclists in about 40 per cent of its span (Lindenberg Lemos and Wicher Neto, 2014). In 2014, several lanes previously designated as parking spaces for cars were replaced by bike lanes. These new lanes totalled almost 40 per cent of the permanent infrastructure built between January 2013 and August 2015 (Lindenberg Lemos and Ramos, 2015).

This chapter explores the physical infrastructure not only through a policy and planning perspective but also by considering the social infrastructure in civil society that made these changes possible. The fragility of the physical infrastructure, given its subsequent decommissioning after a turnover in political administration, raises our awareness of the vulnerability of many infrastructure transitions and the need to think through a lens of spatial justice when considering the linkages between physical and social infrastructures (see Cox, Chapter 1, this volume). Using secondary sources and semi-structured interviews carried out with selected members of the public, this chapter analyses both the agency of actors and the political context in each moment of their struggle. It does not purport to give a conclusive account of the processes that advanced the cycling agenda, but seeks to provide a window into the battles by members of Civil Society to include cycling in the urban mobility network of São Paulo and show the societal-state interaction that took place and enabled the implementation of cycling policies. Infrastructure in the built environment is enmeshed with both social and political infrastructures.

Civil society and the State

Brazil was under a dictatorial regime during two periods of its history, from 1930 until 1945 and from 1964 until 1985. The second transition to democracy was led by a robust social movement that also contributed to the Constitution enacted in 1988. Gurza Lavalle et al (2017) point out the importance of civil society organisations (CSO) and social movements (SM) to help understand the relationship between the State and its citizens and the participatory innovations in Latin America ['Social movements' here refers to coalitions of civil society organisations that are united around shared causes, and may also include other members of the public who are not formally affiliated with any civil society organisation but who are allied with the same cause].

Unlike in the realm of the labour rights, there is no consensus as to the collective interests for CSOs and SMs, and which organisation(s) should speak on their behalf, although there is recognition that there are interests that need to be represented. The public status of these organisations, as well as the institutionalised spaces that are created to engage in dialogue with the State, are plural and 'clearly vulnerable and unstable in comparison to corporate institutions' (Gurza Lavalle et al, 2017: 9). The literature on social movements, in its turn, focuses on 'the building of influence and the potential institutionalisation of the interests of the actor focused by it' (Gurza Lavalle et al, 2017: 10), but there is disagreement about the effects of this process.

Re-democratisation in Brazil, achieved after years of pressure by social movements on the military regime, 'established a set of principles for the participation of civil society' (Dagnino, 2004: 141) and pluralised the forms of interaction between the State and the Civil Society 'with formal and institutionalised arrangements and also informal experiences' (Almeida, 2014: 98). That created the possibility for civil society actors to enter into the State's bureaucracies and bring with them a progressive agenda into the sphere of the State, as well as a bet on the possibility of 'joint action for the further development of the democracy' (Dagnino, 2004: 141). Understanding the policy outcomes of the activity of social movements became relevant in this context because of the 'proliferation of participation arenas and public oversight in different public policies areas', as well as the increased institutionalisation of civil society participation, and the involvement of civil society actors 'in the process of production and implementation of public policies' (Carlos et al, 2016: 2).

While discussing the 'outcomes and the political and institutional consequences of the social movements' (p. 3), Carlos et al (2016) describe the social movements' organisational forms as 'hybrid', because they present a variety of patterns of interaction. According to these authors, there are two essential dimensions for analysing and explaining collective action in relation to public policies: 'the *dynamics* of the movements and their *interaction* with the political context' (p. 3, emphasis in original). The authors argue that studies on the effects of social movements have evolved to encompass a recognition 'that both the societal configuration and the political context matter when explaining the outcomes' (Carlos et al, 2016: 3). They propose to use the 'polity approach,' a framework that is based on the idea that there is a relationship between Civil Society and the State and that they are mutually constituted.

Following line of thought, Abers and Tatagiba (2014) have made efforts to overcome the idea of separation between the State and Civil Society. The authors analysed the actions of feminist actors during Dilma Rousseff's administration (2011–14) and showed that these activists were not only inserted into the State bureaucracies, but also received support, criticism and challenges from the groups with which they were previously associated.

Amenta et al (2002) argue that a better understanding of the State is necessary to understand the effects of the activity of social movements insofar as these actors 'seek to influence the State, challenge the public policies, the bureaucracies, and the rules and institutions in order to gain 'collective benefits' for those they represent' (Carlos et al, 2016: 12). The authors argue that the State 'is often a key target of social movements who seek to influence it directly or to apply pressure on other targets' (Amenta et al, 2002: 69) through it. According to them, the 'success' of the social movements in gaining advantages, access or increased power has been the focus of the literature about the consequences of their actions, but to understand the impact of challengers on the State, 'the ideas need to be better connected to specific State structures and processes' (Amenta et al, 2002: 71). The impact of civil society mobilisations in their various forms described here illustrates the importance and power of social infrasructures in social change. Through collective action and identification, activist movements provide the means by which structural change can be effected.

Bicycling in the early 20th century

Bicycles arrived in São Paulo as imports from Europe at the end of the 19th century. They were first used for sport among local elites, but were almost immediately also adopted for commuting in the city (Souza, 2016). The focus of urban mobility policies throughout the 20th century, however, was the automobile, which dominated the historic city centres as early as 1920 (Freire, 1926). For cycling, the public space in the central region of the city was restricted to the Velodrome, commissioned by local aristocrats for the pleasure of their peers and where the elites practised sport cycling – demolished in 1915 to make way for a new street (Souza, 2016).

During the Juscelino Kubitschek administration, between 1956 and 1961, Brazil underwent an intense modernisation period characterised by rapid industrialisation. The automobile industry had a prominent role in this process and became the foundation for economic growth (Caputo and Melo, 2009). São Paulo experienced tremendous population growth throughout the 20th century (Oliveira, 1982), facilitated by mobility policies that promoted an accelerated uptake of automobiles for the upper classes and the use of buses for the lower classes, the latter frequently being privately operated and unregulated. These mobility policies prompted an impressive geographic spreading of the city, making it increasingly dependent on motorised modes

(Vasconcellos, 1999; Rolnik and Klintowitz 2011; Gomide and Galindo, 2013).

The oil crisis and the first plans for cycling

During the 1970s, the oil crisis pushed the Brazilian Government to search for new solutions to the fuel shortage. Brazil was then under a military dictatorship, and political decisions were highly centralised at the national level. The GEIPOT (Grupo Executivo de Integração da Política de Transportes [Executive Group for the Integration of Transport Policies]), created in 1965, published several documents, among them a manual entitled 'Planning for cycling – a policy for bicycles'.

In São Paulo, the city explored cycling as a possible solution to the lack of infrastructure for leisure and sports, but also considered it as a way to mitigate the problems deriving from the oil crisis. In the mid-1970s, the first bike path was built and was less than two kilometres in length and located along the median strip of a newly created avenue. It was also intended to serve as a pilot project that could eventually lead to the construction of bicycle lanes or paths on other streets around the city (*O Estado de São Paulo*, 28 October 1975). In addition, in the beginning of the 1980s the recently created Traffic Engineering Company (TEC) [the public body responsible for traffic] in São Paulo produced and published the first plans for cycling policies.

The national government, however, was simultaneously developing a nationwide Pro-Ethanol program, the objective of which was to develop a renewable energy source that could replace fossil fuels. Its success resolved the immediate fuel problem, resulting in a vast retrofitting and replacement of car technology to allow vehicles to run on ethanol. From an environmental perspective, it was considered to be an outstanding achievement of Brazilian scientists, not only for being renewable but also because it was believed to be a non-polluting fuel source (Ceneviva, 2017, personal interview, 4 August).

More recently, researchers have found that the use of ethanol (E85) increases the emission of gases other than carbon dioxide and that 'a future fleet of E85 may cause a greater health risk than gasoline' (Jacobson, 2007: 4156). Furthermore, while it strengthens the use of productive land for monocultural sugarcane production in Brazil (a well-established agricultural tradition in the south-east of the country), it precludes the possibility of transitioning these areas into farms to feed the population, promoting natural biodiversity, converting farms to uncultivated uses or adopting permaculture. In addition, because the focus was on gasoline shortage, once a new fuel was developed the problem was deemed solved and the automobile-based mobility model was left unchanged, even strengthened.

Re-democratisation brings a new context to civil society

During the 1980s, Brazil faced prolonged economic crisis, leading to a series of protests that brought demands for re-democratisation and direct presidential elections (such as the Direct Elections Now movement) to the forefront of the national political conversation. Following the end of the dictatorship and with democracy newly restored in Brazil, there was a pluralisation of the means by which the State and Civil Society interacted. The Urban Reform Movement led the campaigns for urban space and the Right to the City, which were translated into demands for housing and public services – like schools, daycare services and health care facilities. With regard to urban mobility, the focus was placed on the public transit system, especially buses (Gomide and Galindo, 2013). The Urban Reform Movement was also tightly engaged in the drafting of the new Constitution and worked to include urban issues in its text, setting the foundation for the creation of the Ministry of the Cities in 2003, where cycling policies would eventually be reconsidered.

Although a segment of society was starting to organise around cycling issues, these actors were not directly involved in the Urban Reform Movement and the re-democratisation agenda. Nor was cycling a central issue for the leftists that were part of the Movement and who were creating the Workers Party (Alcorta, 2018, personal interview, 23 March). Additionally, because the dictatorship had previously promoted policies, plans and infrastructure for cycling in a top-down fashion, and in light of the change in political context, there was an abatement in the national discussion on cycling policies (Rosin, 2016). Following the loss of importance of the cycling agenda, Jânio Quadros, mayor of São Paulo between 1986 and 1988, demolished the bicycle track pilot project that had been constructed only ten years earlier to make way for a car-only tunnel.

In 1982, during discussions on the drafting of the proposals for Franco Montoro's candidacy for the São Paulo State government, the candidate's son commissioned a plan for 'the alternative path of cycling' to be presented to the group (Alcorta, 2018, personal interview, 23 March). After Montoro was elected he pressed for the proposal to be presented to government staffers, but an engineer in the TEC blocked the plan saying that, according to Alcorta (2018, personal interview, 23 March), 'I won't do it, because I don't want to.' Despite the resistance from inside the bureaucracy, the presentation made during the drafting of Franco Montoro's proposals increased the exposure of several politicians to the concept of cycling, and one of them, Walter Feldman, came to be what Rosin (2016) framed as a 'political entrepreneur' for cycling causes. While Feldman was a city councilman, he proposed and passed two cycling-related laws in the City Council, which were followed by future proposals from other politicians.

Initial activism for cycling policies: the first wave of rhetorical strategising

In addition to the Urban Reform Movement, the first civil society actors advocating the inclusion of cycling in São Paulo's mobility policies also emerged during the 1980s. Ribeiro (2016: 197) defines these cycling activists as 'those cyclists that decided to go beyond the ordinary and individual practice of pedaling, and adopted the use of the bicycle as a cause, disseminating rhetoric and practices that aimed to enact a particular agenda'. Subsequently, Ribeiro identifies three waves of cycling activists' rhetorical strategising (*gerações discursivas*) and described these first actors from the 1980s as arising from 'two different discursive trends' (2016: 199).

The first discursive trend aimed to reinforce the use of utilitarian cycling. The second tendency, which became mainstream, proposed to shift the focus from the use for transportation – which was associated with the poor, and thus not desired – to something more attractive to the wealthy. According to the actors with this second approach, to 'entice the upper classes into using the bicycle' would be 'the most efficient way to gain political power' (Ribeiro, 2016: 199), to pressure the State and to achieve their underlying objective: getting the city to build infrastructure for cycling. Their tactic was to promote the use of the bicycle for sports (Ribeiro, 2016; Alcorta, 2018, personal interview, 23 March). Even though there had been cycling associations and clubs promoting this same use previously, Ribeiro argues that these actors were the first 'to confront the challenge of transforming the image that had been established of the bicycle as "negative"' (2016: 198), directly connected to its utilitarian use by the lower-income population.

The actors who participated in the first wave brought the mountain-bike to Brazil and, by the end of the 1980s, organised night cycling groups in São Paulo, the Nightbikers (Züge Junior, 2015; nightbikers.

com). They expected that the elite members would be 'enticed' into using the bikes for sport and 'would naturally adopt them as means of transport, which in reality did not happen' (Ribeiro, 2016: 202). On the contrary, this tactic ended up creating antagonism between the use of bicycles for sport *versus* their use for transport, the former being conceived of as 'something for the rich' while the latter was relegated as 'something for the poor'. Also, because the infrastructure needs for the utilitarian usage of the bicycling – namely, commuting – are not the same as those for sports (which are done inside parks, at weekends or at night, or on streets that have naturally been emptied of cars), the demand for utilitarian cycling infrastructure 'seemed misplaced and lacking political support' (Ribeiro, 2016: 202). Thus, the pressure that these actors produced during the 1990s had minimal results 'in political terms and in terms of built infrastructure' (Ribeiro, 2016: 203).

The first wave of cycling rhetoric meets environmentalism

In 1992, the United Nations Conference on the Environment and Development was held in Rio de Janeiro, and with it came an increased awareness of the environmental agenda to Brazil and the idea of encouraging cycling (Rosin, 2016). The following year, the Department of Open Space and the Environment (DOSE) was created in São Paulo, and its first director was Werner Zulauf, a long-standing environmentalist. During his years working as a consultant in COSIPA [*Companhia Siderúrgica Paulista* – Metallurgical Company of São Paulo] earlier, he met Gunther Bantel, a Brazilian engineer who had been in Amsterdam for a metallurgy internship during the oil crisis and who witnessed the 1970s transformation (see Chapter 7, this volume). That same year, Zulauf invited Bantel to organise and coordinate the first institutionalised space created in the city of São Paulo to discuss issues related to the use of bicycles in São Paulo: a working group named the Cyclist Project. The DOSE coordinated the project, which included representatives of other departments and participants from civil society (ITDP Brazil, 2015).

In a direct parallel to Abers and Tatagiba's observations of the role of the feminist movement during Rousseff's administration, Bantel was an actor from civil society that had been advocating for the bicycle, who then became part of the State bureaucracy and started promoting 'institutional activism' from within the State. The Cyclist Project was decommissioned in 1997, but some of the outputs of the work done during those years were significant for the institutionalisation of cycling issues later on, including the first plans for some of the bike lanes that would be built during the 2013–16 administration. Also, the 'institutional activism' undertaken by Bantel disseminated pro-cycling ideas within the State, creating what one of Rosin's interviewees described as 'network of infiltrators' inside the bureaucracies that continued to engage in 'institutional activism' long after Bantel left his position in the DOSE.

Bantel was also able to contribute to the drafting of the Brazilian Traffic Code (BTC – Federal Law n. 9.503/1997) that was taking place in the national Congress, and his participation resulted in the inclusion of cycling issues within four articles of the Code. These contributions included the recognition of bicycles as vehicles and the granting of the right for cyclists to ride on streets (Rosin, 2016; Ceneviva, 2017, personal interview, 4 August). There was no institutionalised participation of Civil Society in the discussions surround the drafting of the Code, but through 'institutional activism' (Abers et al, 2014) cycling issues were institutionalised on the national level as a fit (Skocpol, 1992; Carlos et al, 2016; Gurza Lavalle et al, 2017). As a response to the enactment of the Code, the civil society group that had focused its actions on other actors within Civil Society over the previous decade – promoting group bike rides – started demanding changes in cycling policies, and thus redirected its attention towards the State.

The activists created a campaign entitled 'Bicycle Brazil: Pedaling is a Right' and organised a bike ride of more than 1,500 kilometres (between Paraty, a coastal city near Rio de Janeiro, and Brasília), demanding real implementation of the BTC (Züge Junior, 2015). The BTC case shows not only the societal-State interaction but also the restructuring and realignment of civil society actors in response to a change in political context. Achieved via institutional activism, the institutionalisation of cycling at the regulatory level reshaped civil society's actions, exemplifies the mutual constitution of State and Civil Society.

During this period, a few additional laws were passed and some municipal-level plans were produced (Malatesta, 2012; Lindenberg Lemos and Wicher Neto, 2014; ITDP Brazil, 2015), but the bike tracks or lanes built during this period were largely inside of parks. Despite the campaign for the implementation of the BTC, Ribeiro (2016) argues that there was a 'disappointment and dissatisfaction within the cycling activists movement' during the second half of the 1990s when they realised 'the limits imposed by their own discourse' and an 'apparent loss of inertia in Brazilian cycling activism in recent years' of the decade.

The second wave of rhetorical strategising

In the first years of the 2000s, 'in the context of anti-capitalism and anti-globalisation demonstrations,' a second wave of cycle activists' rhetorical strategising arose (Ribeiro, 2016). Their adversaries were multiple: capitalism, hierarchy, militarism, racism, sexism, homophobia, and environmental destruction. At this time, cycling was not the major issue of the claims but was seen as 'an element of consistency within their demands,' since 'in a world dominated by the automobile dictatorship, the bicycle could figure as 'subversive'' (2016: 202–5). In this perspective, they perceived cycling as a revolutionary means of transport.

These were the actors that began the *Bicicletada* (the word used in Portuguese for 'Critical Mass' bike rides) as a demonstration against cars – symbols of capitalism – aiming at 'call[ing] attention to the expropriation of public spaces in the city by the automobile' (Ribeiro, 2016: 206). The *Bicicletada* relates to a 'form of exemplary demonstration' (Abers et al, 2014: 332) – marching on the street –, but with a different performance: using bicycles. In it there is a recognisable linkage not only to 'occupying the street' as in traditional demonstrations, but also to San Francisco's Critical Mass (Bennichio, 2012), which is symbolic for cycle activists. There is no evidence of more tangible or specific demands from these actors, and there is also no evidence that there was an interaction between them and the State apart from demonstrations in the streets. It is likely that this lack of evidence is due to the lack of additional interaction, rather than a lack of documentation.

The actors in this political wave were unable to find 'enough support on their practice' (Ribeiro, 2016: 206) and the *Bicicletada*, which did not engage enough participants, gradually lost strength. The knowledge organised through foreign texts translated into Portuguese or written by these actors about São Paulo, however, helped spread the idea of cycling as an alternative means of transport and became an essential reference for the actors from the third 'discursive generation' (Ribeiro, 2016: 206).

The second wave of cycling rhetoric and environmentalism

In 2005, the local executive branch created a new working group also inside the DOSE under the Clean Air Initiative (CAI), thus clearly linked to the environmental agenda, later to be called the Bicycle

Working Group. Sponsored by the World Bank and with resources from the Global Environment Facility (GEF), the group was directed to develop a project to improve air quality and included promoting cycling as one of the proposed tactics. The proposal involved selecting an area to receive 'an intervention for cycling, the objective of which was to enable the construction of an experiential framework that could go on to subsidise the replication of that model' (Ceneviva, 2017, personal interview, 4 August).

The executive secretary of the CAI – Laura Ceneviva – and a staff member that had worked earlier with Bantel – Ana Hoffmann – organised the group. They included representatives from other government bodies (both city departments and state-owned companies) and actors from the civil society. Bennichio, who some years later came to be one of the founders and first director of Ciclocidade, an important cycling association in São Paulo, criticised how these actors were invited to participate because they were not necessarily representative of the society; he therefore calls this 'the NGI (non-governmental individuals) moment' (Bennichio, 2018, personal interview, 23 March).

The following year, the working group was made official by Municipal Ordinance n. 1.918/2006 as the 'Pro-Cyclist Executive Group' (PCEG) inside the DOSE, and although the meetings were 'open and the floor was granted to the citizens' (ITDP Brazil, 2015: 6), the participation of civil society was not formalised. Ceneviva (2017, personal interview, 4 August) justifies the absence of institutionalised social participation by arguing that in the previous groups, societal participation was essential in increasing the degree of maturity on the issue, but for this second moment, which involved developing public policies, in her view the responsibility was of the public authorities and not of civil society. According to her, 'the focus [of the PCEG] was to take' the issue and 'make everything for the thing [the cycling policies] to happen... because from the environmental point of view, the more people cycling, the better' (Ceneviva, 2017, personal interview, 4 August).

The third wave of rhetorical strategising

Alongside these institutional changes during the mid-2000s, increasing numbers of young middle-class riders bicycles formed a third 'rhetorical generation' of cycling activists. According to Ribeiro (2016) there are multiple reasons for this growth, but the most common issues were: 'a great dissatisfaction with the means [of transport] that were offered for them'; a disenchantment with cars; and the disposition to 'engage their body to solve a mobility problem' (Ribeiro, 2016: 210). With this new wave, the *Bicicletada* was resumed, and cycling activism received a new body in São Paulo. According to Züge Junior, the *Bicicletada* became a space for generating connections between activists, broadening their actions to 'occupying the streets, advertising the use of bicycles and engaging in other activities with more media appeal … from pressuring the mayor in each and every event they appeared at, to painting unauthorised traffic signs' (Züge Junior, 2015: 26). The *Bicicletada* started to gather such a large number of cyclists and gain such a profile that the participants of the 2006 *Bicicletada* began to call the place they used as their starting point 'Cyclist Square' (Züge Junior, 2015). This name was made official in 2007, by the Municipal Law n. 14.530. proposed by an alderwoman whose assistant was a cycling activist.

According to Rosin (2016), in the second half of the 2000s, cycling activism matured, featuring both a consolidated 'network of infiltrators' and 'institutional activism.' Bennichio (2018, personal interview, 23 March) reports that by 2007, the *Bicicletada* was stronger, and the participants were starting to become more organised and discuss the possibility of becoming institutionalised as an association. In mid-2009, some civil society actors were working in tandem with public authorities, for example, by offering training courses for bus drivers to teach them about sharing the road with cyclists. It was during the first event in one of these courses that Leandro Valverdes, a cyclist from civil society, questioned why cycling issues were conducted inside the DOSE, and not in the department handling Transportation. According to Valverdes, if civil society wants cycling to be treated as a means of transportation, 'there is nothing more obvious than for the Department of Transportation (DoT) to respond for it' (CHIA, 2009). To this end, the Department committed itself to creating a coordinating body inside the DoT to deal with issues related to the use of the bicycle as a means of transportation.

The PCEG was officially transferred to the DoT in July of 2009, and in November of the same year the Department for Cycling Planning (DCL) was created inside the planning department of the TEC, thus falling under the responsibility of the DoT. Over time, the DCL was consolidated as the body 'responsible for the development and coordination of projects related to mobility with bicycles' (ITDP Brazil, 2015: 8). However, some years later actors within civil society started to realise that the change from DOSE to the DoT had a downside because it 'ended up sequestering a policy process' from 'involved several different actors who possessed significant knowledge about the issue' (Rosin, 2016: 30). Furthermore, even though participation was not institutionalised, when the issue was handle by DOSE, actors from civil society were allowed to participate and express their thoughts, but after the transfer to the DoT civil society's access to the discussions became more limited and the meetings less frequent, which resulted in the demobilisation of the PCEG (Bennichio, 2018, personal interview, 23 March).

The debate among cyclists whether they should or should not engage in institutionalised settings intensified in 2009 (Bennichio, 2018, personal interview, 23 March). The group split, and the two most significant associations were created with different approaches, even as they both participated in pressuring and dialoguing with the State: CicloBR and Ciclocidade. The first focused mostly on promoting rides, the car-free-day modal challenge, and bike repair services during the Operational Bike Lanes on Sundays, thus aiming their methods and rhetoric at civil society in order to encourage cycling. The latter has also undertaken actions and participated in programs aimed at civil society, but has focused its energy more intently on advocacy, declaring as one of their primary objectives to work 'to develop public policies and initiatives that address bicycle mobility' (www.ciclocidade.org.br/quem-somos).

New opportunities for cycling activism

In 2012, two events created new opportunities for cycle activists. The first was the enactment of the National Policy for Urban Mobility (NPUM), which legally defined that active (non-motorised) modes have priority over motorised modes in the mobility system and, as with collective modes, that they have priority over private motorised modes. This provided leverage for those seeking changes in mobility policies, and cycling activists began to use the NPUM to support their claims.

Although there was no direct pressure from civil society to include active mobility in the NPUM (Silva, 2018, personal interview, 10 April), Rosin (2016) argues that the process of drafting the NPUM was related to a broader movement for urban mobility, to which the cycle activists were, and still are, connected. Malatesta (2018, personal interview, 4 August), a former staff member of the TEC, claims that the ANTP (National Agency for Public Transport), a civil society entity focused on promoting public transit systems, and to which cycle activists also contributed, was responsible for drafting the proposal for this legislation (Maletesta, 2018). Consequently, there is no evidence of a direct causal correlation between the pressure from cycle activists and the drafting of this legislation, but the two processes are not disconnected.

The second opportunity for the cycle activists was the 2012 Mayoral elections in São Paulo, which brought the possibility for change of both the municipal administration and the political context, and thus prospects for new synergies. The cycling activists were already highly institutionalised and organised and carried out a campaign demanding a commitment from the candidates to the cycling agenda. The activists succeeding in getting almost every candidate to sign a letter of commitment to cycling policies, including the one who was ultimately elected, Fernando Haddad. The agenda was included in Haddad's campaign proposals and later in the administration's Goals Program, with a promise to build 400km of dedicated tracks and lanes during the four years of his administration (São Paulo, 2013). The Goals Program is a document that must be prepared in the first 90 days of the municipal administration and must include strategic actions, metrics and goals. The requirement to present such a program was proposed by a civil society entity and passed as a municipal law, improving the accountability of the local executive branch. It is thus a mechanism to link political administrations with civil society and to emphasise participation.

The Haddad administration in São Paulo (2013–16)

The Haddad administration differed from previous administrations in two respects that are relevant to cycling policies. The first was with regard to the opening up of institutionalised spaces to societal participation. The space that had previously been used to debate issues related to cycling, the PCEG, was not formally extinct, but after the Protests of June and the municipal administration change, the Municipal Council for Traffic and Transport (MCTT) had demobilised the group, and the meetings ceased to be held (Bennichio, 2018, personal interview, 23 March). The MCTT was reconstituted as a trilateral council involving city representatives, transit operators and civil society. As a result, only 21 of the 63 seats were designated for civil society members, and of these only one was designated for cyclists. Aiming at broadening their voices in the MCTT, the cyclists aligned themselves with other agendas, especially those for pedestrian mobility, public transit, environment, and consumer protection. Leveraging this broader connection with other societal actors, they created a campaign entitled 'Occupy MCTT' comprised of several entities, among them Ciclocidade, Cidade a Pé, and Mobilizse, to 'defend the interests of pedestrians, cyclists and public transit users' (mobilize.org).

Although MCTT was created to deal with mobility in general, as an outcome of this campaign it provided cyclists with a specific space in which to assert their demands. According to an evaluation by Rosin (2016: 52), 20 per cent of the unique contributions made during the MCTT meetings until 2015 'were related to cycling, bicycle paths, and/or were made by speakers representing cyclists'. Using the MCTT, the cyclists succeeded in creating a space specifically to deal with issues related to cycle mobility: the Special Committee for Bicycling (SCB – in Portuguese, *Câmara Temática da Bicicleta*). The SCB was a 'fit' produced by cycle activists. It became an access point to the State, including regular meetings with the mayor, and granted cyclists access to decision-making: the design of cycling policies, the drafting of legislation with direct impacts for this group (such as the Mobility Plan of São Paulo), and actual policy implementation, particularly as it relates to the installation of infrastructure.

The second way in which the Haddad administration diverged from others is in regard to the type and scale of the built infrastructure. During the Kassab administration (2009–12) the TEC mostly adopted infrastructure models that fundamentally preserved existing space for cars. Chief among these were (1) Operational Bike Lanes, (2) poorly marked bike routes and (3) bicycle infrastructure in marginal spaces, such as along railway lines (see Lindenberg Lemos and Wicher Neto, 2014). Starting in 2013, the space available to cars was fundamentally affected for the first time. Forty per cent of the new cycling infrastructure consisted of bike lanes painted on spaces that were previously dedicated for parking cars (Lindenberg Lemos and Ramos, 2015). Even though the 400km of dedicated cycle lanes and tracks added up to less than 2 per cent of the 17,000km of streets and roads, the replacement of parking spaces with bicycle lanes broadened the debate about the share of urban space for circulation by different transportation modes and had widespread repercussions, both supportive and oppositional, in media and in public opinion.

One of the few bicycle tracks created to be completely separated from motorised traffic was built on Paulista Avenue by the 2013–16 administration. This track became an important symbol in the conservative resistance to the implementation of multi-modal transportation policies and infrastructure, and was eventually the target of a legal action carried out by the Public Prosecutor (in Portuguese, *Ministério Público*) of the State of São Paulo (mpsp.mp.br).

This case also showcased the diversity of responses from civil society. By publishing manifestos and organising a *Bicicletada* (https://vimeo. com/123478276), bicycle activists generated crucial support for the municipal administration, allowing the policy implementation to continue. [Two notes made by activists stand out (http://vadebike. org/2015/03/acerto-e-erro-acao-ministerio-publicosuspensao-ciclovias/ andwww.ciclocidade.org.br/noticias/643-nao-aceitaremos-nenhum-passo-nosentido-contrario-ao-de-uma-cidade-mais-ciclavel-humana-segura-inclusiva-e-justa), and one from academia (https:// observa sp.wordpress.com/2015/03/31/implantar-as-ciclovias-e-superar-os-seus-entraves/)].

Cycling policies still in dispute

While the Haddad administration seemed to have made progress towards utilitarian cycling policies, some issues still stand to be examined. Even though the 400 kilometres of bike lanes had been incorporated in the Goals Program for the 2013–16 administration, one of the main proposals within the urban policies program was the Arc of the Future, a proposal for urban transformation along the floodplains of the major rivers and of a primary rail line of São Paulo. Considering this, it is fitting to ask why the cyclists' agenda – as well as that of buses – achieved such a central position in São Paulo's urban policies. Rosin argues that there was 'a change in the paradigm of mobility policies starting of 2012' (2016: 36), but according to this hypothesis there is no explanation for the resumption of automobile-oriented mobility policies in the next administration. In addition, if there had been a change in paradigm starting in 2012, there is still the unanswered question as to why cycling and bus policies were implemented only at the end of 2013. According to Rosin (2016), the turning point that sheds light on the timeline for the implementation of cycling policies was a visit by the mayor and the secretary of transportation to Buenos Aires. During this visit, they saw the Porteño solution: to remove street parking and designate bike lanes, thus creating space for cycling without removing space for car circulation. But even if this were the case, this explanation ignores the broader context of 2013, which must be taken into account.

The first issue to consider is the political context in which Haddad's administration began. There were tight budget constraints and he was unable to advance his agenda for urban transformation projects. This was partly due to the intensification of corruption-related legal actions that hamstrung construction contractors (the most important actors in enabling and executing large urban projects), hampering the ability to further develop the Arc of the Future plan. Haddad was also pressured by part of civil society – especially the housing movement – to re-draft the Strategic Master Plan (SMP) for the city, which had been done by the previous mayor without observing the proper procedures for public participation. The process of drafting the new SMP demanded months of work and delayed the planning for the Arc of the Future.

During the first half of 2013, and also in the realm of pressures from civil society, the cyclists maintained pressure on the local executive branch, holding street protests and demanding dialogue with the recently elected mayor. It was in June, however, triggered by the bus fare increase, that the pressure from civil society shook politics. The MPL (Movement for Free Fares; in Portuguese, *Movimento Passe Livre*), a social movement that demands that transportation be treated as a fundamental right 'so that it may enable of other rights, to the extent that it grants access to other services' (MPL, 2013: 26), held street demonstrations that unfolded into an avalanche of protests and marches. Thus, the mayor was facing budgetary constraints and intense pressure from civil society for mobility policies that facilitated active and collective modes. It seems that the bike lanes (and bus lanes) were solutions with low budgetary impacts which had the potential to respond to a social constituency that showed strength in June 2013.

Most of what was deployed during the 2013–16 administration were bike lanes (Lindenberg Lemos and Ramos, 2015), consisting basically of painting pre-existing asphalt without resurfacing the roads. In addition to the simplicity of the infrastructure, the policy was quite limited and did not include a broad parking provision or even connections between travel segments, resulting in unconnected fragments of bike tracks and lanes. These connections would have incurred an extra political cost, since it would have been necessary to use more intensely contested spaces on roadways. Further, to allow the policy to be quickly implemented, the administration 'off the record' reorganised the relational position of the DCL inside the bureaucracies of the TEC, attaching it directly to the Department's office, according to information provided by TEC staff member at the time, Glaucia Pereira (2018, personal interview, 6 March).

Nevertheless, because Haddad brought the mobility agenda for active and collective modes closer to him, not only implementing policies but also giving priority to these issues during the administration – in terms institutional reorganisation as well as in terms of the agenda for public participation – he ended up establishing these issues as his signature policies, or as his administration's brand. As a consequence, the mobility agenda for active and collective modes became a target for opposition politicians. The new mayor did not confront the cyclists directly, but he also did not create proposals for cycling policies, and consistently carried out an evasive kind of dialogue while gradually emptying the MCTT and the SCB. The DoT turned its focus towards trying to re-signify Haddad's cycling policies, with proposals for a 'new look' for the bike lanes, but it ultimately resumed the models from the previous Kassab administration (2009–12): Operational Bike Lanes and cycling routes, frequently proposed as replacements for bike lanes that were supposedly not being used.

Final remarks

The recent politics of cycling infrastrcture in São Paulo is a politics of both hard and soft inftrastructures it engages with individual and collectives, both inside and outside of the formal strucutres of governance, and illustrates the degree of permeability of these boundaries. The implementation of hard infrastructure as part of the city's provisioning is an outcome of complex and long-standing manoeuvering, as shown in common with the study of Amsterdam (Chapter 7, this volume). The implementation of the new bicycle lanes reads ambiguously. On the one hand there is the triumph of the concerted effort and of consecutive generations of activists, which produced a meaningful response from the administration. On the other hand, the implemented measures were relatively minimal in comparison with the overall city budget and ensured that there would be no real confrontation with the dominant paradigm of automobile-oriented mobility. Indeed, the outcomes can be viewed as having set the scene for their subsequent revoking.

The societal actors have accumulated considerable collective knowledge over the years and have produced new forms of interaction between civil society and administration. Until 2012, for example, the public forums for societal-State interaction to oversee the cycling policy agenda did not cede space to civil society in a manner that was balanced with the State's power, but rather only permitted that the societal actors used them as access points. While using these spaces as leverage, the activists were able to institutionalise their agenda and slowly gain political advantages. Since 2013, these actors succeeded in legitimising themselves before the State; although there is still a question over representation in civil society, they have broadened their leverage and gained agency in using the spaces created for them to interact with the public authorities about mobility broadly, and more specifically regarding cycling issues.

Cycling policies and societal–State interactions were not immune to the pendular swings of politics, particularly because Haddad became closely identified as the patron of the cycling cause. Thus, the next administration, which was openly opposed to Haddad, tried to re-signify the policy. The backlash (bikelash, as cycle activists call it) of cycling policies that started in 2017, which included the removal of infrastructure and the emptying of participatory spaces, warrants additional research.

Acknowledgements

I wish to acknowledge financial support by Fapesp (Fundação de Amparo à Pesquisa do Estado de São Paulo) in the preparation of this chapter, as part of a more extensive PhD project at the Department of Architecture and Urban Planning, University of São Paulo.

References

Abers, R.N. and Tatagiba, L.F. (2014) Institutional Activism: Mobilizing for Women's Health from Inside the Brazilian Bureaucracy. *38° Encontro Anual da ANPOCS*.

Abers, R.N., Serafim, L. and Tatagiba, L.F. (2014) 'Repertórios de Interação Estado-Sociedade em um Estado Heterogêneo: A Experiência na Era Lula', *Dados*, 57(2), 325–57.

Almeida, D.R. (2014) 'Pluralização da representação política e legitimidade democrática: lições das instituições participativas no Brasil', *Opinião Pública*, 20(1): 96–117.

Amenta, E., Caren, N., Fetner, T. and Young, M. (2002) 'Challengers and states: toward a political sociology of social movements', *Sociological Views on Political Participation in the 21st Century*, 10: 47–83.

Amenta, E., Caren, N., Chiarello, E. and Su, Y. (2010) 'The political consequences of social movements', *Annual Review of Sociology*, 36: 287–307.

Araújo, M.R.M., Sousa, A.A., Oliveira, J.M., Jesus, M.S., Sá, N.R., Santos, P.A.C., Macedo Junior, R. and Lima, T.C. (2009) 'Andar de bicicleta: contribuições de um estudo psicológico sobre mobilidade', *Temas psicol*, 17(2): 481–95.

Bennichio, T. (2012) 'Critical mass is dead. Long live critical mass!' in C. Carlsson (ed) *Shift Happens! Critical Mass at 20*, San Francisco: Full Enjoyment Books.

Caputo, A. and Melo, H. (2009) 'A Industrialização Brasileira nos anos 1950: Uma análise da introdução 113 da SUMOC', *Estudos Econômicos*, 39(3).

Carlos, E., Dowbor, M. and Albuquerque, M.C.A. (2016) Movimentos sociais e seus efeitos nas políticas públicas: proposições analíticas e desafios metodológicos, *40° Encontro Annual da ANPOCS*, Caxambu, MG.

CHIA, R. (2009) '3×2 com Leandro Valverdes, cicloativista'. Available at: https://pedaladas.wordpress.com/2009/07/17/3x2-com-leandro-valverdes-cicloativista/. Accessed: 27 February 2018.

Dagnino, E. (2004) 'Construção democrática, neoliberalismo e participação: os dilemas da confluência perversa', *Política & Sociedade*, 5: 139–64.

Daly, E. (2014) *The Social Implications of Bicycle Infrastructure: What it Means to Bike in America's Best Cycling Cities*. Geography Honors Projects, Macalester College.

Dill, J. (2009) 'Bicycling for transportation and health: the role of infrastructure', *Journal of Public Health Policy*, 30: 95–110.

Fernández-Heredia, A., Andrés Monzón, A. and Jara-Díaz, S. (2014) 'Understanding cyclists' perceptions, keys for a successful bicycle promotion', *Transportation Research Part A Policy & Practice*, 63: 1–11.

Flusche, D. (2012) *Bicycling Means Business: The economic benefits of bicycle infrastructure*. Available at: https://bikeleague.org/sites/default/files/Bicycling_and_the_Economy-Econ_Impact_Studies_web.pdf. Accessed: 27 February 2018.

Freire, V. (1926) 'The Town of São Paulo. Report 38'. *Permanent International Association of Roads Congresses Vth Congress*, Milan.

Gomide, A.Á. and Galindo, E.P. (2013) 'A mobilidade urbana: uma agenda inconclusa ou o retorno daquilo que não foi', *Estudos Avançados*, 27(79): 27–39.

Gurza Lavalle, A. and Szwako, J. (2015) 'Sociedade civil, Estado e autonomia: argumentos, contra-argumentos e avanços no debate', *Opinião Pública*, 21(1): 157–87.

Gurza Lavalle, A., Carlos, E., Dowbor, M. and Szwako, J. (2017) Movimentos Sociais, Institucionalização e Domínios de Agência, *Série Textos para Discussão*. Centro de Estudos da Metrópole.

Hoffmann, M.L. (2016) *Bike Lanes are White Lanes: Bicycle Advocacy and Urban Planning*, Lincoln: University of Nebraska Press.

Houtzager, P. (2003) 'From polycentrism to the polity', in P. Houtzagere and P.P. Moore (eds) *Changing Paths: The New Politics of Inclusion in International Development*, Ann Arbor: University of Michigan Press, pp 1–31.

ITDP Brazil (2015) *Política de Mobilidade por Bicicletas e Rede Cicloviária da Cidade de São Paulo: Análise e Recomendações*. ITDP, November.

Jacobson, M. (2007) 'Effects of ethanol (E85) versus gasoline vehicles on cancer and mortality in the United States', *Environmental Science & Technology*, 41(11): 4150–7.

Lefebvre, H. (1968) *O Direito à Cidade*, (Portuguese translation 2009) São Paulo: Centauro.

Lindenberg Lemos, L. and Wicher Neto, H. (2014) 'Cycling infrastructure in São Paulo: impacts of a leisure-oriented model', *12th Annual Conference of the International Association for the History of Transport, Traffic and Mobility* (T2M).

Lindenberg Lemos, L. and Ramos, I.B. (2015) 'Bicicletas em São Paulo: uma avaliação do estado da arte', *Simpósio internacional Tecnologías y movilidades, miradas históricas y contemporâneas*. Santiago do Chile, Chile, outubro.

Malatesta, M.E.B. (2012) *A História dos Estudos de Bicicletas na CET*, Boletim Técnico 50. São Paulo: Companhia de Engenharia de Tráfego.

Mobilize.org (no date) Available at: http://www.mobilize.org.br/noticias/9732/mobilidade-ativa-lanca-candidatos-a-conselho-em-s-paulo.html

MPL (Movimento Passe Livre) (2013) 'Não começou em Salvador, não vai terminar em São Paulo', in: Vainer, C. et al (eds) *Cidades Rebeldes*: Passe Livre e as mobilizações que tomaram as ruas do Brasil. São Paulo: Boitempo, Carta Maior.

mpsp.mp.br (no date) Available at: http://www.mpsp.mp.br/portal/pls/portal/!PORTAL.wwpob_page.show?_docname=2560427.pdf

Oliveira, F.O. (1982) 'Estado e o Urbano no Brasil', *Espaço & Debates*, 6: 36–54.

Pezzuto, C.C. (2002) 'Fatores que influenciam o uso da bicicleta', Dissertation (MSc in Transport Engineering), Universidade Federal de São Carlos, São Carlos.

Ribeiro, R. (2016) 'Gerações discursivas do cicloativismo no Brasil: sport, transporte e mobilidade', in R. Rolnik and A. Fernandes (eds) *Cidades*, Rio de Janeiro: Funarte.

Rolnik, R. and Klintowitz, D. (2011) '(I)Mobilidade na cidade de São Paulo', *Estudos Avançados*, 25(71): 89–108.

Rosin, L.B. (2016) *Difusão de novos paradigmas de mobilidade urbana: a institcionalização do uso de bicicleta na cidade de São Paulo*. Relatório Iniciação Científica do Programa.

Sá, T.H., Pereira, R.H.M., Duran, A.C. and Monteiro, C.A. (2016) 'Diferenças socioeconômicas e regionais na prática do deslocamento ativo no Brasil', *Rev Saúde Pública*, 50: 37.

São Paulo (2013) *Programa de Metas da Cidade de São Paulo 2013–2016*, Prefeitura de São Paulo.

Skocpol, T. (1992). *Protecting Soldiers and Mothers: The Political Origins of Social Policy in the United States*, Cambridge, MA: Harvard University Press.

Sousa, P.B. (2012) 'Análise de fatores que influem no uso da bicicleta para fins de planejamento cicloviário', Thesis (PhD in Planning and Operation of Transport Systems), Escola de Engenharia de São Carlos, Universidade de São Paulo, São Carlos.

Souza, Y. (2016) 'Quando as rodas conquistam a cidade: cultura, tensões, conflitos e ações na prática do ciclismo em São Paulo', Dissertação (Mestrado), Pontifícia Universidade Católica, São Paulo.

Stein, S. (2011) 'Bike lanes and gentrification: New York City's shades of freen', *Progressive Planning*, Number 188.

Taino M., Nazelle, A.J., Götschic, T., Kahlmeier, S., Rojas-Rueda, D., Nieuwenhuijsen, M.J., Sá, T.H., Kelly, P. and Woodcocka, J. (2016) 'Can air pollution negate the health benefits of cycling and walking?', *Preventive Medicine*, 87: 233–6.

Tatagiba, L.F. (2014) '1984, 1992 e 2013: Sobre ciclos de protestos e democracia no Brasil', *Política & Sociedade*, Florianópolis, 13(28) set/dez.

Tavolari, B. (2016) 'Direito à Cidade: uma trajetória conceitual', *Novos Estudos*, Cebrap, 104, março, pp 92–109.

Vasconcellos, E.A. (1999) *Circular é preciso, viver não é preciso: a história do trânsito na cidade de São Paulo*, São Paulo: Annablume, Fapesp.

Züge Junior, O. (2015) *Cicloativismo paulistano: uma investigação jurídico-fenomenológica*. Tese (Doutorado em Filosofia e Teoria Geral do Direito) – Faculdade de Direito, Universidade de São Paulo, São Paulo.

Conclusion: politicising infrastructure or sustainable mobility?

Peter Cox and Till Koglin

The politics of cycling infrastructure

In her work *Mobility Justice*, Mimi Sheller (2018) devotes a whole chapter to 'Infrastructural Justice' highlighting the degree to which infrastructure shapes not only the quality of life, but more fundamentally locates one within social structures of (in)equality. Differential provision and differential life chances are intertwined. Sheller writes of *infrastructuring* as an active process, involving *kinopolitical struggle* in order to build *infrastructures of hope* for just and sustainable futures. Kinopolitical struggle is the work done to create the politics of mobility justice: mobility practices have the capacity to change people's lives for better or for worse and Sheller demands that infrastructuring be undertaken with constant reference to effects of inclusion and exclusion

Many of the narratives in this volume can be re-read as illustrations of those processes of this kinopolitical struggle. To reinforce this point, mobility struggles are not just about the place and existence of physical infrastructural construction, but the mobility practices and the mobile relationships that different arrangements create. The struggles play out through narrative (Freudendal-Pedersen; Koglin) or through organisational structures and processes (Emanuel; Feddes, te Lange and te Brömmelstroet). They are historical (Morgan) and contingent (Plyushteva and Barnfield; Lemos). They work through ideological frames (Brezina, Leth and Lemmerer; Whitelegg).

The richness of the contributions to this volume is that each of them also crosses those categories. A narrative analysis also demonstrates an ideological frame; organisational focuses reveal the contingency of decision-making. Each chapter could easily be reassigned to another form category from the above listing, or defined as a combination of different readings. What they all have in common is the degree to which infrastructures are constantly in flux, contentious and contended. The directness of bodily contact with the physical environments of travel and with other travellers experienced by those who ride cycles lends a particularly passionate and emotional tenor to many of the discussions held about cycling infrastructure. While the politics of cycling infrastructure may be analysed in terms of abstract political discourse and power relations, what all the contributors to this volume also show is the degree to which that politics is also embodied; lived out in the spaces of mundane and everyday travel. One of the notable observations in the discussions of Amsterdam's transformation into a cycling city and in the study of the Øresund Crossing is also that this embodied politics is also about real people. Individual lives and relationships are involved, as Leyendecker and Brezina, Leth and Lemmerer also clearly show. To do justice to the politics of infrastructure we have had to constantly move between empirical study and theoretical analysis. The personal truly is political here, and the obverse is also immediately true, that the political is experienced in the personal. Both policy and discourse concerning infrastructure shape the experiences of those whose mobile lives are lived in the spaces that are a result of political decision making.

Listening to the case studies and presentations of infrastructural provision made by policy makers and designers at the annual Velo-City, Polis and other international conferences that exist to share and highlight good practice, it would be easy to assume the superiority of European cycle infrastructure provision. Generally, European cycle infrastructure has been presented as good or as much better than the infrastructure provided in countries like the United States of America, Canada or Australia. However, this volume has shown that the bicycle infrastructure in countries like Denmark, the Netherlands, Sweden or Austria also fails to fully recognise the bicyclists' needs for active and daily mobility. Opening a space for shared critique, rather than focusing on the search for a mythical universal best practice allows dialogue between perspectives. It also permits (and insists on) analysis of the backstage of infrastructure construction. What processes and assumptions are behind the plans drawn up and the decisions made? Who are the people involved and what considerations drive them? How are these considerations justified?

Locations internationally celebrated for good practice (for example, Copenhagen, Amsterdam) often escape rigorous scrutiny as Sabelis (2015) has argued. Treating them at the same level as less celebrated (or more notorious) cases allows us to open up the complexities of process and to understand that the gains made are not always straightforward, nor result in perfect cycling systems inclusive of all cycling practices.

The empirical chapters by many of the contributors to this volume show the complexity of bicycle infrastructure in cities that have a good general reputation for cycling and cycling infrastructure, like Copenhagen, Bremen or Amsterdam. Nevertheless, this book has shown that those cities also struggle with the implementation of good bicycle infrastructure and dealing with bicycle traffic and mobility by, for example, decreasing space for motorised mode of transport. Bicycle infrastructure, as shown in many of the examples in this volume, not least Johannesburg and Sao Paulo, is inherently political in car-oriented societies and societies that want, consciously or unconsciously, the car to be the dominate mode of transport in planning and in peoples' everyday mobility.

Leyendecker, Feddes et al, and Freudendal-Pedersen have shown clearly that cities with a national and international reputation of being bicycle-friendly continue to face problems concerning infrastructure. The conflicts in Copenhagen between cyclists, and between cyclists and motorised traffic have increased over the years as Freudendal-Pedersen has shown, and in Bremen, as Leyendecker shows, infrastructure provision implemented without consideration of the gendered patterns of cycle mobilities results in the privileging of a majority of journeys made mostly by men over those which are predominantly made by women.

Looking across the contributions highlights the need to think not only about the politics of cycle infrastructure, but about the politics of sustainable mobility. Increasing cycling in the mode share is one very important aspect in a sustainable transport system. However, as the numerous examples show, car traffic and automobility still dominate debates, politics and planning – even when planning for cycle-specific infrastructure. Thus, one has to think about politicising sustainable mobility in the sense that sustainable mobility (cycling) can only be successful if the car society is questioned, criticised and not part of the common discourse in politics and planning.

What is at stake in the politics of cycling infrastructure is also more than the (relative) privileging of cycling as a mode of travel above other mobility forms. As Whitelegg has powerfully shown in this volume and elsewhere (Whitelegg, 2016) the issue that often silently lies behind all mobility planning is the need for a decrease in levels of mobility overall. To reduce the carbon footprint of mobility practices, we need to break cultural addiction to the hypermobility that car travel encourages. As Plyushteva and Barnfield further point out in their chapter, the need is for paradigm shift, not merely the refocusing of concern in infrastructure planning.

Infrastructures for sustainability, infrastructures of hope

This work has been about the past and present of the politics of cycling infrastructure. It also points the way to future work on infrastructural sustainability. In bringing together these chapters we have begun a comparative assessment of existing and historic struggles and note the need to connect with other studies such as the *Cycling Cities* programme (Oldenziel et al, 2016). While we need to be aware of our current situations, how they came about and how people make sense of them, we also need to consider what infrastructures will be needed for future minimal carbon mobilities. To do this requires further work of building a political imaginary commensurate with a paradigm shift. Such thinking needs to begin not with the task of retrofitting cycle lanes or routes to existing transport systems but conceptualising and working out how to make possible the infrastructures of carbon neutral mobilities. We will need to think how cycling might look in terms of normative mobility practices in such a vision and how mobility spaces might be entirely reconfigured to match these aspirations. In other words we do need new visionary thinking or maybe even new utopian thinking when it comes to the future of the politics of bicycle infrastructure.

References

Oldenziel, R., Emanuel, M., Albert de la Bruheze, A. and Veraart, F. (eds) (2016) *Cycling Cities: The European Experience: Hundred Years of Policy and Practice*, Eindhoven: Foundation for the History of Technology.

Sabelis, I. (2015) 'Diversity in cycle policies', in P. Cox (ed) *Cycling Cultures*, Chester: University of Chester Press, pp 43–62.

Sheller, M. (2018) *Mobility Justice: The Politics of Movement in an Age of Extremes*, London: Verso.

Whitelegg, J. (2016) *Mobility*, Shropshire: Straw Barnes Press.

Index